To Father — Happy Birthday

To Father — Happy Birthday

The
Lawless Decade

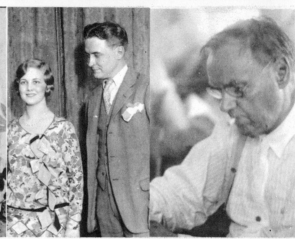

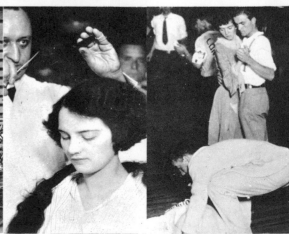

The Lawless Decade

A PICTORIAL HISTORY OF A GREAT AMERICAN TRANSITION: FROM THE WORLD WAR I ARMISTICE AND PROHIBITION TO REPEAL AND THE NEW DEAL

By Paul Sann

Executive Editor, *The New York Post*

PICTURE COLLATION BY GEORGE HORNBY

BONANZA BOOKS · NEW YORK

Designed by George Hornby

Library of Congress Catalog Card Number: 56-11376

© MCMLVII by Crown Publishers, Inc.

Printed in the United States of America

This edition published by Bonanza Books
a division of Crown Publishers, Inc.,
a b c d e f g h

FOR

BIRDYE,

Without

Whom,

etc.

PICTURE SOURCES

Associated Press
98 bl, 100, 197 b

Brown Bros.
18 tr, 21, 24 t, 25 bl, 28 tl, cl, 29 bl, br, 30, 31 b, 35 cr, bl, 38 bl, br, 39 t, bl, 40 tc, cr, 43 t, 50 c, 51 tl, 52 tr, 55 t, 57 b, 58 tr, 59 t, 75 tr, bl, 78, 85 tr, 104 b, 111, 115, 116 t, 117, 166, 168, 169 tr, 176, 177, 178 t, 208, 210, 215, 234

Culver Service
13, 16, 17, 18 b, 19, 23 b, 24 c, b, 25 t, c, br, 26 br, 27 b, 28 tr, bl, br, 29 tl, 33, 34 tl, 38 tl, 39 br, 40 tl, tr, cl, c, bl, br, 40 bc, 41, 42, 44 cl, cr, 45, 48 br, 49 br, 50 tr, 51 tr, bl, br, 53, 54 t, 57 t, 63 tl, 64 br, 66 c, tr, 72 tc, 73, 75 br, 79 tl, b, 80 bl, c, 85 br, 93 b, 94 br, 96, 97 tl, tr, 108 br, 110 bl, 116 b, 132 bl, tr, 135 tl, bl, cr, 136 br, 154 t, 156 br, 157 cl, 171 tr, 179, 181 tr, 182 tl, bl, 198, 203 bl, br, 221, 222 b, 225, 227 br, 228 tl, cl

Harry Grogin
140, 154 br

Harris and Ewing
84 tr

John Held, Jr.
46, 48

International Newsreel
114 tl, 137 bl

International News Photo
18 tl, 20, 23 t, 26 tl, bl, cl, 31 t, 32, 35 tl, 36, 37, 43 bl, br, 44 tc, tr, bc, br, 47 b, 49 bl, 50 bl, 51 tc, 52 tl, 55 b, 56, 58 tl, bl, 59 bl, bc, br, 60, 63 br, 64 tl, 63, 66 tl, 68, 69, 70, 71 b, 72 tl, tr, 74 tl, tr, bl, bc, br, 76, 77, 79 tr, 80 tr, 82, 83, 84, 85 tl, bl, 86, 88, 89, 90, 91, 92, 93 t, 94 bl, 95, 97 tc, bl, br, 99, 101, 102, 103, 104 t, 105, 106, 107, 108 tl, tr, bl, 109, 110 t, 112, 113,

114 tr, br, 118, 119, 120, 121, 122, 123, 124, 125, 126, 127, 128, 129, 130, 131, 132 c, 133, 134, 135 bl, br, 136 cl, 137 tl, cr, 138, 139, 140, 141, 142, 143, 144, 145, 146, 147, 148, 149, 150, 151, 152, 153, 154 cl, bl, 155, 156 bl, bc, 157 tr, bl, br, 158, 160, 161, 162, 163 tr, bl, 164, 165, 167 t, 170, 171 tl, 172, 173, 174, 175, 178 b, 179 tl, 180, 181 c, 183, 184, 185, 186, 187, 188, 189, 190, 199, 200, 201, 202, 203 tr, 204, 205 b, 206, 207, 209, 211, 212, 213, 214, 216, 217, 218, 219, 222 t, 224, 226, 227 t, 228 tr, 229, 230, 231, 232, 233, 234 bl, br

New York Historical Society
193

New York Post
159, 192, 194, 195, 196, 197 t, 232

New York Times
14, 81, 220

Pacific and Atlantic
98 br

Penguin
44 tl, bl, 47, 66 br, 75 tl, 136 tl, cr, 137 tr, 182 br

Boardman Robinson
48

Underwood and Underwood
54 b, 87 br, 163 tl, 167 bl

United Press
34 bl

Variety
223

A. A. Wallgren, Stars and Stripes
15

ABOUT THE BOOK and THE TIME

This is an informal historical excursion back into the Nineteen Twenties.

We call it the Lawless Decade, but it has been known by many names. F. Scott Fitzgerald, using bathtub gin for the ceremonies, christened it the Jazz Age. Westbrook Pegler called it the Era of Wonderful Nonsense. Frederick Lewis Allen, the period's most able observer, talked of the New Era and the New Freedom. Some put it down as the Roaring Twenties, others as the Get-Rich-Quick Era. To the sports journalists it was the Golden Age. And to the bluenoses, may they rest in peace, it was the Dry Decade—a name born of 100-proof fancy. There was nothing dry about the twenties.

This is one of the reasons—only one—why we call it the Lawless Decade. The law that had the greatest impact on the wide and wonderful land evoked the least obedience from the people. Liquor—good, bad, indifferent or deadly—flowed like a giant waterfall all during the thirteen wobbly years of the thing Herbert Hoover called "an experiment . . . noble in purpose." But the bootlegger was not alone; he dealt only in the happy juice. His errands made Prohibition a sopping-wet farce but there were many other laws ground into the dust during the vibrant and tumultuous years from the Armistice to Repeal. Criminal laws, moral laws, civil laws, social laws, political laws, religious laws—name them.

The great postwar shocks of the twenties left very little sacred and very little unturned; most of the old playing rules were rewritten.

It was in this time and in this way that the country made itself ready for all the previously-unthinkable changes and complete turnabouts of the thirties and forties: going off the gold standard, the New Deal and the NRA, the end of isolation, the United Nations, the Atom Bomb. In the Lawless Decade the barriers of tradition and custom were broken down. The government, business, the people were no longer inhibited by the Past—for better or for worse.

When we speak here of the Lawless Decade we don't mean lawless in the Wild West sense. America didn't go back to the untamed ways of the frontier; it went forward. It threw off the shackles. Prohibition invaded the American's right to pamper—or ruin—his own insides, so he flouted it.

The semi-Victorian morals of the horse-and-buggy days inhibited his right (and hers) to enjoy a long night out after all the sacrifices involved in making the world safe for democracy, so the old codes were discarded. Grandpa's penny-a-day ideas about thrift, tipped with gold dust at the compound interest window, went out the window too; the road to sudden riches ran through the Florida sands to the pavements of Wall Street.

It was a time to plunge, on all the levels; that was the new American way. It was a time for superlatives —for the Million Dollar Gate and the Million Dollar Body (all aquiver on the silent screen). It was a time for deeds of derring-do—Lucky Lindy astride the Atlantic in "The Spirit of St. Louis" and Trudy Ederle conquering the English Channel with her hands and feet. It was a time, then as now, for preserving American institutions from foreign invaders—thus the Red Raids and the tragedy of Sacco and Vanzetti. It was a time for sex spectaculars in the courts—Hall-Mills and Snyder-Gray and don't spare the details. It was a time for innovations — radio, mah-jongg and Freud. It was a time to ask questions out in public—Darrow and the monkey versus Bryan and the Book at Dayton.

The best way to tell it seemed to us to lie in the stories of the people who made the time or were made by it. Thus our emphasis is on the human record. There's something to learn from Ella Boole and from Clara Bow, too, from Eugene Debs and Woodrow Wilson, from Jack Dempsey and the Barons of Wall Street, from Al Capone and Al Smith, from Warren Harding and Nan Britton too, from Aimee Semple McPherson and Rudolph Valentino, from Shoeless Joe Jackson and from Calvin Coolidge and Gentleman Gene Tunney— and from Babe Ruth and the many, many others who made one kind of mark or another in that frenzied moment in our history.

Here, then, is the Lawless Decade, and any resemblance to persons living or dead is the clear intention of the author.

PAUL SANN

Riverdale, New York
April, 1957

TABLE OF CONTENTS

The
Lawless Decade

New York City, November 11, 1918.

"All the News That's Fit to Print."

The New York Times.

THE WEATHER

VOL. LXVIII...NO. 22,206. .... NEW YORK, MONDAY, NOVEMBER 11, 1918. TWENTY-FOUR PAGES. TWO CENTS

ARMISTICE SIGNED, END OF THE WAR! BERLIN SEIZED BY REVOLUTIONISTS; NEW CHANCELLOR BEGS FOR ORDER; OUSTED KAISER FLEES TO HOLLAND

SON FLEES WITH EX-KAISER

Hindenburg Also Believed to be Among Those in His Party.

ALL ARE HEAVILY ARMED

Automobiles Bristle with Rifles as Fugitives Arrive at Dutch Frontier.

ON THEIR WAY TO DE STEEG

Belgians Yell to Them, "Are You On Your Way to Paris?"

LONDON, Nov. 10.—Both the former German Emperor and his eldest son, Frederick William, crossed the Dutch frontier Sunday morning, according to advices from The Hague. The former German Emperor's party, which is believed to include Field Marshal von Hindenburg, arrived at Eysden, [midway between Liege and Maastricht,] on the Dutch frontier, at 7:30 o'clock Sunday morning, according to Daily Mail advices.

Practically the whole German General Staff accompanied the former Emperor, and ten automobiles carried the party. The automobiles were bristling with rifles, and all the fugitives were armed.

Kaiser Fought Hindenburg's Call for Abdication; Failed to Get Army's Support in Keeping Throne

By GEORGE RENWICK.

AMSTERDAM, Nov. 10.—I learn on very good authority that the Kaiser made a determined effort to stave off abdication. He went to headquarters with the deliberate intention of bringing the army around to his side. In this he failed miserably.

His main support consisted of a number of officers, nearly all of Prussian regiments, who formed themselves into two regiments and placed themselves at his Majesty's disposal. To do anything with such support was more, of course, to be Gilbertian.

During the night the Kaiser called the Crown Prince, Hindenburg, and General Gröner to him, and the consultation lasted a couple of hours. Both officers strongly pressed the Kaiser to look to the inevitable, and Hindenburg informed him that any more delay in coming to a decision to abdicate would certainly have the most terrible consequences and lead to serious events in the army. For those consequences Hindenburg said he must refuse responsibility.

The Crown Prince, it is said, was the first to give way. General Gröner fully supported Hindenburg's view, but when the conference broke up the Kaiser remained unconvinced of the advisability of abdication. He is said to have come to his final decision an hour or so later, after several communications had reached him from Berlin and after another short and stormy talk with Hindenburg.

Meanwhile, his son-in-law, the Duke of Brunswick, for himself and his heir, had abdicated. "Brunswick's Fated Chieftain" was forced without fighting to abdicate. Reports have it that the republican movement in Brunswick, which long before the war was chafing under autocratic conditions, began to be noticed even before it was set in motion at Kiel.

Kaiser Shivered as He Signed Abdication

LONDON, Nov. 10.—Emperor William signed his letter of abdication on Saturday morning at the German Grand Headquarters in presence of Crown Prince Frederick William and Field Marshal Hindenburg, according to a dispatch from Amsterdam to the Exchange Telegraph Company.

The Crown Prince signed his renunciation of the throne shortly afterward.

Before placing his signature to the document, an urgent message from Philipp Scheidemann, who was a Socialist member without portfolio in the Imperial Cabinet, was handed to the Emperor. He read it with a shiver. Then he signed the paper, saying:

"It may be for the good of Germany."

The Emperor was deeply moved. He consented to sign the document only when he got the news of the latest events in the empire.

The ex-Kaiser and former Crown Prince were expected to take charge of their troops on Saturday, but nothing had then been settled regarding their future movements.

GERMAN DYNASTIES BEING WIPED OUT

King of Wuerttemberg Abdicates—Sovereign of Saxony to Follow Suit.

MORE WARSHIPS JOIN THE REDS

Four Dreadnoughts in Kiel Harbor Espouse the Revolutionary Cause.

BERLIN TROOPS JOIN REVOLT

Reds Shell Building in Which Officers Vainly Resist.

THRONGS DEMAND REPUBLIC

Revolutionary Flag on Royal Palace—Crown Prince's Palace Also Seized.

GENERAL STRIKE IS BEGUN

Burgomaster and Police Submit—War Office Now Under Socialist Control.

LONDON, Nov. 10.—The greater part of Berlin is in control of revolutionists, the former Kaiser has fled to Holland, and Friedrich Ebert, the new Socialist Chancellor, has taken command of the situation. The revolt is spreading throughout Germany with great rapidity. Dispatches received in London today announce these startling developments. The Workmen's and Soldiers' Council is now administering the municipal government of the German capital.

The War Ministry has submitted, and its acts are valid only when countersigned by a Socialist representative. The official Wolff telegraphic agency has been taken over by the Reds.

The red flag has been hoisted over the royal palace and the

Socialist Chancellor Appeals to All Germans To Help Him Save Fatherland from Anarchy

BERNE, Nov. 10. (Associated Press.)—In an address to the people, the new German Chancellor, Friedrich Ebert, says:

Citizens: The ex-Chancellor, Prince Max of Baden, in agreement with all the Secretaries of State, has handed over to me the task of liquidating his affairs as Chancellor. I am on the point of forming a new Government in accord with the various parties, and will keep public opinion freely informed of the course of events.

The new Government will be a Government of the people. It must make every effort to secure in the quickest possible time peace for the German people and consolidate the liberty which they have won.

The new Government has taken charge of the administration, to preserve the German people from civil war and famine and to accomplish their legitimate claim to autonomy. The Government can solve this problem only if all the officials in town and country will help.

I know it will be difficult for men to work with the new men who have taken charge of the empire, but I appeal to their love of the people. Lack of organization would in this heavy time mean anarchy in Germany and the surrender of the country to tremendous misery. Therefore, help your native country with fearless, indefatigable work for the future, every one at his post.

I demand every one's support in the hard task awaiting us. You know how seriously the war has menaced the governing of the people, which is the first condition of the people's existence. The political transformation should not trouble the people. The food supply is the first duty of all, whether in town or country, and they should not embarrass, but rather aid, the production of food supplies and their transport to the towns.

Food shortage signifies pillage and robbery, with great misery. The gloomiest will suffer the most, and the industrial worker will be affected hardest. All who illicitly lay hands on food supplies or other supplies of prime necessity or the means of transport necessary for their distribution will be guilty in the highest degree toward the community.

I ask you immediately to leave the streets and remain orderly and calm.

COPENHAGEN, Nov. 10.—The new Berlin Government, according to a Wolff Bureau dispatch, has issued the following proclamation:

Fellow-Citizens: This day the people's deliverance has been fulfilled. The Social Democratic Party has undertaken to form a Government. It has invited the Independent Socialist Party to enter the Government with equal rights.

cers were concealed shots were fired from the windows. The Reds then began shelling the building. Many persons were killed and wounded before the officers surrendered.

When the cannonade began the people thought the Reichsbank was being bombarded, and thousands rushed to the square in front of the Crown Prince' palace. It was later determined that other buildings

in the solution of demobilization problems.

Serious food difficulties are expected in Germany, owing to the stoppage of trains. The Council of the Regency will take the most drastic steps to re-establish order.

In the new German Government there will be only three representatives of the majority parties, namely, Erzberger, Gothein, and Richthofen, says a dispatch from Copenhagen. The other posts will be occupied by Socialists and independents.

WAR ENDS AT 6 O'CLOCK THIS MORNING

The State Department in Washington Made the Announcement at 2:45 o'Clock.

ARMISTICE WAS SIGNED IN FRANCE AT MIDNIGHT

Terms Include Withdrawal from Alsace-Lorraine, Disarming and Demobilization of Army and Navy, and Occupation of Strategic Naval and Military Points.

By The Associated Press.

WASHINGTON, Monday, Nov. 11, 2:48 A. M.—The armistice between Germany, on the one hand, and the allied Governments and the United States, on the other, has been signed.

The State Department announced at 2:45 o'clock this morning that Germany had signed.

The department's announcement simply said: "The armistice has been signed."

The world war will end this morning at 6 o'clock, Washington time, 11 o'clock Paris time.

The armistice was signed by the German representatives at midnight.

This was it. The Great War was over. Four days earlier wild celebrations had swept the nation on Roy W. Howard's premature exclusive from Paris: *UNIPRESS NEW YORK URGENT ARMISTICE ALLIES GERMANS SIGNED ELEVEN SMORN-ING HOSTILITIES CEASED TWO SAFTERNOON.* The publisher got the story from Admiral Henry B. Wilson, Commander of the U. S. naval forces in France, but the Germans had not yet come through our lines to lay down their swords. The next morning the front was still aflame and a terrible hangover descended on the home front. When the real thing did come, the people managed to summon up energy for a new round of riotous demonstrations.

LIGHTS OUT

BONE DRY

JUST IN TIME!

PROHIBITIONIST

DYING CAMEL

U.S.

MY HOW SHE HAS CHANGED

Shadows of dead men
Stand by the wall,
Watching the fun
Of the Victory Ball
They do no reproach,
Because they know,
If they're forgotten,
It's better so.

—From ALFRED NOYES' poem,
A Victory Dance

Johnny Comes Marching Home

It was a glorious homecoming.

There were parades on all the Broadways and all the Main Streets. There were brass bands and wild, cheering throngs that had to be held back by the horse cops. There were long and lavish tributes from overstuffed men in top hats . . . councilmen, judges, congressmen, mayors, even governors and senators. There were miles of ticker tape, and Red Cross ladies with coffee and hot buns. And there were nameless girls (later to be known as flappers) to hug Johnny to their bosoms and maybe light up his troop-ship pallor with a kiss that left a vivid red stain—lipstick.

And there was always Old Glory, waving from all the same windows—and from 130,000 windows that had a

new decoration glittering in the sun: the Gold Star, for the boy who did not come marching home but lay in Flanders Field or on some lonely knoll Over There. That was a Blue Note—130,000 Blue Notes—and there were others, too.

For all the hurrahs and all the hosannas, Johnny would find something less than wonderful about the America of 1919. It was not the same place he had left in '17. It was changed, and changing still; there would be agony in peace, as in war. In a word, Johnny had some shocks coming when he flecked off the confetti and packed away his hero's khaki.

The Postwar Blues

"The American business man . . . devel-

oped a fervent belief that 100-per-cent Americanism and the Welfare of God's Own Country and Loyalty to the Teachings of the Founding Fathers implied the right of the business man to kick the union organizer out of his workshop . . ."

—FREDERICK LEWIS ALLEN, *Only Yesterday*

Johnny didn't march back into the short day and high pay he was enjoying when Uncle Sam tapped him to go make the world safe for democracy. Oh, no. The prosperity of 1914-1918 dried up as fast as the signatures on the Armistice. There would be two years of depression and more than five million unemployed before the economy could adjust itself to peace. The Hun quit too soon; our factories were

The *Leviathan* brings the doughboys home from France. . .

overexpanded, our shelves glutted, our foreign markets devastated by the years of havoc and destruction, our price structure shot.

The wartime honeymoon between labor and capital blew up in fearful strife. Four million men hit the bricks in 1919 alone: the unions didn't want to go back to the long week and low wage of the prewar years, nor to the Open Shop cherished by the patriotic defenders of free American enterprise. Strikes swept the nation by the thousands, hitting steel, the meat packers, the railroads, the building industry, the garment trades, even the vaudeville houses. John L. Lewis took 435,000 miners out of the pits and relaxed with Homer's *Iliad* as Detroit closed its freezing schools and factory owners everywhere talked of banking their furnaces. Seattle was crippled by a general walkout. On the Atlantic Seaboard, striking longshoremen shut down the ports. Blood ran, too. Pennsylvania's coal and iron police bent clubs over strikers' skulls and U.S. troops ran interference for U.S. Steel's scabs in

Some of our troops were still coming home long after the Big Parade. This is the *Santa Teresa*.

The 1919 Victory Parade in New York, hailing the return of General John J. (Black Jack) Pershing and his *AEF* troops, passes the reviewing stand on Fifth Avenue.

Gary, Indiana. In West Virginia, the Weirton Steel Company's private police force made 118 strikers kneel and kiss the American flag; in the temper of the time, with the Government's Red Raids picking up steam, you were a Bolshevik if you shouldered a picket sign. "The American businessman," said Frederick Lewis Allen in *Only Yesterday,* "was quite ready to believe that a struggle of American laboring men for better wages was the beginning of an armed rebellion directed by Lenin and Trotsky, and that behind every innocent professor who taught

that there were arguments for as well as against socialism there was a bearded rascal from eastern Europe with a moneybag in one hand and a smoking bomb in the other."

So Johnny found that the festival of homecoming ended with the Big Parade. The dreams he had in the mud and the trenches were wafted away by very hard realities. Maybe he heard about the twenty thousand millionaires—up from a prewar sixteen thousand—and the legions of the New Rich on the native hearth. He was more likely to qualify for the New Poor. To

begin with, the dollar in his discharge pay was worth only forty-five cents in the inflated postwar economy. Maybe he thought he would settle down in a new home or a new apartment when he got back; he found housing short and rents sky-high. He might wind up in the shabby "temporary" barracks built for wartime and kept standing for years afterward because the construction industry couldn't catch up. Maybe he thought he was coming home to a tranquil shore; he woud find race riots in Chicago and Washington and a rebirth of the Klan in the South.

Sergeant Alvin C. York, out of the Tennessee backwoods, was the war's most decorated hero. He led a seventeen-man patrol that killed twenty to twenty-five enemy soldiers, captured 132, and knocked out forty-five machine-gun nests, breaking up a counter-attack the Boches were about to launch in the Argonne Forest in October, 1918. "I wasn't skairt any during the scrap," Sergeant York said later. "I feel it was God took me through. It was Him who took us all through."

Transition of a doughboy: From France to transport, to parade, to work, to strike, to strong-arm methods. The Republic Steel Co. was among those hit by the walkouts in heavy industry as labor fought to hold its wartime gains. This picture was made at Republic's Monroe, Michigan, plant after tear gas was thrown at the strikers.

The Ku Klux Klan was on the march in the early twenties. Strongest in the South, it had branches in Long Island, New Jersey, Ohio, and in almost every Northern state as well.

Mademoiselle from Main St.

"The American puella is no longer naïve and charming; she goes to the altar of God with a learned and even cynical glitter in her eye. The veriest schoolgirl of today knows as much as the midwife of 1885, and spends a good deal more time discharging and disseminating her information..."

—H. L. MENCKEN, 1916

On the more practical levels of his day-to-day existence the soldier home from the wars did find something to cheer about—unless he happened to be an Honor Scout or otherwise excessively strait-laced. Johnny found his American Beauty drifting away from the prim morality of the pre-1914 world even faster than Henry Ford's Model T would carry her. The girl who kissed him demurely at the depot, while her skirt swept the dusty floor, had been working harder and harder on the New Freedom in his absence. When he got home she wanted to be more like the Mademoiselle from Armentières—not to mention some of the real-life fast-steppers Over There. She wanted to be the life of the party —indoors, or in the open roadster parked on the lonely road.

Let's face it: The girl hadn't sat out the war. The process of emancipation that set in before '17 quickened perceptibly while the boys were away. The revolution in underwear offered perhaps the most vivid case in point. The old cotton undergarments, layer upon layer, gave way to the much sexier, much more feminine, silk. The long black stockings gave way to sheer hose that exposed the leg—and some of the girls weren't averse to rolling 'em below the knees when the band turned on that hot fox trot tempo. Skirts went up six inches from the ground. The high-laced shoe started toward the museum, replaced by low pumps that showed off the well-turned ankle. Bobbed hair arrived, consigning the old fashioned bun and long locks to the beauty parlor floor. (In the beginning, that took courage; there were those who associated short hair with free love and radicalism, but the best families permitted it after a while.) Rouge was on the way, too.

Thus Johnny found a social scene that was much more varied—and surely more interesting—than the one he had left. The curtain had come down on the girl he used to know. She was a flapper now, raring to go. She was en-

The girls looked different. They, too, had learned something, had loosened up, during the war. This was bold and daring, for those days.

tirely ready for her role in the Lawless Decade. She was even ready for the speakeasy, which happened to be at hand. If Johnny complained, only the stuffier historians recorded it.

The Ordeal of "Meester Veelson"

"From the day he landed in Hoboken he had his back to the wall of the White House, talking to save his faith in words, talking to save his faith in the League of Nations, talking to save his faith in himself, in his father's God . . . (if anybody disagreed, he was a crook or a red; no pardon for Debs)."

—JOHN DOS PASSOS, 1919

The people of France laid a crimson carpet for him at Brest and hailed him as "Meester Veelson," the savior of Europe. But when the powers among the twenty-seven victor nations got down to the hard bargaining, Woodrow Wilson found himself around a table in the Palace of Versailles with three very tough men who didn't share his ideals at all. The gentle forgiveness of Wilson's Fourteen Points had no place in the better world envisioned by Britain's Lloyd George, France's

Georges Clemenceau and Italy's Guido Orlando. They wanted a winner's peace, Germany on her knees. The high-minded American had to trade the best part of his first thirteen points to put over No. 14—the cherished dream of a League of Nations.

Another trio awaited Woodrow Wilson back in Washington, in its way even more formidable than the one that trimmed his wings in the Hall of Mirrors. Home from the ceremony of peacemaking with his illusions dented but his will as strong as ever, the President had to match his ardor and his oratory against such senatorial giants as Henry Cabot Lodge of Massachusetts, William E. Borah of Idaho and Hiram Johnson of California. They wouldn't buy the fancy-sounding League of Nations (a quarter of a century ahead of its time). They had enough of Europe and its bickerings and bloodletting: no entangling alliances; let the foreigners sweat for themselves.

Wilson took his case to the people. He went into the whistlestops and laid his burning ideals on the line. "The

President and Mrs. Wilson on the bridge of the S.S. *George Washington*, March, 1919.

whole world," he said, "is now in a state where you can fancy that there are hot tears upon every cheek, and those hot tears are tears of sorrow. They are also tears of hope." Not many Americans took the glistening words to heart. The cool reception made a mockery of the pencil-scrawled message the President had put before the nation at 3:00 A.M. on November 11, 1918, when the guns were stilled in Europe: "Everything for which America fought has now been accomplished. It will now be our fortunate duty to assist by example, by sober, friendly counsel, and by material aid in the establishment of just democracy throughout the world." If you needed a world organization to bring about "just democracy," the people in the richest and most powerful nation of them all would just as soon sit it out.

The graybeard Lodge and his isolationist cohorts on Capitol Hill—"A little group of willful men," Wilson called them—knew it. They knew the returning doughboy and his family had no appetite for the League of Nations, just as the cynical men in Louis XIV's marble halls had known that the masses below them wanted a victor's spoils and not the nice peace of Woodrow Wilson.

So the earnest schoolmaster lost. His heart broke first and then his body. He came back sick from his cross-country journey and a stroke paralyzed his left side. He served out the last seventeen months of his term an invalid in a wheel chair, all but crushed. Then Warren Gamaliel Harding arrived in the White House and "Meester Veelson," a hero in Europe and a villain in his own land, went to the big house on S Street to await the solace of death.

UNCLE SAM'S WATER WAGON

Billy Sunday (shown here on the right): "The reign of tears is over..."

The Lawless Decade opened on a dreary note—unless you happened to be a Dry.

The New Year floated in on an ocean of whiskey, the last good whiskey most Americans would taste for thirteen years, but it was not a time for unconfined revelry. There was another binge in the making. The Eighteenth Amendment was going into effect at 12:01 A.M. on July 16, 1920. The more dedicated allies of the Demon Rum set aside this historic night for the "last" bender but it didn't live up to its advance notices. There were just some maudlin scenes in the drinking emporia as men wept into their Scotch or rye and proclaimed the end of the wet and happy world they knew.

There was no weeping in the enemy camp.

In Norfolk, Virginia, the Rev. Billy Sunday presided over mock funeral services for John Barleycorn in high glee. He sent the condemned man off in a horse-drawn twenty-foot coffin and ten thousand bone-dry followers cheered his words: "Good-bye John. You were God's worst enemy. You were Hell's best friend . . . The reign of tears is over."

The evangelist looked into the bright Dry future, too. "The slums soon will be only a memory," he cried. "We will turn our prisons into factories and our jails into storehouses and corncribs. Men will walk upright now, women will smile, and the children will laugh. Hell will be forever for rent."

The Anti-Saloon League of New York foresaw a much better America with the cork on the bottle. "Now for an era of clear thinking and clean living!" said the League. "Shake hands with Uncle Sam and board his water wagon." In no time at all, as it happened, a great many Americans would be much too rocky on bootleg hootch to make their way aboard any kind of wagon.

The Demon Rum Indicted

"Wine is a mocker,
Strong drink is raging:
And whosoever is deceived thereby
Is not wise."

—Proverbs XX, 1

Drink always has been a problem—especially to the Drys. The bluenoses have traced the Poisoned Cup all the way from Noah's Ark (can you think of a time when a man needed a shot more than that?) to Colonial America to our own vale of tears.

1920

American Issue, a Dry organ, summed up the Puritan record very darkly: "Drink was godfather at every christening, master of ceremonies at every wedding, first aid in every accident and assistant undertaker at every funeral. It had come with the Spanish to St. Augustine in 1565. It had carried the Virginia election for John Smith in 1607. It was the 'Dutch courage' of Manhattan Island in 1615. It led the prayers on Plymouth Rock in 1620 . . . It was the first organized treason in the whiskey rebellion of 1791. It has been the *fata morgana* of many millions of immigrants to this day."

It is sometimes said that the Puritans passed laws against almost everything a man could enjoy except liquor, but this is not so; and Virginia "outlawed" drunks in 1619, the year before the Mayflower brought all those people. That was the first liquor law in the New World. (The first all-out prohibition went back to the ban on selling spirits to the Indians but not many palefaces observed it.) The Colonial guzzler had a nice choice of spirits—Jersey Lightning, an applejack; Strip and Go Naked or Blue Ruin, gin drinks; Kill-Devil, a rum, and some blackstrap rum-and-molasses mixtures. The stuff could knock mules down, no less mere men. Thus the Colonies became increasingly concerned about drunkenness. Governor John Winthrop of Massachusetts banned toasts in 1630, presumably because people were toasting too many things. Maryland in 1642 levied a fine

21

"NOW THEN. ALL TOGETHER. 'MY COUNTRY 'TIS OF THEE'"

Cartoonist Rollin Kirby, in the *New York World*, gave the nation this lasting image of Mr. Prohibition in action. It was a devastating portrait.

The first wake for King Alcohol was held on June 30, 1919, because Wartime Prohibition—ineffective because there was no enforcement machinery until the Volstead Act was passed the following year—was going into effect the next day.

of 100 pounds of tobacco on anyone caught blotto in a public place. Connecticut in 1650 limited tippling to a half hour per sitting. Maryland started putting drunkards in the stocks in 1658. New Jersey in 1668 banned all drinking after 9:00 P.M. New York in 1697 ordered all saloons closed on Sundays. New Hampshire in 1719 made it illegal to sell a drink to anyone already under the influence.

None of those laws did much good.

The American of Colonial days drank at seed time and harvest time and in-between. He drank to pass the time of day with a neighbor—or to pass the time of day alone. In Portland and other New England villages the town bell was sounded at 11:00 A.M. to remind him to cease his labor and have a refreshing jolt. Employers recognized the need of spirits. An advertisement in the *New York Gazette* of December 4, 1769, offered a job to "An hostler that gets drunk no more than twelve times in a year." Provided he came well recommended, of course.

Early-day bluenoses in Georgia managed to get a Prohibition Act on the books in 1735, but the hills ran with hootch. South Carolina rum runners and other good neighbors made up any slack the local moonshiners couldn't fill. So Georgia's Dry law expired in 1742.

The enemies of the bottle took heart in 1785 from a pamphlet reporting on *An Inquiry into the Effect of Spirituous Liquors on the Human Mind and Body*. The author was a substantial citizen—Dr. Benjamin Rush, Surgeon-General of Washington's Continental Army—and his little essay was devastating. He found no food value (or any other value) in the hard stuff, no sir. The doctor said liquor would make a man a drunkard or something akin to an ass, a mad bull, a tiger, a hog, a he-goat—or maybe a killer. And he said it had other faults too.

The pamphlet gave such impetus to the earliest Dry movements that Dr. Rush came to be known as "The Father of Temperance Reform," and even to-

day the bluenoses look back on him with much longing. He was the first to furnish medical testimony against the Demon Rum. Before then (and even afterwards) some doctors prescribed a snort for practically anything that ailed a man.

"Get Away from those Swinging Doors!"

"A reformer is a guy who rides through a sewer in a glass-bottomed boat."
—JAMES J. WALKER

The first of the silver-tongued temperance orators was John Henry Willis Hawkins, a reformed alcoholic. Hawkins developed a taste for spirits in the 1830's while apprenticed to a Baltimore hatter who dealt liquor rations to his workmen to keep them happy. This was a common practice among employers in those days.

The hatter said he reeled through fifteen years all but mad on rum but quit the habit cold one wintry day when his little daughter Hannah pleaded, "Papa, please don't send me for whiskey today." Hawkins said the evil of his ways penetrated the alcoholic fog at that very moment and made him a Dry. The next year, 1841, he roamed far and wide out of Baltimore bespeaking the virtues of abstinence. He got 100,000 elbow-benders to sign no-drink pledges for the Washington Temperance Society while Hannah, bless her, achieved lasting fame as the heroine of a hair-raising true-life booklet called *Hannah Hawkins, or, The Reformed Drunkard's Daughter,* written by the Rev. John Marsh.

State Prohibition laws began to appear within ten years after John Hawkins demonstrated that the woods were full of men who could live without bottled stimulants. Maine blazed the trail in 1851 under the persistent hammering of Mayor Neal Dow of Portland, New England's leading Dry, and by 1855 that first Prohibition wave had taken in New Hampshire, Vermont, Delaware, Michigan, Indiana, Iowa, Minnesota, Nebraska, Connecticut, Rhode Island, Massachusetts and New York. The water wagon broke down along the way, however. In some states Prohibition was declared unconstitutional. In others the abolition fight and the Civil War put temperance in the

This prophetic Dry slogan—in electric lights, no less — was dedicated in a Baptist church in 1914.

discard. The movement then languished until the weaker sex breathed some fire into it.

"Mothers, to the Barricades!"

"Here sighs, plaints and voices of the deepest woe resounded through the starless sky. Strange languages, horrid cries, accents of grief and wrath, voices deep and hoarse, with hands clenched in despair, made a commotion which whirled forever through the air of everlasting gloom, even as sand when whirlwinds sweep the ground."

—DANTE, *The Inferno*

The way Ella A. Boole looked back on it in 1929 from her lofty pinnacle as president of the Women's Christian Temperance Union, the nineteenth century was a most dismal time. Indeed, she said Blue Monday wasn't so-called because the girls had to do the wash, but because the men were barely over their week-end binges and either didn't get to work or couldn't eke out a day's wages if they did get there.

And that was far from the worst of it.

"The poorhouses were filled with old men and old women, rendered penniless by drink," Dr. Boole said. "There were women who disgraced themselves and their families by getting drunk, for a drunken woman was always repulsive—then, as now. The saloon filled the brothel; the brothel filled the saloon." But salvation lay around the corner, in our time, as Dr. Boole reconstructed it in 1929 in her book, *Give Prohibition Its Chance*: "Women prayed for deliverance; they prayed in the home, they prayed in the midnight hours; they prayed with their hearts breaking, and their eyes filled with tears. And God hearkened to, and answered their prayers!"

God or no, a crusade did spring from the rum-and-blood-soaked soil as the nation licked its Civil War wounds. The Woman's Crusade of 1873, in Ella Boole's words, "swept across Ohio and the Middle West like a prairie fire of the pioneer days." It swept clear to New York, where Dr. Dioclesian Lewis organized it into the WCTU. Pretty soon embattled women were descending on drinking resorts, armed only with Bibles and boundless zeal, and shaming grogshop proprietors into pouring the Devil's Brew into the gut-

The speakeasy opened as fast as the doomed saloon closed. Federal raiders sometimes used axes—Carry Nation had to be content with a hatchet—to demolish the illegal oasis.

The carriage trade had its pick of the swanky drinking resorts set up in New York's old brownstone dwellings. All you needed to get in was the password (or you could say you were friends of Mr. Sweeney) and the price.

Any town, any city, any state—before Prohibition and after. Note the brass footrail and the spittoons.

ters; here and there the cobblestones ran with the stuff.

One battalion of Crusaders tilted with a resolute defender of the drinker's faith in Cincinnati. This saloon-keeper set up a cannon in the town square as the bone-dry delegates advanced for a prayer meeting. Mrs. Annie Wittenmyer, the WCTU's first national president, set down for the record the flaming defiance of a Mrs. Leavitt, otherwise unidentified, who glared into the mouth of the artillery

Dr. Benjamin Rush's anti-liquor pamphlets stirred bone-dry hearts way back in Revolutionary times.

Frances E. Willard stood for temperance and brotherhood, too. And keep away from tobacco while you're at it.

piece and spoke as follows: "If God wants to take me, as He took Elijah, to heaven in a chariot of fire, I would just as soon go that way as any other."

Nobody touched off the cannon, so the issue was not joined.

Frances E. Willard, Mrs. Wittenmyer's successor, was a strong believer in words as well as deeds in the battle on the Poisoned Cup. She made at least one speech a day for ten years. In 1883 she managed to carry the Dry word into each and every one of the states and territories, preaching not just temperance, but also brotherhood —*sober* brotherhood—between capital and labor. She composed this pledge for her youth battalion, the Loyal Temperance Union:

*I promise not to buy, sell or give
Alcoholic liquors while I live;
From all tobacco I'll abstain
And never take God's name in vain.*

For youngsters reluctant to save America by joining the Crusade, Mrs. Willard had this item prepared:

*Young man, why will you not sign
  the pledge,
And stand with the true and brave?*

*How dare you lean over the
  dangerous ledge,
Above the inebriate's grave?*

The children also had a slogan built just for them:
*Tremble, King Alcohol, we shall
  grow up!*

King Alcohol proceeded to tremble almost at once. A second Prohibition wave, in the eighties, produced some scattered state Dry laws, though they didn't hold up.

The WCTU registered a small victory in 1892 when it turned back at the very gates a delegation of alleged maidens sent here to introduce the English barmaid system to our backward nation. In 1903, the WCTU got liquor banished from the Senate and House restaurants in Washington, and at Ellis Island, too. The women long had fretted about the drinking capacities of new arrivals. Dr. Boole, also known as "The Iron Chancellor of Prohibition," talked about the need for special diligence by the Drys "among foreigners who brought with them from other lands drinking habits and customs and needed to know the curse of the liquor

"I cannot tell a lie—I did it with my little hatchet!" Carry Nation is at the left, in person. The cartoon is the Utica (N.Y.) *Globe's* impression of her one-woman crusade against the Demon Rum. Mrs. Nation, once married to an alcoholic, staged a violent campaign against the saloons that were flouting the Kansas Prohibition law in 1900. Then, middle-aged, she came out of the West and turned her Dry fury on the legal drinking emporia in the Wet states. The police often had to confiscate the Nation hatchet when her vast evangelical zeal got the best of her. She passed from the scene in 1911 but suffered considerable embarrassment in the grave four years later: the revenuers turned up a tremendous moonshine layout on her father's old farm in Missouri.

traffic." That theme would be sounded all through the Prohibition Decade. The Drys invariably found a way, however slick, to air the view that it was the immigrant much more than the 100 per cent American who needed the splendid discipline of Prohibition.

The WCTU found itself a formidable ally in 1913. The Anti-Saloon League—"an army of the Lord to wipe out the curse of drink"—had been content for twenty years to fight for nothing more ambitious than local option laws and statewide Prohibition. Now the WCTU and the League elected to make common cause in a nationwide assault on Mr. Barleycorn, and the joining of the sexes paid off fast. The Drys, controlling huge blocs of votes, loaded Capitol Hill with men pledged to their cause (at least in principle). Now they could push the third Prohibition wave, which had started in 1907 and made much headway in Southern legislatures, onto the national scene. They made quick work of it: the Eighteenth Amendment rode through Congress with healthy majorities in December, 1917. It would take another year for the necessary thirty-six states to ratify, still another for Rep. Andrew J. Volstead of Minnesota to put across his enforcement act, and still another for the billion dollar liquor, wine and beer industries to walk the Dry plank. And what would happen after that? This is the way Herbert Asbury looked back on it in his history of Prohibition, *The Great Illusion*:

"The American people . . . had expected to be greeted, when the great day came, by a covey of angels bearing gifts of peace, happiness, prosperity and salvation, which they had been assured would be theirs when the rum demon had been scotched. Instead they were met by a horde of bootleggers, moonshiners, rum-runners, hijackers, gangsters, racketeers, trigger men, venal judges, corrupt police, crooked politicians, and speakeasy operators, all bearing the twin symbols of the Eighteenth Amendment — the Tommy gun and the poisoned cup."

That was Prohibition, American style.

Ella Boole was plump, gray and motherly, and for fifty years she fought not only drink, but even dancing, theater-going and card playing.

Rep. Andrew J. Volstead pushed the Prohibition enforcement statutes through Congress.

William E. (Pussyfoot) Johnson, one of the more colorful Dry heralds, was not above taking a drink himself when it would help convert a skeptic to the cause. As the nation got wetter and wetter in the twenties, he retired from the battle. "The devil often gets the best of it," he said.

Bishop James Cannon, Jr., acid-tongued voice of the Dry lobby, with entry to the White House itself, did as much as any man (or even woman) to put the Eighteenth Amendment across. But in 1928 it turned out that he had hoarded flour and other scarce foodstuffs during the war and had lately cleaned up a fortune in bucket-shop gambling operations in stocks. The Southern Methodist Church mercifully forgave the Bishop his errant ways but his influence as a moral leader took what you might call a dip.

THE RED RAIDS

Give me your tired, your poor,
Your huddled masses, yearning to breathe free,
The wretched refuse of your teeming shore.
Send these, the homeless, tempest tossed, to me;
I lift my lamp beside the golden door.

—From the *Emma Lazarus* poem
on the Statue of Liberty

The Mother of Exiles must have blinked her eyes in astonishment as the New Year dawned in 1920. Across the citadel of freedom the minions of Attorney General A. Mitchell Palmer were swooping down on the huddled masses. The Great Red Raid opened on January 1 with two hundred arrests and went into high gear the next day: two thousand were dragged into the net in thirty-three cities. In Hartford, Connecticut, a new device padded the catch: visitors who came to see the jailed "subversives" were arrested on the spot on the theory that they, too, must have some connection with Communists.

The raids were orderly. Palmer didn't like blackjacks and brass knuckles. He just told his men to take along "strings, tags and envelopes"—the better to wrap and classify such evidences of revolution as they encountered.

The raids were legal, too. Never mind the freedoms set forth in the First Amendment, nor the fact that nothing like this had happened in America since Thomas Jefferson's classic battle against the Sedition Law of 1798. The Espionage Act of 1917 and the much-tougher Sedition Act of 1918 made it a crime to say anything at all critical about the war effort or the Wilson Administration. And as if these rigid enactments were not adequate to preserve American institutions, a double-edged Alien Act barred the "golden door" to anyone the Secretary of Labor deemed a radical, no matter how thin the evidence.

The Red fever took a powerful hold on the people, and a handful of fanatics and bomb throwers helped it retain its grip. Palmer's own home was dynamited in 1919; the only casualty was the man who planted the explosive. A TNT bomb planted across the street from the House of Morgan in New York on September 16, 1920, killed thirty people in a noonday Wall Street crowd and injured hundreds. Wobblies (members of the Independent Workers of the World) defending the IWW hall at Centralia, Washington, killed four American Legionnaires on Armistice Day of 1919 and paid dearly—one IWW man mutilated and hanged, and seven others jailed for twenty to forty years. An alert New York post-office clerk, Charles Caplan, intercepted sixteen paper-wrapped bombs addressed to J. P. Morgan, John D. Rockefeller, Justice Oliver Wendell Holmes, and to Palmer and other government officials.

There were larger factors in the anti-Red hysteria, too. The Bolshevik uprising in Russia terrified the super-patriots here, as did the revolutionary outbreaks in Germany and Hungary. The bitterness stored up during the war also helped fan the flames; the leftover hatred of the Hun, who quit too soon, was turned on Miss Liberty's "tempest tossed." The alien, butt of the Prohibition lobby's worst gibes for years, now became the target for the whole country's pent-up fury and frustration. Even Johnny, marched home a hero, got in on the kill. He cracked a few skulls breaking up Socialist meetings and let a haymaker fly in a sortie against the IWW now and then: they

Mounted police patrol road to struck mill outside of Pittsburgh.

The two men in the felt hats are Big Bill Haywood and Carlo Tresca (right). Haywood led the Wobblies (IWW) and the Western Federation of Miners in the early labor wars out West. Caught up in the postwar Red Raids and charged with a variety of offenses against the Republic, he drew a twenty-year sentence from Judge Kenesaw Mountain Landis, but jumped bail and fled to Russia. The Workers' Fatherland rubbed the wrong way against Haywood's flaming independent spirit and he died there an unhappy man. Tresca, an Anarchist during the twenties, emerged later as one of the more relentless anti-Fascist fighters. He was shot to death on lower Fifth Avenue in New York in 1943 and the crime was never solved. The deed was widely credited to agents of Mussolini.

A. Mitchell Palmer: Woodrow Wilson's Attorney General, he wielded a big stick during the early twenties.

Alexander Berkman, Anarchist leader, addressing a Union Square rally in New York.

John Reed came out of Harvard a romantic rebel—fiercely dedicated to the world's underdogs. He became a newspaperman and got thrown into jail for exhibiting strong partisan tendencies on labor's side while covering the great Paterson Textile Strike in 1913. As a war correspondent, he was in Petrograd during the October Revolution and put that violent drama into his famous book, *Ten Days That Shook the World.* Back in the States writing for the left-wing magazine, *The Masses,* he turned his crisply eloquent prose against the excesses the government was committing under the Espionage and Sedition Acts. Then, drawn by what was being advertised as the dictatorship of the proletariat, he went to Moscow. He died of typhus in 1921 and was buried in the Kremlin.

William J. Burns' detective agency frequently functioned as the strong right arm of management during the labor-capital struggles. When the Red Raids came he emerged as an authority on subversion, estimated that America harbored 422,000 native Communists.

Wielding clubs, police disperse a crowd during a Philadelphia strike. In the mood of the time, pickets generally were regarded as dangerous radicals and were treated accordingly.

were all Bolshies and bomb throwers and he wanted none of them loose in his United States. He was for filling the jails with them, and Palmer, Woodrow Wilson's "Fighting Quaker," was just the man to do it. Political prisoners went behind bars by the thousands. Newspapers (but not big ones) were shut down for publishing items deemed to be critical of the regime. College professors were expelled for teaching "subversive" doctrines out of the standard textbooks they had always used.

It was the time of the Big Whisper, duplicated thirty years later in the Security Follies of the 1950's. Palmer dwelt on the sanctity of the American farm and home and on American bank deposits and American Liberty Bonds and enlisted 200,000 worried citizens as volunteers in his crusade to send the Bolsheviks "back where they came from." Even the soldier home from the wars might find his own neighbor cocking an ear his way to see if he had smuggled any dangerous ideas back from France. The Palmer Doom Book simply bulged with suspect names. For the ex-doughboy who cared about such things, there must have been a terrible irony in all this; the "just democracy" preached by Woodrow Wilson lay in the dust right here at home in the wake of the war to make the world safe for democracy.

Eugene V. Debs, the labor leader and Socialist chieftain, languished in the Federal Penitentiary at Atlanta for opposing the war. Victor L. Berger, the Wisconsin Socialist, beat a twenty-year espionage sentence and got elected to Congress three times but the House wouldn't let him take his seat.

Striking telephone operators pose while doing picket duty in Boston in 1919.

Courtroom scene in Montesano, Washington, where eleven IWWs were on trial for the fatal Armistice Day battle at Centralia.

In New York, Speaker Thaddeus C. Sweet of the State Assembly directed the sergeant-at-arms to present the five newly-elected Socialist members before the bar to be expelled because their party had been deemed "a disloyal organization composed exclusively of perpetual traitors."

To such historians as Charles and Mary Beard the Palmer raids and their offshoots across the land "recalled the fateful days of 1692 in Salem." And for what? The Beards in *The Rise of American Civilization,* published in 1930, drew two conclusions from the Red Raids:

"The first is that not a single first-class German spy or revolutionary workingman was caught and convicted of an overt act designed to give direct aid and comfort to the enemy. The second is that, as in England during the period of the French revolution, the occasion of the war which called for patriotic duties was seized by emotional conservatives as an opportunity to blacken the character of persons whose opinions they feared and hated."

There were some revolutionary nests in operation, of course. The scattered bombings indicated as much. But the five thousand arrests in the Palmer crusade turned up a total of three pistols from among the hordes supposedly plotting to overthrow the government by violence. It makes one wonder, looking back, what all the fuss was about. Perhaps these two headlines from the *Boston Herald* summed up the time:

BOLSHEVIST PLAN FOR CONQUEST OF AMERICA!

BRIDE THINKS REDS KIDNAPED MISSING GROOM

It turned out that neither story needed to be taken seriously.

Scene outside the Sub-Treasury Building after the Wall Street bomb disaster. The fatalities were high—30 dead and hundreds injured—but the crime was never solved.

A mounted militiaman on duty in the Boston police walkout of 1919 stops to chat with one of the few non-striking patrolmen.

"One Born Every Minute..."

*"Capitalist production is not merely the production of commodities;
it is essentially the production of surplus value."*

—Karl Marx, *Das Kapital*

This is what Charles Ponzi looked like when he sat for a police portrait on an early conviction for forgery.

This is Ponzi the financial wizard, posing in his Boston office at the height of his fame as a Get-Rich-Quick merchant.

In Boston in 1920 a man came up with something that was more fun than mah-jongg or petting in parked cars. The man was Charles Ponzi ("The Great Ponzi," he liked to say) and he had the next best thing to a machine that made dollar bills. He shipped your money across the oceans and had his agents buy International Postal Union reply coupons at depressed rates and then sell them in other alien outposts which paid a higher exchange. Presto. Profit. Big profit. Ponzi offered investors $2.50 for every $1.00 they put in, payable in ninety days, if not sooner.

You didn't believe it? The first financial writer who suggested that no juggling of foreign currencies could produce any such staggering windfalls drew a fast libel suit from Ponzi. The dandy little forty-two-year-old "financier" — ex-sixteen-dollar-a-week clerk, bankrupt in a small fruit-and-vegetable business, failure as a forger and a mess as a smuggler of aliens—sued for $5,000,000 in damages.

Maybe financial writers and other educated skeptics doubted Ponzi; the people didn't. Everybody, it seemed, rushed to get in on the killing. Money poured in out of bank accounts, stockings, piggy banks and cookie jars. It came from 40,000 people, mostly little people, and it added up to $15,000,000 —all within eight months. There was more to be had, but Ponzi couldn't handle the traffic, not even with branch offices scattered over New England, New York and New Jersey. The get-rich-quick legion massed at the State House in Boston one day when the flashy money-trader was called in to answer some questions about his operations. This exchange on the steps illustrated his popularity:

VOICE IN CROWD: You're the greatest Italian of them all.

PONZI: No, no. Columbus and Marconi. Columbus discovered America. Marconi discovered the wireless.

VOICE: Yes, but you discovered money!

The fact is, Ponzi hadn't. He was simply pocketing the cash as it poured into his hole-in-the-wall office on

School Street. He paid old notes with the proceeds of new notes and hoped the day of judgment would never come. His overseas agents, if any, had little to do but sip wine in the sidewalk cafés. He bought and redeemed no more than thirty dollars in foreign postal coupons during his one-man gold rush.

Ponzi was at his crest, hauling in $200,000 a day from the new-found gamblers among New England's charwomen, elevator boys, peddlers, truck drivers, short-order cooks, shopkeepers, pensioners and what-have-you, when the *Boston Post* dug up his criminal record. The dismal revelation that the Wizard of School Street had done time in Montreal for forgery and in Atlanta for smuggling aliens blew the lid off. Ponzi's paper empire collapsed, dragging with it the Hanover Trust Co., the bank he had favored with his trade. His books, such as they were, showed a deficit of $5,000,000. The federal government exacted from Ponzi a four-year term in the bastille at Plymouth for using the mails to defraud. Then the Commonwealth of Massachusetts got him sentenced to seven to nine years as a "common and notorious thief." While out on bail pending appeal, Ponzi dropped down to Florida to repair his purse in the real estate

Day of reckoning: the run on Ponzi's bank.

boom there, but instead picked up another year's sentence for fraud. Massachusetts finally collected him and put him away until 1934. "I bear no grudges," he said as he emerged from prison, "and I hope the world forgives me."

The world may have; the government didn't. Ponzi was deported to Italy, made his way to South America and died in a charity ward in Rio de Janeiro in 1949. Whatever happened to the cascading fortunes that passed through his sticky fingers in the first year of the Lawless Decade, no one ever said.

This photo records one of the rare untroubled moments in the sad and curious romance of Ziegfeld star Fannie Brice and the dapper but dishonest Nicky Arnstein, shown on the beach with their son and daughter. While the Boston authorities were poking into the affairs of The Great Ponzi, New York had its hands full with a band of thieves that was acquiring substantial wealth with guns, rather than con games. This ring relieved Wall Street messengers of $5,000,000 in negotiable stocks and bonds and turned the lion's share over to Arnstein for conversion into the coin of the realm. Arnstein was a fugitive in the case for two years, while the broken-hearted Miss Brice played out her comedy routines on Broadway and sang the magnificent "My Man," a ballad of undying loyalty. Arnstein surrendered in spectacular fashion, falling into the rear of a police parade in a shiny blue Cadillac landaulet and driving down Fifth Avenue in considerable splendor before proceeding to the District Attorney's office. He served a mere twenty months in the bond haul and the law never got its hands on much of the loot. Miss Brice, never lucky in love, stood by her elegant jailbird while he was in Leavenworth but divorced him in 1927 when it appeared that he was beyond reform, socially or domestically.

MEANWHILE—BACK IN NEW YORK

"Say it ain't true, Joe"

"Men do not confide themselves to boys, or coxcombs, or pedants, but to their peers . . ."
—RALPH WALDO EMERSON

Shoeless Joe Jackson

Eddie Collins, the classy second baseman of the Chicago White Sox, was simply awash with confidence before the 1919 World Series against the Cincinnati Reds.

"There never was a better ball club," Collins told the baseball journalists. "We've got everything . . . Cicotte and Williams are two of the greatest pitchers that ever planted a foot on the slab, and our gang can field and hit. We ought to win."

But the lowly National League entry, 4-1 underdogs, upset the White Sox.

It was no fault of Eddie Collins'; he played his heart out. But Eddie Cicotte and Claude Williams pitched as if they had lost their stuff and some of the other Sox played like sandlot kids.

The truth didn't come out until the 1920 season.

Only one game behind first-place Cleveland, with three left to play, Charles A. Comiskey, the "Old Roman" who owned Chicago, suddenly suspended Cicotte, Williams, left fielder Shoeless Joe Jackson, center fielder Oscar (Happy) Felsch, shortstop Charles (Swede) Risberg, pinch hitter Fred McMullin and third baseman George (Buck) Weaver. Comiskey had no alternative. Cicotte, Jackson, Williams and Felsch, under relentless investigation, had just admitted to a Chicago Grand Jury that the 1919 World Series had been dumped to Cincinnati in a betting coup. The jury indicted the seven stars and first baseman Arnold

(Chick) Gandil, who had left the team during the winter in a salary row. The true bill stunned the nation. Baseball, then as now the great American game and also a multimillion-dollar business, tottered on the brink.

One of the classics in the annals of American sport came out of the scandal. The day the ball players emerged from the Grand Jury room a crowd of small boys awaited them. One of them went up to Shoeless Joe.

"It ain't true, is it, Joe?"

"Yes, boys," the stylish outfielder replied, "I'm afraid it is."

Four baseball writers testified to the exchange, but down through the years the men who fix up our folklore, whoever they are, touched up the small boy's plaintive sentence until it came out, "Say it ain't true, Joe" or, at other times, "Say it ain't so, Joe." You never see it written any more the way the boy said it.

The eight tarnished athletes stood trial in the summer of 1921. The jurors

Buck Weaver

Eddie Cicotte

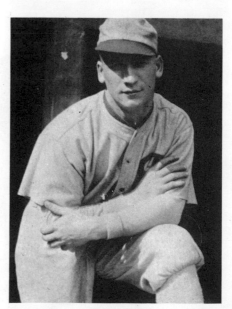

Happy Felsch

not only acquitted Cicotte & Co. but carried some of the defendants out of the courtroom on their shoulders. The baseball magnates did not share the jurors' high glee, however. The man they made the $50,000-a-year czar of the game, Judge Kenesaw Mountain Landis, never let Comiskey's wayward stars don uniforms again.

The Sellout

"Don't you know that wheel is crooked?"
"Sure, but it's the only wheel in town . . ."
—OLD OPTIMIST'S LAMENT

Eddie Cicotte and Chick Gandil suffered a touch of the Get-Rich-Quick virus and came to New York after the White Sox won the 1919 American League Pennant. In the wicked city they talked to Sleepy Bill Burns, a former pitcher for the Sox and the Reds, and Billy Maharg, an ex-fighter, about blowing the World Series for a bundle of money. The next day Burns approached Arnold Rothstein at Jamaica Racetrack and let it be known that the fine American institution known as the October Classic could be fixed for a mere $100,000. Some say the famous gambler, moneylender to the under-world, put up the necessary currency to nail down the fix. Others say the shrewd Rothstein saw no need to contribute to the delinquency of the Chicago stars and simply elected to bet on Cincinnati and pocket some sure winnings without running into high overhead costs in the ugly form of bribe money.

Rothstein, in any case, never had to stand trial in the scandal. The man accused of masterminding it was Abe Attell. The ex-featherweight champion—Damon Runyon called him one of the five great fighters of all time—happened to be a betting man. And he also happened to be in the Hotel Sinton in Cincinnati when the big money on the Reds was floating around.

William J. Fallon, the celebrated criminal lawyer (and one of Rothstein's favorites when he wasn't drinking), helped Attell beat the case. Gene Fowler's biography of Fallon, *The Great Mouthpiece*, furnished a vivid account of the behind-the-scenes betting operations as the White Sox—thereafter the Black Sox—floundered through the series.

Attell & Co. wagered heavily on Cincinnati the first day. They won. A representative of the corrupt

Charles A. Comiskey

players called to collect the promised moneys—$20,000 being the fee stipulated for each losing game.

The caller saw stacks of bills on every horizontal plane of the suite, excepting the ceiling. Dresser tops, tables, and chair seats held yellow-backs. Mr. Attell, buried in currency, was perspiring with prosperity and behaving like a farm hand making love in a haystack.

"Don't bother me now," Mr. Attell said. "I need all the dough I can lay my hands on. We got to make a cleanup tomorrow. It takes capital, partner. It takes capital."

The collector teetered on his heels. "The players are gettin' worried."

"What *they* got to worry about?"

"They was promised twenty grand at the end of each game."

"You go back," said the former champion, "and tell them not to burn."

"But when does the ghost walk?"

"Tomorrow."

Cicotte lost that first game. His invincible "shine ball" failed him so badly that the Reds knocked him out in the fourth with a five-run outburst which even included a triple by the opposing pitcher, Dutch Reuther. But Cicotte didn't lose for nothing: he admitted that he found $10,000 in small bills under his pillow that night. If Attell didn't put it there, the windfall may have been dealt off by another set

Swede Risberg

William J. Fallon defended Abe Attell.

Arnold Rothstein: Did the New York gambler have anything to do with the Black Sox scandal? He always denied it . . .

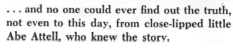

. . . and no one could ever find out the truth, not even to this day, from close-lipped little Abe Attell, who knew the story.

Judge Kenesaw Mountain Landis was called in to keep baseball free of impurities.

of the errant Sox's gambling partners to keep them in the proper frame of mind for missing easy grounders and fouling off fat pitches.

Fowler said Attell shelled out $10,000 after Chicago dropped the second game. But if he did the little fellow's $10,000 contribution went for naught. Chicago won the third game, presumably to teach the gamblers a lesson for being so penurious. Attell told the New York *World* the athletes got from $60,000 to $70,000 in the process of losing the series, 5 games to 3 (best 5 out of 9 won in those days). He would never holler cop on the workings of the fix but he did say that Rothstein made $60,000 betting with the smart money on the Reds. Rothstein insisted that he never made a dime on it, presumably because he was too suspicious to risk his money on dishonest baseball players.

The scandal could have killed baseball except for the iron hand and incorruptible mien of Judge Landis and the great brawn of George Herman Ruth. The Babe started breaking down ball-yard fences in earnest just when the fish-eyed paying customers needed that kind of distraction.

As for sports in general at the time, never mind the dastardly Black Sox. The Golden Age was at hand. The giant Ruth was not alone. There were others in the wings: Red Grange, Jack Dempsey, Gene Tunney, Walter Hagen, Gertrude Ederle, The Four Horsemen, Big Bill Tilden, Helen Wills, Bobby Jones . . . There would be no lack of headlines to divert the attention of the growing boy who asked Shoeless Joe Jackson that tear-stained question outside the halls of justice in Chicago.

WHO KILLED JOSEPH ELWELL?

Mr. Elwell

The ex-Mrs. Elwell

The Murder House

Once Joseph Elwell was a hardware sales-man, struggling along on sixty dollars a month and trifling commissions. Then, blessed with a phenomenal memory and a fine card sense, he took up bridge and whist. Pretty soon he was moving both among the high players and high society. His book, *Elwell on Bridge*, outstripped less stimulating works of non-fiction but he made his big money playing cards rather than writing about them. Indeed, the Elwell share-the-wealth program brought such rich rewards that he was able to branch out into Wall Street and the horse race marts. Beyond that, he acquired a string of two-legged fillies, causing Mrs. Helen Derby Elwell to leave his bed and board in a jealous tantrum.

As the dawn peeped into Manhattan's West Seventieth Street on June 11, 1920, somebody put a .45 calibre slug into Joe Elwell's handsome head while he was reading a letter in his study. The murder furnished the New York press with the first sex-and-sin mystery of the twenties. It had all the necessary ingredients: the stylish gambler's bachelor retreat yielded up a card file listing no less than fifty-three women, many of them boasting strong social affiliations alongside their purely feminine lures. The tabloids called this interesting roster a "love index." The slain playboy's effects also contained a nice selection of milady's silk underthings in assorted sizes, including a dainty monogrammed bed jacket with the initials strangely cut out. Another cache produced forty wigs and one pair of false teeth, revealing to a startled populace that the celebrated man-about-town had aged—but in much secrecy—beyond his forty-five summers.

The investigation turned up nothing more than a strong variety of women and girls—and even irate males—who appeared to have one reason or another to take a gun to Joe Elwell. In a word, there were too many suspects because, as one of the papers noted, "a persistent scarlet thread of passion shot through the warp and woof of Elwell's life fabric." The murder was never solved.

Marie Larsen, the Elwell housekeeper, hid a pink kimono while the doctors were attending to her employer but the girl who owned it proved she wasn't on the premises when the man was shot.

This is the cab—some were open in those days—that drove the bridge expert home from his Manhattan rounds to his rendezvous with sudden death.

Elly Hope Anderson was questioned in the case because she was in a party that encountered Elwell at the Ritz and at the New Amsterdam Roof (the *Midnight Frolic* was on the playbill) on his last night.

The Rise and Fall of Big Jim

"The higher the type of man, the greater the improbability that he will succeed."
—NIETZSCHE

Luigi Colosimo's boy Jim shined shoes on the Chicago streets to help his immigrant family eat. He sold papers. He ran errands for the smalltime hoodlums of the South Side slums. He stole. He carried water for a railroad section gang. He worked as a street cleaner. He got into ward politics and the rackets. He became the maestro of a brothel. He married Victoria Moresco, his childhood sweetheart, and made her a madam—in an Armour Avenue house, that is. As he prospered, he branched out into bootlegging (a pretty good trade even before Prohibition) and the saloon business.

By 1920, Big Jim Colosimo was a walking ad for the new American nobility. He was wearing diamonds—on his tiepin, his studs, his suspenders and belts, his watch fob, and even on his garters. And he had a respectability befitting his station in life. His restaurant at Wabash Avenue and Twenty-second Street, in the Red Light district, became a Chicago showplace. There in the late hours you might see the Great Caruso, or Luisa Tetrazzini, or Amelita Galli-Curci, or Flo Ziegfeld, or George M. Cohan, or Gentleman Jim Corbett, or John McCormack. Everybody knew about the splendid vino and Italian dishes at Colosimo's and everybody knew the genial proprietor, especially the opera people. Big Jim, who carried a cane and wore a Homburg, loved the opera with passionate devotion. He loved a fine voice. That could have been what killed the first of the Windy City's overlords of crime in the Lawless Decade.

A songbird named Dale Winter came into town one icy winter in search of a living. An Ohio girl, she had sung light opera in New York, San Francisco, and Australia. Now she was out of work. Somebody brought her to Colosimo's café. Big Jim liked the voice —and the flesh, too. He put Miss Winter on the night shift in his café, enrolled her in the Chicago Musical College with Caruso's help, and had her do part-time choir duty in the South Park Avenue Methodist Church to keep her vocal cords polished at all times. The church connection didn't last long. A straying elder saw Miss Winter in the gilded Colosimo dive and tattled. The pastor defended the girl but the songbird fled anyway.

In March, 1920, Big Jim shed his wife Victoria, the light of his life in poverty and in riches, in favor of Dale Winter. "This is the real thing," Colosimo told Johnny Torrio, who replied, "It's your funeral, Jim." The forty-nine-year-old gangster settled $50,000 on Mrs. Colosimo and married his beautiful young thrush. The oddly-matched pair spent a quick honeymoon at French Lick (Indiana) and repaired to the Colosimo mansion on Vernon Avenue. They had barely settled down for the long matrimonial pull when, on May 11, Big Jim excused himself to meet someone on "urgent business" before his restaurant opened. The business proved to be murder—and the victim was Colosimo.

There were numerous theories behind the slaying. The first had to do with the deceased's amours. It was said

Mr. Colosimo and Dale Winter.

that his casual discarding of Victoria Moresco had suggested to the underworld that no vestige of loyalty or dependability remained in the man, so everybody would be better off without him. It was also said that he had fallen out with Torrio, his very own lieutenant, and that Torrio himself had summoned him to his rendezvous with death. And it was said that the long arm of vengeance simply had caught up with the diamond-studded flesh peddler. Police had linked Big Jim to twelve murders in the years of his rise, including the violent departure of three Black Hand agents who once demanded that he present himself under a South Side bridge with a goodwill offering of $5,000. The shakedown crew expired under the bridge in the fire from two Tommy guns, one supposedly held by Colosimo himself.

Big Jim had the first of the gangland funeral extravaganzas of the twenties —a $50,000 affair that drew a good representation from the ranks of Chicago officialdom and its cultural life, along with the underworld nobility and its hangers-on. There were judges, policemen, aldermen, pimps, opera stars and actors, but little John Torrio shed the most noticeable tears. "We was like brothers," Torrio said as the ex-whitewing was lowered into the grave.

The estate was supposed to come to $2,000,000 but only $40,000 turned up for the records. The widow Dale spurned her share and instead relied on the golden tones that her late husband's *goombah*, Caruso, liked so much. She did a long run in *Irene* on Broadway and then married well and disappeared from the public prints.

The principal benefactor of Colosimo's greater wealth, which lay hidden in its vast potential, was the brainy Torrio. He picked up the scepter following his brief show of public mourning for the man who had brought him to Chicago to put him on the golden ladder. It was the eve of the Prohibition-time boom in the rackets. Torrio had an empire to build. And, like Colosimo before him, he sent to New York for a good right bower to keep him healthy, or at least bulletproof. He sent for Al Capone.

The early crystal sets entranced the old and young alike and came as a boon to the shut-ins.

"The Saxophones Begin at 7"

"What hath God wrought!"
—The first telegraph message,
Washington to Baltimore, 1844

It happened on November 2, 1920. The Westinghouse Electric & Manufacturing Company broadcast the election returns from a specially built penthouse on its highest plant building in Pittsburgh. Very few people had receiving sets then and not too many would need to be told, in any case, that Warren Harding had beaten the Democratic candidate for the Presidency, James M. Cox; it was a no-contest race. But that broadcast from station KDKA was a momentous thing just the same: it marked the birth of Radio.

From that day on a man wouldn't have to leave his home to be entertained, to hear about the remarkable virtues of soap or cigarettes or Ford cars, to chuckle over jokes and witty sayings, to enjoy live singing (short- or long-haired), to acquire a touch of spoken culture, to hear why he must vote for so-and-so if he really loved the U.S.A. or to pamper his soul with a sermon. Radio changed our way of life when it came squeaking and blaring into our living rooms.

You have to go back to Guglielmo Marconi to fix the blame. The Italian invented wireless telegraphy in 1901 and Reginald A. Fessenden, Sir John Ambrose Fleming, Dr. Lee de Forest and Edwin H. Armstrong took the succeeding steps to make it possible for voices to assail you out of the blue.

But never mind the pioneers: the man who shoved the intruder into your home was Dr. Frank Conrad, Westinghouse's chief engineer, and he was only trying to sell some Westinghouse products. It came about by chance.

Dr. Conrad that summer of 1920 had started to send out two-hour broadcasts to the nation's amateurs—"hams"—every Wednesday and Saturday from his garage in East Pittsburgh. He broadcast music and baseball scores and the hams—there were about 12,000—pleaded for more. Something else also occurred: the local store which was lending music to Dr. Conrad discovered that the records he played outsold all the others. This meant that

Dr. Frank Conrad, who started something.

Dr. Conrad's home broadcasting station, set up over his garage in East Pittsburgh.

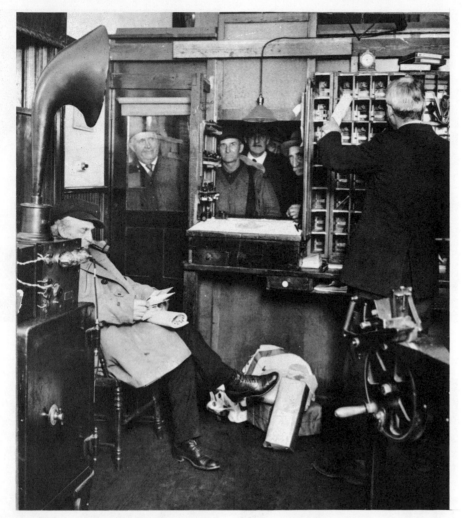

Few homes had receiving sets in radio's early days, so men often gathered in such public places as post-office stations to hear what the free air was producing.

Major J. Andrew White tunes a crystal set for Jack Dempsey in training camp before the Dempsey-Carpentier fight—the first one aired blow-by-blow. White did the broadcast.

Graham McNamee broadcasting the 1924 World Series in which the Washington Senators ("now pitching . . . Walter Johnson") beat the New York Giants.

even without commercials you could sell products over the air as well as through the printed page. In September, 1920, another local store advertised low-priced crystal receivers to pick up the homemade Conrad broadcasts—and the receivers sold well.

It took one giant step to go from there to KDKA and the first broadcast. Westinghouse happened to manufacture radio receiving equipment and here was a chance to set up a ready-made, captive market. The move must have caused some faces to turn red at the Marconi Wireless Telegraph Company, where an assistant traffic manager, David Sarnoff, had been talking about a radio "music box"—not just for hams but for everyone—since 1915. Sarnoff held that radio was something bigger than a hobby for hams trading idle chatter and casual information, but he couldn't get the Marconi company to take a chance on a broadcasting station.

Radio didn't just grow; it flew. There were 220 stations on the air eighteen months after KDKA took the plunge. People lined up for receiving sets—at $50 to $150 for the first of the more elaborate models—and 3,000,000 homes had them by 1922. Consoles were on the way, running into hundreds of dollars, and soon the test of a man's affluence would be whether his future included one of those fancy pieces of furniture as well as a Ford. Radio sets, parts, and accessories brought in $60,-000,000 in 1922, $136,000,000 in 1923, and $852,000,000 in 1929, when most people ran out of spending money. Radio reached into every third home in its first decade. The listening audience was put at 50,000,000 by 1925.

How could anyone resist? The million-dollar Dempsey-Carpentier fight came blow-by-blow into the home in 1921, courtesy of RCA . . . Floyd Gibbons spit out news at 217 words per minute . . . Grantland Rice broadcast the 1922 World Series between the Giants and Yankees . . . There were songs by the Cliquot Club Eskimos, the Ipana Troubadours, the A&P Gypsies, Vaughn de Leath . . . The Happiness Boys (Billy Jones and Ernie Hare) . . . The booming voice of William Jennings Bryan from the Democratic National Convention of 1924, calling Radio "a gift of Providence" (he liked to be heard) . . . There was the Connecticut Yankee with "The Maine Stein Song": Rudy Vallee, lead-

Vaughn de Leath

The Happiness Boys, Billy Jones and
Ernie Hare

Jessica Dragonnette

Smilin' Ed McConnell

Norman Brokenshire's velvety tones put him
in the first rank of radio announcers from the
very start.

Wendell Hall, one of the early singers, got
lots of mileage out of a number called "It
Ain't Gonna Rain No Mo'."

Little Jack Little

The Cliquot Club Eskimos

Ruth Etting

ing the parade of the crooners ... Amos 'n' Andy in 1929 (and still going as this is written) ... Milton Cross, Ted Husing and Norman Brokenshire ... Ed Wynn doing bits from *The Perfect Fool* ... Wake-up exercises at 6:45 A.M. ... Paul Whiteman drawing $5,000 for an hour of popular music ... Walter Winchell's gossip and news, machine-gun style ... Al Jolson, Harry Richman, Fred Allen, Jack Pearl (*"Vass you dere, Sharlie?"*), Joe Penner (*"Wanna buy a duck?"*), Jack Benny ... The Philharmonic from Carnegie Hall ... Red Godfrey, the Warbling Banjoist, later King Arthur of CBS ... Kate Smith ... The Goldbergs, with Molly Berg ... College football ... Market reports ... Your favorite congressman ... Herbert Hoover appealing for European relief (1921) ... Will Rogers impersonating Calvin Coolidge and drawing indignant letters ... Maurice Chevalier ... Willie and Eugene Howard ... Jolson saying Clara Bow slept "cater-cornered" and drawing complaints from listeners ... Walter Damrosch ... Your favorite pastor ...

What was the mixture? Was Radio spreading culture, or jazz and snappy sayings? Charles Merz looked and listened and found that ten bigger stations in a given week were devoting 28 hours to talks, 77 to serious music and 189 to syncopation. He found that ten bigger stations—such as WEAF and WJZ in New York; KDKA; WGN in Chicago—had 56 hours of talks, 42 hours of good music and 259 of the other kind. Merz had this to say in *The Great American Bandwagon* in 1928:

"The predominance which jazz enjoys is even more impressive than these figures show ... the usual procedure is to get the serious part of the program done with, fairly early in the day, so as to have the evening free for sheer enjoyment. It is during the daytime hours, when listeners-in are relatively scarce, that most of the talks on teeth, the discussions of the Dawes plan, the courses in French and the violin solos take the air—and during the evening hours, when millions of people are listening in, that the friendly jazz-bands blare ...

"This much seems sure: however marvelous the mechanics of the radio, however unlimited its future and however splendid its chance of becoming in due course of time a great national talking-machine from which an enraptured public will extract sheer disembodied knowledge, its chief function for the moment is more limited, more easily realized and much more entertaining.

"The saxophones begin at seven."

Merz, later Editor of *The New York Times*, a force for education and culture if there ever was one, took a dim view of all this.

"Into a nation that lives at top speed most of the day and comes home much too wide-awake to settle down, the radio brings a stimulus for tired nerves and something to distract us from the dull business of staying put at home. We tune in, and let it play while we wash the dishes, read the evening's news, or entertain a neighbor on the porch. We tune in—in a mighty rhythm to which millions of people are marking time, the pulse-beat of a nation. All over the country the trombones blare and the banjos whang and the clarinets pipe the rhythm. All over the country the same new tunes that will be generations old before the week is out are hammered home at the same vast audience from a hundred different places. Oom-pah-pah, oom-pah-pah, I got the blue-hoo-hoos, I got the blue-hoo-hoos, I got the oom-pah-pah, the oom-pah-pah ...

"This is our counterpart of the drum the black man beats when the night is dark and the jungle lonely. Tom-tom."

That was Radio in the Lawless Decade. It's better in our time. It got older and wiser. It found you could sell soaps and lotions with all kinds of programs — from Rock 'n' Roll to Dr. I. Q. to Clifton Fadiman.

There are some familiar faces in this early All-Star band. The saxophonist on the left is Glen Gray. Andre Kostelanetz is at the piano and Rudy Vallee on the bass. Ozzie Nelson is third from the end, and the last man is Ted Lewis ("Is Everybody Happy?")

Let's Dance

". . . the flapper came in to the tune of 'I'll Say She Does'—and frequently she did . . ."
—LLOYD MORRIS, *Incredible New York*

The Methodist Episcopal Book of Discipline had always contained a ban on dancing and games of chance and on such kindred diversions of "questionable moral tendency" as theaters, race tracks and circuses. The penalty for straying from these hard concepts was expulsion from the church.

In March, 1920, the New Jersey Methodist Episcopal Conference voted to raise the moral curtain and eliminate its most drastic provisos. The Book of Discipline was revised, after much soul-searching, to permit "such diversions" as "thoughtful and instructed conscience" might dictate. All good Methodists were enjoined to shun like the plague anything not fit to be used in "the name of the Lord Jesus, of course." But the old order was going —and going fast—just the same.

America had been dancing something besides the minuet since 1912, when such "wild" items as the fox trot and the tango began to sizzle the boards. And by 1920, as Frederick Lewis Allen noted in *The Big Change*:

". . . The war had pulled millions of young men and women out of their accustomed environments, and given them a taste of freedom under circumstances in which it didn't seem to matter very much what Mrs. Grundy said. With many of these young people the postwar reaction took a special form: it was easy for them to think of themselves as a generation who had been condemned to go through the hell of war because of the mistakes of their elders, whose admonitions on any subject must therefore be suspect. At any rate, by 1920 the rebellion against puritanism and stuffiness was widely visible, and it gained in impetus as the decade progressed."

Lloyd Morris, in *Incredible New York*, had this to say about the girls:

"If your concern was paternal, the flapper was a problem. Otherwise, she was a pleasure. Jauntily feather-footed in her unfastened galoshes, her flesh-colored stockings rolled below the knee and her skirt barely touching it,

slender and boyish, the flapper came in to the tune of 'I'll Say She Does'— and frequently she did. Her seniors soon caught on. The women you saw shopping on Fifth Avenue didn't suggest matrimony and motherhood. Their shingled hair was peroxided or hen-

naed, their eyebrows were plucked and penciled, their eyelids were beaded, their cheeks and lips were piquantly rouged. Except for their silver-fox or mink jackets, the sum of what they wore could almost have been packed into their handbags. Smart leather-

Paul Whiteman was the King of Jazz in the Lawless Decade and hung grimly on down through the years, surviving the music world's countless detours. Even such wild excursions as Rock 'n' Roll, in our time, failed to dislodge the big bandmaster. Nothing, of course, ever could dim the eminence associated with Whiteman's name as the man who introduced George Gershwin's "Rhapsody in Blue." The concert which launched that American jazz classic at New York's Aeolian Hall on February 12, 1924, entailed a $7,000 deficit, even with an SRO sign hung out. Whiteman paid the losses out of his own pocket—and never had occasion to regret it.

Rudy Vallee—Hubert Prior Vallee when he came out of Yale—was the first of the crooners. His soft nasal tones, rounded with the help of a megaphone, chained women to their radios in droves and caused the frail singer to be embraced as the nation's "Vagabond Lover." The romantic description came from the song of the same name, as sung by the college-bred troubadour. Vallee also put "The Maine Stein Song" on the map and was still singing it in guest appearances on television a quarter of a century later. Between radio, vaudeville, night clubs and movies— the crooner garnered many millions. He also made a reputation for holding on to same.

There are some notable musical personalities in this picture. Paul Whiteman is the man with the violin, Vincent Lopez is at the piano, and band fans will recognize several others.

This is Duke Ellington, below is Fats Waller and on the next page is Louis (Satchmo) Armstrong. All three played important roles in the long fight to smash down racial barriers put in the way of Negro musicians and entertainers.

Fats Waller

George M. Cohan, the song-and-dance man, formed a successful producing partnership with Sam H. Harris (right) on Broadway.

Victor Herbert, Irving Berlin, John Philip Sousa—three diverse talents, three lasting names in music.

Two of the brightest talents of the twenties, shining on unto eternity: George Gershwin and Jerome Kern.

B. A. Rolfe conducts a string ensemble broadcasting over NBC.

Meyer Davis and one of his orchestras. In time, he built a sort of monopoly as the Number One conductor for High Society's soirées.

Louis Armstrong

Fred and Adele Astaire were popular favorites but the sister-and-brother dance act broke up when Adele married Lord Charles Cavendish of the British nobility and quit the stage.

On twinkling toes, Marilyn Miller was the rage of the musical comedy stage.

goods shops were advertising the novelty of an 'overnight case.' It seemed a primary requisite for women who, in the current phrase, were bent on 'leading their own lives.' . . . Sex appeared to be a ubiquitous commodity, as accessible as chewing gum. Amateur competition drove the streetwalkers indoors, except around Times Square."

Maybe so, but across the river in New Jersey the city of Paterson barred "shadow" dancers and "shimmies" in public places. And the Women's War Economy League stood four-square not just against liquor but against jewels or other ornaments deemed useless and also against cigarettes, fancy clothes and parties in the homes.

On the literary front, if you could call it that, Bernarr Macfadden's *True Story* magazine sold well by holding aloft flaming torches to warn the girls against the perils of the time. Some sample stories:

THE DIAMOND BRACELET SHE THOUGHT HER HUSBAND DIDN'T KNOW BUT—

THE RISE OF LIZ O' THE LANE THE LIFE STORY OF A GIRL WHO WOULDN'T STAY DOWN SHE WANTED TO BE CLEAN

BLACK EYED SUSAN'S STORY KEEP TO THE RIGHT, THE RIGHT WILL KEEP TO YOU, HER MOTTO

WHEN MARY CHANGED HER MIND SHE FOUND OTHER GIRLS MIGHT BE SOMETIMES RIGHT AFTER ALL

In the case of married girls, the Macfadden journal conceded that a change of mind might conceivably be in order now and then. A true-to-life document in the Christmas issue of 1920 carried this cheerful title:

WHY I'M GLAD I LEFT MY HUSBAND

Irene and Vernon Castle, performing before World War I, did much to launch the ballroom dancing craze which made huge strides in the twenties. Castle wasn't around to see the popular dance come of age. He flew a fighter plane for England during the war and came through it alive, only to die on a training flight in Texas after the United States went in.

Mrs. Castle is credited with starting the bobbed-hair style. The story is that some of her hair was burned accidentally and she had to cut it short. On her it looked good, and she pioneered an enduring fashion.

John Held, Jr., titled this cartoon "THE DANCE-MAD YOUNGER SET" by way of making the point that petting really took precedence over terpsichore in those days.

The bathing beauties on the screen got away with swimming suits that were considered dreadfully scanty even for the Torrid Twenties. In real life, some girls got arrested for showing up at the beach looking like Mack Sennett girls; the lower photo was made outside a public beach in Chicago. It is noteworthy that police were so engaged in the Windy City at a moment when the gangsters were running wild and drawing nothing more than perfunctory attention from the law.

COMPARATIVE ANATOMY

In this cartoon by Boardman Robinson the elderly lady is represented as observing of the flappers that "It isn't only their clothes—they're built different."

ZOOLOGY

John Held, Jr. drew the classic portraits of the flapper and Joe College. His cartoons, appearing in *College Humor*, in the old *Life* and in many other periodicals and books did much to establish the types and to make "flapper" and "Joe College" part of the language. The cartoons above appeared in a layout in the old *Life*, marking the start of a new school year.

Alice White as the typical flapper. See a variation on the theme on the next page.

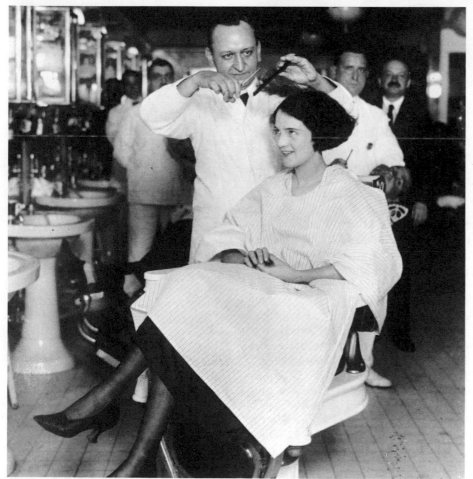

This one, from a movie, illustrates the Flaming Youth theme, a step beyond the flapper idea.

If you didn't have your hair bobbed you were an old-fashioned girl.

Alice White, shown here in flapper costume, played Dorothy in the early Paramount version of Anita Loos' *Gentlemen Prefer Blondes*. This photo can be classified as a mild forerunner of the "cheesecake" art the New York ship news photographers ultimately turned into a never-tiring specialty.

IT HAPPENED IN 1920...

New York closed out the war, fourteen months after the Armistice, with a parade for the last six hundred AEF troops to come home . . . The Cook County Jail in Chicago made two hundred prisoners view the hanging of a desperado so that they would learn to behave themselves . . . A "Rum Rebellion" in Michigan was put down without bloodshed . . . For the first time in five months, President Wilson was well enough to go for an automobile ride . . . The House decided that Prohibition was enforceable and voted $1,500,-000 to enforce it . . . The Senate again voted down Mr. Wilson's Treaty of Versailles . . . A movement to wear overalls to bring down high clothing prices spread over the nation from the South . . . Cornelius Vanderbilt, Jr., and Rachel Littleton were married and the bride counted a million dollars' worth of gifts . . . A Dartmouth College boy killed another student in an argument over whiskey . . . The Prohibition Party nominated William Jennings Bryan for President . . . Ray Chapman, Cleveland shortstop, was killed by a pitched ball . . . A man in the Polo Grounds dropped dead from excitement as Babe Ruth hit his forty-third homer of the season.

John D. Rockefeller gave $63,763,357 to charity and brought his total benefactions to $475,000,000 . . . President-elect Harding went fishing to relax himself for the labors ahead . . . Georges Carpentier knocked out Battling Levinsky . . . Jack Dempsey stood trial as a draft evader and beat it . . . John and Lionel Barrymore appeared on Broadway together in *The Jest* and then John did his first Shakespearean role, in *Richard III* . . . Chaplin made *The Kid* with Jackie Coogan . . . Eugene O'Neill's *Beyond the Horizon* won the Pulitzer Prize for drama . . . The

H. L. Mencken

Man O'War burned up the turf.

Poor White and Edith Wharton's *The Age of Innocence*. In non-fiction, John Maynard Keynes' *The Economic Consequences of the Peace* was near the top of the list, but H. G. Wells' *The Outline of History* would sell very strongly right through 1924 . . .

* * *

H. L. Mencken didn't like all the back-slapping in the business community. "The first Rotarian," said the Sage

Hatfield-McCoy feud in Kentucky produced several deaths . . . Man O'War ran a mile and a quarter in 2:03 for a purse of $75,000 and a gold cup . . . Mrs. Harding and Mrs. Wilson had tea at the White House . . . Franklin Delano Roosevelt ran for Vice-President against Calvin Coolidge and went down in the Harding landslide . . . H. S. Truman was a civilian again . . . Henry Ford established the *Dearborn Independent*, America's leading anti-Semitic journal . . . The best-sellers in fiction were Zane Grey's *The Man of the Forest* and Peter B. Kyne's *Kindred of the Dust*, but there were some other books moving too: Sinclair Lewis' *Main Street*, F. Scott Fitzgerald's *This Side of Paradise*, Sherwood Anderson's

Family outing—Ku Klux Klan style.

Harry Truman in World War I.

F. Scott Fitzgerald

George White

Sinclair Lewis

Chaplin and Jackie Coogan in *The Kid*

Sacco (right) and Vanzetti

of Baltimore, "was the first man to call John the Baptist Jack" . . . George White paid George Gershwin fifty dollars a week to write tunes for the *Scandals of 1920* . . . Babe Ruth, Jack Dempsey and Georges Carpentier went before the Hollywood cameras. The pay was high, the product low . . . The Ku Klux Klan came back—with a large distaste for Negroes, Catholics, Jews, and the foreigners in the big cities . . . A jury in Hammond, Indiana, acquitted a man who killed an alien for saying "To hell with the United States."

In Massachusetts, there was an incident that would reverberate around the world for seven years and write a sorry chapter into our history. Nicola Sacco and Bartolomeo Vanzetti were charged with shooting down two guards during a payroll holdup in Braintree. The nation paid no attention. Sacco and Vanzetti were just two more Anarchists hauled into the net—for an alleged murder rather than a political misdeed. It was not a time to get excited when two foreigners got thrown into jail.

Mr. Harding

Q. Mr. Daugherty, you don't really think Harding has a chance, do you?
A. Well, boys, I'll tell ya what I think. The convention will be deadlocked. After the other candidates have failed, we'll get together in some hotel room, oh, about 2:11 in the morning, and some 15 men, bleary-eyed with lack of sleep, will sit down around a big table. When that time comes Senator Harding will be selected.
—MEET THE PRESS, 1920

"Gee, What A President He'd Make!"

Mr. Daugherty

That's what Harry M. Daugherty said the day he laid eyes on Warren Gamaliel Harding. He didn't know the man. He just liked what he saw. Harding was tall and handsome and the soul of the American middle ground, standing there beside the hotel bootblack in rustic Marion, Ohio. By God, he *looked* like a President! Daugherty knew it— and this was twenty years before the man got to the White House. Daugherty knew it and he would wait; you don't run into a ready-made, built-in President every day, no sir.

The lawyer Daugherty was high in Republican state politics and going higher (and wider and handsomer). Harding published the *Marion Star* and enjoyed much contentment despite a loveless marriage to rich Florence King. The confident Daugherty introduced himself as Harding yielded his seat on the shoeshine stand. Then he proceeded to take his man slowly and surely up the ladder—from the Ohio Senate in 1900 to lieutenant governor in 1904 to a bid for governor in 1910 to the United States Senate in 1915. In Washington, the Roman idol from Ohio voted the party line, yea or nay, and stirred up absolutely nothing on his own. He made the papers so infrequently that his beautiful face almost always escaped public recognition—a decidedly handy item in his case, as later events would show.

The absence of a meaningful record made Harding quite attractive as the Republican National Convention of 1920 assembled in Chicago. The Grand Old Party needed nothing more than an upright American who couldn't be

1921

pilloried for past deeds or misdeeds. "Any good Republican can defeat any good Democrat," said Pennsylvania Boss Boies Penrose, and it figured. The people had returned Mr. Wilson to power under the slogan "He kept us out of war" but were hip-deep in it three months later, and now had the postwar miseries — strikes, towering prices, depression, high rents, and "Bolshevik" plots. It was time for a change.

Harding, who was happy enough in the club known as the United States Senate, had to be talked into setting up headquarters at Chicago. But Daugherty knew what he was doing. He expected General Leonard Wood and Frank O. Lowden, the front-runners, to knock themselves out. He put Harding in as Ohio's favorite son and waited for the lightning to strike. Sure enough, when the balloting deadlocked, the Republican elders collected in the Blackstone's Room 401—the

Colonel George B. M. Harvey was one of the kingmakers in the smoke-filled room at Chicago in 1920. Senator Boies Penrose (right), the powerful Republican boss from Pennsyl- vania, was widely credited with engineering the Harding nomination, but he was quite ill at home when that hand was being dealt to the party and the people.

smoke-filled room of legend—and agreed that Harding would do fine.

Colonel George B. M. Harvey, an apostate Democrat who had shifted with the postwar tide, was delegated to put the one big question to the prospective nominee: "We think you should tell us, on your conscience and before God, whether there is anything that might be brought up against you that would embarrass the party, any impediment that might disqualify you or make you inexpedient, either as candidate or as President."

The question stunned the dignified, gray-haired paragon from the Buckeye State. There was an agonized pause. Could he think it over, please? Colonel Harvey directed the big fellow to another room. Harding came back ten minutes later and said no, there was nothing that might disqualify him from the nation's highest honor . . . no impediment.

The bosses' choice sent the delegates home hung over with joy. They had a sure winner. As Senator Frank Brandegee of Connecticut said, "Harding is no world-beater but he is the best of the second-raters." (The very same Senator turned up in the Poker Cabinet later.) Mrs. Harding, called Flossie in Ohio and "The Duchess" along the Potomac, was hardly elated. "I can see but one word written above his head if they

make him President," she said, "and that word is Tragedy." The woman was right; he would not live through his term and scandal would stalk his grave. Harding himself couldn't quite harness the lightning. "I feel like a man who goes in with a pair of eights and comes out with aces full," he said. He was worried.

The election ran according to forecast. Harding's 16,000,000 votes nearly doubled James M. Cox's and he carried thirty-seven states—without benefit of a real campaign. The Republican pin-up boy confined himself largely to his own front porch and stood—or sat— more or less squarely on his classic Boston utterance of May, 1920: "America's present need is not heroics, but healing; not nostrums but normalcy; not revolution but restoration . . . not surgery but serenity." The one unserene note in the campaign—an allegation that the Hardings had Negro blood tracing back to a mysterious West Indian in the family—evaporated under examination.

Harding took office in March, 1921, with many misgivings. He really didn't feel equal to the job. "Talk to God about me every day by name," he besought a friendly bishop, "and ask Him somehow to give me strength for my great task."

He took the same theme to the peo-

ple. "It will help," he said, "if we have a revival of religion . . I don't think any government can be just if it does not have somehow a contact with Omnipotent God." He tried to keep his own contact with The Man Upstairs through the Psalms of David, the Four Gospels and Solomon.

The Bible didn't help.

Harding got some respectable names into his Cabinet—Andrew Mellon in the Treasury, Charles Evans Hughes as Secretary of State, Herbert Hoover in Commerce, John W. Weeks in War, Will Hays in the Post Office, Henry C. Wallace in Agriculture—but his government was full of leaks. Harry Daugherty was his Attorney General and Albert M. Fall was his Secretary of Interior and the place crawled with slick operators, boodle boys and bag men. The Ohio Gang and its recruit legion was in the White House woodwork from the start.

The tolerant Harding may not have known it—no one ever accused him of being a big brain—but he must have suspected it. "My God," he told William Allen White, "this is a hell of a job. I have no trouble with my enemies. I can take care of them all right. But my damn friends, White, they're the ones that keep me walking the floor nights."

That wasn't the whole truth. The President didn't walk the floor much, but rather stayed up late sweating over a hot card table with the strangest assortment of highbinders that ever passed through the White House portals.

The Poker Cabinet included some hands whose aces-in-the-hole were to disgrace Harding in the grave. Colonel Charles R. Forbes would do time behind bars for frauds running into the millions when the Veterans Bureau was under his charge. Albert M. Fall and Harry F. Sinclair would go to jail in the Teapot Dome scandal. Harry Daugherty would barely beat a prison term and his mysterious right-hand man, Jess Smith, would commit suicide. Indeed, the two poker pals fated to come out the cleanest would be the whacky millionaire, Ned McLean, and the White House bootlegger, Mort Mortimer. No one ever accused them of dispensing anything but fun, frolic and spirits.

Alice Roosevelt Longworth, longtime arbiter of what was right and wrong in Washington's social life, took

James M. Cox, Harding's badly-defeated opponent, shown with Woodrow Wilson.

President Harding and his Cabinet—the President at the head, Vice-President Calvin Coolidge at the foot of the table. At the President's right: Charles Evans Hughes, John W. Weeks, Will Hays, Albert M. Fall, Herbert Hoover. At the President's left: Andrew W. Mellon, Harry M. Daugherty, Edwin Denby, Henry C. Wallace, James J. Davis.

A close-up view of Harry M. Daugherty.

a dim view of the goings-on in the White House study under the Bible-spouter from Ohio. Mrs. Longworth put it this way in her memoir, *Crowded Hours,* in 1933:

"Though violation of the Eighteenth Amendment was a matter of course in Washington, it was rather shocking to see the way Harding disregarded the Constitution he was sworn to uphold. Though nothing to drink was served downstairs, there were always cocktails in the upstairs hall outside the President's room . . . While the big official receptions were going on, I don't think the people had any idea what was taking place in the rooms above. One evening . . . a friend of the Hardings asked me if I would like to go up to the study. I had heard rumors and was curious to see for myself what truth was in them. No rumor could have exceeded the reality; the study was filled with cronies . . . the air heavy with tobacco smoke, trays with bottles containing every imaginable brand of whiskey stood about, cards and poker chips ready at hand—a general atmosphere of waistcoat unbuttoned, feet on the desk and the spittoon alongside."

Mrs. Longworth observed acidly that between the White House of Coolidge and Harding "the atmosphere was as different as a New England front parlor from a back room in a speakeasy." But when Harding went out into the hinterlands to "bloviate" (a word he coined along with "normalcy"), he dealt sternly with illicit drinking. His bloviations often included impassioned demands for a rigid enforcement of Prohibition. He pulled no punches. He was for a Dry America, bone-dry, all the way.

Except, of course, on the first floor of the stately mansion on Pennsylvania Avenue, or the "Little Green House" on H Street where the Ohio Gang liked to horse around, or in the locker room at the golf club, or on the Presidential special . . . Or in the dim and lonely love nests where that pretty blond child, Nan Britton, waited in the backstreet of Warren Harding's life . . . Nan Britton, mistress of a President, mother of his daughter, would tell that story to the world in 1927 . . .

Albert M. Fall and E. L. Doheny.

THE MILLION DOLLAR GATE

Jack Dempsey

"Of course we will fight him again. We will fight anybody."

—JACK KEARNS, *after Firpo fight*

Nat Fleischer, an authority on the heavyweights, said the young hobo had the punch of Sullivan, the speed of Corbett, the cunning of Johnson and the strength of Jeffries. He said the boy had "a neck like a bull, a granite jaw and fists like iron." He was talking about Jack Dempsey.

William Harrison Dempsey, Irish with a dash of Cherokee on his Mormon mother's side, came out of the West like a cavalry regiment. As a five-dollar-a-day mucker in the copper mines, and a lumberjack and dance hall bouncer, he got into fights all the time —and won them all. He pocketed $2.50 for his first professional bout, knocking out an oversized blacksmith in Montrose, California, in 1915. Before Gentleman Gene Tunney retired him twelve years later he had drawn $10,000,000 past the turnstiles—$4,000,000 went to the penny-poor boy from Manassa, Colorado — and he had taken boxing out of the smelly wayside arena into the big-city ball park. He made boxing respectable—and also a gold mine.

Dempsey came up fast. He beat everyone in sight. In 1918, he knocked out Fred Fulton and Battling Levinsky and he was ready for a shot at Jess Willard's title. He got it on July 4, 1919, in Toledo. The Pottawatomie Giant towered five inches over the twenty-three-year-old upstart, outweighing him by 58 pounds and had a 5½-inch advantage in reach. But Willard was over the hill. Dempsey floored him seven times in the first round, heard Referee Ollie Pecord count him out and left the ring on the arm of a radiantly happy manager—Jack (Doc) Kearns had bet $10,000 to $100,000 on a first round KO. But the fight wasn't over. In the roar of 19,000 voices, the referee had counted Willard out *after* the

bell. Dempsey, called back, slashed away at the gallant champion for two more rounds. Then the bloody, hulking bruiser sank onto his stool — jaw broken, right eye closing, cheekbone split, two teeth gone — and murmured through swollen lips to his seconds, "I guess I'm beaten." He couldn't come out for the fourth, and an ex-hobo, lately under attack for not fighting in the war, was heavyweight champion of the world and the Million Dollar Gate was at hand.

Dempsey said he'd be a fighting champion, but he defended his title only five times in seven years: against Georges Carpentier in 1921, Elizar Rioux in 1922, Tommy Gibbons and Luis Firpo in 1923, and Gene Tunney in 1926.

The Carpentier fight, an afternoon waltz at Boyles' Thirty Acres in Jersey City, extracted $1,626,580 from 91,000 fans. It was hailed as the Battle of the Century, but that fit the gate better than the fisticuffs. Carpentier was only a fair light-heavyweight and didn't belong in the ring with Dempsey. Tex Rickard had him train in secrecy lest his shortcomings attract undue notice in the papers. And before the fight the promoter dropped into the champion's dressing room. "Listen, Jack," he said, "the best people in the world are here today and this is just the beginning. Don't knock down the show. Don't kill the sonuvabitch."

Rickard's view of the beautiful challenger happened to be less bearish than that of George Bernard Shaw, who called him "the greatest boxer in the world" and made him a 50-1 favorite against Dempsey on the strength of his victory over Joe Beckett, the English champion.

The band played "The Marseillaise" and then Dempsey cut up the soldier

of France with short hooks to show him that the Yanks were in charge. Carpentier landed with a right in the second and some of the boxing journalists hailed it as a "staggering" blow, but H. L. Mencken, sitting among all the perfumed ladies at ringside, counted twenty-five hard punches by Dempsey in one thirty-second exchange after he had supposedly been hurt. Mencken said any notion that Carpentier had damaged Dempsey in any way was "apocryphal, bogus, hollow and null, imbecile, devoid of substance."

Heywood Broun offered a suitable explanation. "It was impossible for us to root for Dempsey," Broun said in the *New York Tribune*. "He was too methodical and too efficient. It would have been like giving three long cheers for the guillotine as Sydney Carton went to meet it where it waited."

The third round was very bad for Carpentier and the end came in the fourth. Dempsey put the gallant Frenchman down for nine with a right to the jaw and finished him with a left

Jess Willard, the massive champion Dempsey deposed, stands for a portrait.

Willard down in the ring at Toledo in 1919 as the heavyweight title was changing hands. The referee is wearing a cap to protect his head from the broiling July sun. Also note the broad empty spaces in the stands—boxing didn't move up into the big money until after this fight.

A policeman escorts promoter Tex Rickard (left) and Jack Dempsey out of New York's Flatiron Building after a weigh-in.

In Hollywood to make a quickie called *Daredevil Jack*, the champion shows an illegal pointer to Douglas Fairbanks.

Harry Wills, a fine heavyweight, never won a shot at Dempsey, much as he deserved it. Wills got the run-around for years, evidently because the so-called better minds in government and boxing (A) didn't want a mixed title bout while postwar racial tensions were high and (B) didn't want a Negro champion.

The wartime shipyard photo that figured in the slacker outcry against Dempsey. The champion happened to be wearing patent leather shoes while supposedly toiling away in the defense effort. It was a publicity stunt—surely the most ill-advised of the time. In court, Dempsey beat draft evasion charges.

The Million Dollar Gate—Dempsey vs. Carpentier, Jersey City, July 2, 1921.

Estelle Taylor and Dempsey, married in his prime, appeared on the stage together.

Jack Kearns—cash on the barrel head.

Hannah Williams, the singer, succeeded Miss Taylor and bore Dempsey's two daughters.

Dempsey is shown here with other Coast Guard officers.

when he got weakly to his feet. "Carpentier," Mencken wrote, "decayed like an autumn leaf in Vallambrosia. Gently and pathetically he fluttered down." It took four or five minutes to revive the courageous idol of France and the crowd hailed him even as he lay bleeding on the canvas. Joe Humphreys had introduced Dempsey as a man "on whom every red-blooded American pins his hopes this day," but the red-blooded Americans in the wooden soup bowl liked the Frenchman better because he had served in his country's army.

Dempsey always paid dearly—too dearly, perhaps—for staying out of the war, even after a San Francisco jury took but ten minutes to clear him of evading the draft. White-haired Cecilia Dempsey testified that her boy was the sole support of a big brood come on hard times in '17 and '18 and Dempsey produced evidence that the Secretary of the Navy asked him to stay in civilian clothes because he could do more good for the war effort that way; he did raise $200,000 for the Red Cross. What hurt Dempsey, down through the years, was a wartime publicity photo showing him supposedly at toil in a Philadelphia shipyard. He had overalls on but his feet were shod in patent leather. The picture, naturally, was published very widely. Nat Fleischer, Dempsey's biographer, always defended him on the slacker charge but conceded in later years that many boxers had ducked World War I.

"They considered a bayonet a poor substitute for the padded glove and were loath to risk life and limb in a quarrel without gate receipts," Fleischer said.

Dempsey had to wait a quarter of a century to redeem himself. He went into World War II as a Coast Guard commander. He was detailed to the physical training program but went into Tarawa under fire—an "old man" in his late forties among a bunch of boys.

As champion, Dempsey had two other items operating against him. He took to emoting on the stage—for $7,000 a week or more—or living high with his wife, Estelle Taylor, when he should have been in the ring. And he was under ceaseless attack for not giving Harry Wills a crack at the title. Wills—the Dark Menace, the Brown Panther, or the Dark Prince: take your pick—stalked Dempsey all the time.

Why didn't they fight? It would be wrong to imagine that the champion was afraid of the bruising ex-stevedore from New Orleans. Dempsey was a great fighter. He had golden fists and a good jaw and the killer instinct. Yet he was in the position of ducking Wills, the most formidable contender, year after year.

"I would have fought Wills," Dempsey recently told Al Buck, the *New York Post's* boxing writer, "but nobody would promote it. When Wills challenged, Tex Rickard would have nothing to do with the fight. He said he had instructions from Washington not to promote a mixed bout for the heavyweight title."

That may well have been the answer. Jack Johnson held the title from 1910 to 1915 and his easy victories over a string of white contenders in that period were unpopular—among whites, that is. Moreover, come the twenties, the hooded gentry was riding high, bed sheets flapping in the wind, and lynching fever was strong in the South. The bigger brains in Washington quite likely did fear that a mixed heavyweight fight would fan the flames.

The New York Boxing Commission, well this side of the Mason-Dixon line and with the eloquent James A. Farley to carry the gloves, plumped hard for the fight. Dempsey always believed this stemmed more from a large respect for the Negro vote in New York than anything else. "The thing became a political issue," Dempsey told Buck. It remains a shame, first for its sinister racial implications and second for the blot it left on Dempsey's record. He was surely one of the truly great heavyweights—the Firpo and Tunney fights would settle that—and he put much of the glitter into the Golden Age of Sports.

"KNOWN BUT TO GOD..."

They sent Sergeant Edward F. Younger into a musty little chapel in the French village of Chalons-sur-Marne on October 24, 1921, with a bouquet of flowers. In the dimly-lit room lay the remains of four American soldiers counted among the unidentified dead in the World War. The sergeant stood in the middle of the chapel for a moment and then walked resolutely to one of the coffins and laid the bouquet on it. That plain pine box was put on a battleship and sent to Washington to be entombed in Arlington National Cemetery, in the shadow of the peaceful Potomac Hills, with this inscription:

"Here rests in honored glory an American soldier, known but to God."

President Harding put the Medal of Honor and the Distinguished Service Cross on the casket. A British dignitary added the Victoria Cross. Decorations from France, Italy, Rumania, Czechoslovakia and Poland followed. Then a general from Belgium emotionally ripped from his tunic the Medal of Valor pinned on him by his own King and put that down where the American soldier's chest should have been.

Kirke L. Simpson of the Associated Press won the Pulitzer Prize for his story that day. It started this way, and it belongs in any history of the time:

"Under the wide and starry skies of his own homeland, America's unknown dead from France sleeps tonight, a soldier home from the wars.

"Alone he lies in the narrow cell of white stone that guards his body; but his soul has entered into the spirit that is America.

"Wherever liberty is held close to men's hearts, the honor and the glory and the pledge of high endeavor poured out over this nameless one of fame will be told and sung by Americans of all time . . ."

There would be other unknown soldiers, all lower case. Looking back, that's where the pathos lay.

"A FREE SOUL IN JAIL..."

"I will never consent to the pardon of this man ..."
—WOODROW WILSON

SOCIALIST PARTY
FOR PRESIDENT

EUGENE VICTOR DEBS

No. 9653—Candidate for the Presidency.

Eugene Victor Debs, a grocer's son from Terre Haute, Indiana, worked on the railroad in his teens. He became secretary-treasurer of the Brotherhood of Locomotive Firemen a few years later but quit to set up the American Railway Union because he believed in industrial organization. A strike he staged in 1894 stopped James J. Hill from cutting pay on the Great Northern. Then he crippled freight and passenger service west of Chicago by calling out his men in sympathy with Pullman Company strikers who were fighting a 25 per cent pay cut. Federal troops clashed with the strikers and thirty men died. Debs did time in jail for violating an injunction George Pullman got out against the union. The strike was crushed and the union folded and Gene Debs turned to Socialism. He was the party's candidate for President in 1912 and drew 901,872 votes against 6,286,214 for Woodrow Wilson, 4,216,020 for Theodore Roosevelt (Progressive) and 3,483,922 for William Howard Taft.

When the war came, Debs opposed it fiercely. The Espionage Act, meant to silence all anti-war sentiment, merely added fire to his spirit. He mounted one public rostrum after another and denounced "the master class" and "the junkers of Wall Street." He defied arrest. "I would a thousand times rather be a free soul in jail than to be a sycophant and coward in the streets," he said. The government obliged him in 1918. He was tried in Cleveland in September. When Prosecutor F. B. Kavanagh completed his case, Debs congratulated him on his oratory and said he had no defense witness but would address the jury himself. He started by saying that he would not deny any of the utterances ascribed to him and held subversive by Uncle Sam.

"I admit being opposed to the present form of government," Debs told the twelve good men and true (and very solid citizens, too); "I admit being opposed to the present social system. I am doing what little I can to do away with the rule of the great body of people by a relatively small class and establish in this country industrial and social democracy ... You may hasten the change; you may retard it; you can do no more to prevent it than you can prevent the coming of the sunrise on the morrow."

The verdict, of course, was guilty.

Debs addressed the court before sentence:

"Your Honor, years ago I recognized my kinship with all living things and I made up my mind that I was not one bit better than the meanest of the earth. I said then, I say now, that while there is a lower class I am in it; while there is a criminal element, I am of it; while there is a soul in prison, I am not free."

The sentence was ten years.

When Debs came out of the courtroom a little girl rushed up to him with

62

Debs poses in the Atlanta Penitentiary yard
with the young daughter of a supporter.

vindicate the cause of civilization, this man Debs stood behind the lines, sniping, attacking and denouncing them . . . I know there will be a great deal of denunciation of me for refusing this pardon. They will say I am cold-blooded and indifferent, but it will make no impression on me. This man was a traitor to his country and he will never be pardoned during my Administration."

This was two years and two months after the war. The old fighter in Atlanta, who wouldn't ask for clemency himself, turned an equally bitter tongue on the President.

"It is he, not I, who needs a pardon," said No. 9653. "If I had it in my power I would give him the pardon which would set him free. Woodrow Wilson is an exile from the hearts of his people . . . the most pathetic figure in the world. No man in public life in Amer-

some American Beauty roses—his favorite flower—and then fainted. Debs carried the child into an anteroom and stayed until she was revived.

The war ended before the Supreme Court acted on the Socialist leader's appeal — Justice Oliver Wendell Holmes wrote the opinion denying Debs' contention that the Espionage Act violated freedom of speech—and Debs went behind bars. He couldn't be put in a federal lockup, because Attorney General Palmer had them chock full of enemies of the Republic. Debs went into the State Penitentiary at Moundsville, West Virginia. It was April, 1919.

"I enter the prison doors a flaming revolutionist—my head erect, my spirit untamed, and my soul unconquerable,"

the eloquent Socialist said at the gates. He was 64, tall, gaunt, worn by struggle, tortured by lumbago. In June they found room for him in the federal prison at Atlanta and there in May, 1920, a delegation called on Number 9653 to notify him that his party again had nominated him for President. He got permission to issue one bulletin a week to the news services by way of a campaign; he drew 915,302 votes, proportionately way below his 1912 totals.

Palmer urged Woodrow Wilson to free Debs on Lincoln's Birthday in 1921. "Denied," Wilson wrote over the recommendation. "I will never consent to the pardon of this man," the ailing President told his secretary, Joseph P. Tumulty. "While the flower of American youth was pouring out its blood to

Eugene Victor Debs.

Debs and his wife, Kate.

President Wilson and Attorney General Palmer, who led the Red raids.

ican history ever retired so thoroughly discredited, so scathingly rebuked, so overwhelmingly impeached and repudiated as Woodrow Wilson."

Warren Harding committed himself to a general amnesty during the campaign and soon after he took office, in March, Attorney General Daugherty sent for Debs, presumably to see for himself whether American institutions might perish if the sick old man were let out. Debs came alone from Atlanta,

on his honor, and impressed Daugherty as a safe risk. Come Christmas Day, Harding let him out, asking him to drop by the White House. "I have heard so damned much about you, Mr. Debs," the President said, "that I am very glad to meet you personally."

Then Debs went home to Terre Haute to his wife, Kate.

He lingered five years. He died on October 20, 1926. Someone recalled a line from the speech in Canton, Ohio,

that led to his indictment: " . . . they cannot put the Socialist movement in jail."

It turned out to be true.

The Congress of the United States down through the years has passed all kinds of laws but it never passed one that succeeded in putting an idea—good or bad—behind bars. That was Gene Debs' point.

IT HAPPENED IN 1921 . . .

There was good news from Washington one fine day in 1921. Attorney General Palmer looked into the Prohibition law and found that it would be legal for doctors to prescribe beer as medicine. He told the tortured masses — awful sick hangovers came from needle beer—that his ruling would mean "beer at soda fountains but never again over the saloon bar."

Colonel Jacob Ruppert, the New York brewery-and-baseball potentate, hailed Palmer's discovery. "It is the most cheerful news in a business way I have heard in five years," the colonel said. "We are ready on a moment's notice to put out real beer." Alas, real beer did not drive chocolate soda and two-cents-plain from the drugstore spigots. The Internal Revenue people said no, that wasn't what the Attorney General meant. They said he meant beer could be dispensed as medicine in 2½-gallon quantities—under prescription, of course. Even so, the Drys got very angry. The others called the family doctor: they had developed aches and pains that could be relieved only by Colonel Ruppert's foaming medicine.

* * *

The ex-Kaiser charged that in losing the big fight Germany betrayed itself, its God, and the Kaiser . . . Colonel George Harvey, the plain-spoken American Ambassador to the Court of St. James, told the Pilgrim Society of London that we had gone into the war "solely to save the United States of America, and most reluctantly and laggardly at that . . . We were afraid not to fight . . . So we came along toward the end and helped you and your Allies shorten the war." This candid and cynical view of history drew a storm of protests, even on our side of the ocean.

* * *

A woman in Danville, Illinois, fighting a lone battle against the Lawless Decade, went on a forty-eight day fast

The open-handed Urban (Mr. Zero) Ledoux, who ran soup kitchens for the needy, dreamed up his own solution for the bad times. With the best of intentions, he undertook to auction jobless men to prospective employers but the New York police didn't like the idea and hauled him off to jail.

Frank Bacon—he had the SRO sign out on Broadway for a record run in *Lightnin'*.

to make her husband quit smoking and swearing and join the church . . . The Chicago Crime Commission counted 10,000 crooks in the Windy City and said they were stealing $12,000,000 a year . . . In New York, the Committee of Fourteen reported that Baghdad-on-the-Hudson had less *open* crime than any other big city in the whole wide world . . . President Harding ordered himself a bed five feet wide and eight feet long . . . In Dallas, Texas, playful Klansmen flogged a Negro and branded "KKK" on his forehead . . . Boston banned *The Birth of a Nation* . . . On Long Island, Laura Bromwell, 23, looped the loop 199 times in a plane and got killed trying to better that record . . . Race riots in Tulsa, Oklahoma, killed twenty-one Negroes and nine whites.

* * *

Babe Ruth drew a $100 fine and a day in jail for speeding but the judge let him out at 4:00 P.M. so that he could get into that day's game at the Polo Grounds in the sixth inning. December was more expensive for the Home Run King. Judge Landis took away his World Series check, $3,362.26, for playing a post-season barnstorming tour without permission . . . Princeton students voted Woodrow Wilson the University's foremost graduate . . . Caruso died in Naples . . . Champ Clark died . . . Iowa legalized the sale of cigarettes to adults . . . U.S. Steel cut wages back to the prewar 30 cents an hour . . . 100,000 New Yorkers gathered to wave farewells to Frank Bacon and his *Lightnin'* company as the show took to the road . . . Edith Rockefeller divorced Harold F. McCormick and gave him $3,000,000 for title to their homes on Lake Shore Drive, Chicago, and plush Lake Forest, Illinois.

The people were being told that psychoanalysis, something new, could cure what ailed them . . . The White

The Michigan Supreme Court ruled that the husband was master in the home . . . The President got himself a radio . . . Men began to speak of women as "skirts" . . . In Braintree, Massachusetts, Judge Thayer denied Sacco and Vanzetti a new trial . . . Atlantic City staged the first Miss America Bathing Beauty contest.

＊ ＊ ＊

On Bedloe's Island, New York, the Mother of Exiles witnessed a contrary scene: the exiles were going the other

Evelyn Nesbit wanted to die.

House ordered the Klan looked into . . . Evelyn Nesbit Thaw, star of the 1907 courtroom drama in which Harry K. Thaw escaped the electric chair in the slaying of Stanford White, took twenty grains of morphine but survived . . .

Fritz Lieber and Betty Blythe in a friendly moment from William Fox's *Queen of Sheba*. For those who fret over the acres of flesh bared by modern screen sirens, this point may be illuminating: As the Queen of Sheba, the well-rounded Miss Blythe appeared in some scenes wrapped in nothing much more than a few veils and a mess of imitation pearls.

Rudolph Valentino starred in *The Four Horsemen of the Apocalypse*.

way. The Army Transport *Buford*—also called the Soviet Ark—sailed down the harbor on December 21 with 249 Russians "going back where they came from." It was part of the government drive to cleanse the states of such unwholesome guests as Anarchists, and the *Buford* carried Emma Goldman and Alexander Berkman, among others. There would be many more to follow, though hardly of such imposing repute . . . Henry Ford ordered the *Dearborn Independent*, his own paper, to stop printing all those articles blaming everything on the international Jews.

＊ ＊ ＊

Main Street topped the fiction bestsellers . . . Zane Grey stayed up there with *The Mysterious Rider* . . . John Dos Passos' *Three Soldiers* came out, and F. Scott Fitzgerald's *The Beautiful and the Damned* . . . Edith M. Hull's

The youthful John Barrymore, from the portrait by John Singer Sargent.

The Sheik, which would make Rudolph Valentino the decade's Great Lover, did very well and *Life* complained that "any writer who can pull off the same old sex stuff, and make it look new, is always rewarded by the public" . . . Douglas Fairbanks starred in *The Three Musketeers* . . . Mary Pickford played *Little Lord Fauntleroy* . . . On Broadway, W. C. Fields starred in the *Ziegfeld Follies*, John Barrymore in *Clair de Lune*, Helen Hayes in *Golden Days*, Walter Hampden in *Macbeth*, Hedda Hopper in *Six Cylinder Love*, Lenore Ulric in *Kiki*, Katharine Cornell in *A Bill of Divorcement*, Otis Skinner and his daughter Cornelia in *Blood and Sand*, George Arliss in *The Green Goddess*, Julia Marlowe in *Twelfth Night*, Lynn Fontanne in *Dulcy*, Ina Claire in *Bluebeard's Eighth Wife* and E. H. Sothern in *The Taming of the Shrew*. It was a good year on the Great White Way.

Lenore Ulric as the vamp in *Frozen Justice*, one of the more perishable films of the time.

SAND, SEX AND SCANDAL

"We feel a great injustice has been done him."
—The jury that freed Fatty Arbuckle

Fatty Arbuckle: Before the Fall.

On April 12, 1922, Roscoe Conklin Arbuckle emerged from a courtroom in San Francisco and told the press:

"This is the most solemn moment of my life. My innocence of the hideous charge preferred against me has been proved . . . I am truly grateful to my fellow men and women. My life has been devoted to the production of clean pictures for the happiness of children. I shall try to enlarge my field of usefulness so that my art shall have a wider service."

That's not the way it worked out. Hollywood never let Fatty Arbuckle enlarge his "field of usefulness" until it was too late. The round comedian's $5,000-a-week career had actually ended September 5, 1921, during a boozy midday party in a suite in the St. Francis Hotel in the City of Hills. It ended when Arbuckle, conveniently attired in pajamas and bathrobe, adjourned to a bedroom with pretty Virginia Rappe, a delicately beautiful actress and model. The girl, twenty-three, died four days later and the State of California blamed it on "external pressure" applied by

Arbuckle during a sexual adventure. The cause of death was peritonitis. following a rupture of the bladder.

The incident rocked Hollywood on its foundations. The silent screen counted 35,000,000 cash customers per week at the time and the studios weren't relying solely on the kiss-proof, drink-proof, sin-proof Western hero to lure them in. Not at all. The fan who wanted something more current than the 200 per cent purity of William S. Hart or Jack Holt had a nice selection of bedroom epics to draw from. Hollywood somehow knew about the revolution in manners and morals right from the start; the cameras had been grinding away on the New Freedom since the war's end. The once-delicate subject of divorce and the general loosening of the marital ties had produced some spicy items on celluloid and with

1922

them some caustic comments from women in clubs and men in cloth. Fighting the twin threats of boycott and censorship, the studios dreaded a live scandal even more than their own juicy canned product. The irony was that the big blow finally came not from one of the screen's more frolicsome lover boys but from a hefty comic whose work on film was the soul of good clean Mack Sennett slapstick.

Fatty Arbuckle's ordeal—and Hollywood's—lasted through not one but three trials. The star contended all along that Miss Rappe's torn bladder grew out of a chronic condition aggravated by bootleg hootch, but the State's witnesses furnished more lurid headlines. Miss Bambina Maud Delmont testified that there were screams from the hotel room and then Arbuckle emerged, giggling, with the girl's hat tilted on the side of his head, and said, "Go in and get her dressed and take her back to the Palace. She makes too much noise." The witness said she found Miss Rappe all but naked, moaning "I'm dying, I'm dying," and writhing in pain. Alice Blake, a showgirl, supported Miss Delmont's story. "We tried to dress her," she said, "but found her clothing torn to shreds. Her shirtwaist, underclothes and even her stockings were ripped and torn so that one could hardly recognize what garments they were."

The women thought Miss Rappe might have had too much to drink, among other things, so they put her into a cold bath. Doctors called by the defense testified that the bath could have ruptured the bladder. The actress, while she lingered, had furnished no clues to the bedroom scene beyond telling a nurse that she had been intimate with the fun-loving 320-pound comedian. The first jury stood 10-2 for acquittal after 43 hours, so a mistrial was declared. The second stood 10-2 for conviction and was dismissed after 44 hours. The third panel took just 6 minutes to clear the pink-faced defendant of manslaughter and observed:

"Acquittal is not enough for Roscoe

Virginia Rappe: Arbuckle's career died with her.

Roscoe Arbuckle's Wedding Day. But Buster Keaton, at the right, is dead-pan even on this joyous occasion.

The comedian (second from right at counsel table) on trial for manslaughter.

Arbuckle. We feel a great injustice has been done him and there was not the slightest proof to connect him in any way with the commission of any crime."

Miss Rappe's fiancée, director Henry Lehrman, saw it another way from the start.

"Virginia had the most remarkable determination," Lehrman said, "She would rise from the dead to defend her person from indignity. As for Arbuckle, this is what comes of taking vulgarians from the gutter and giving them enormous salaries and making idols of them. Some people don't know how to get a kick out of life, except in a beastly way. They are the ones who participate in orgies that surpass the orgies of degenerate Rome."

The studios, watching the box office, indorsed the Lehrman view not just by blacklisting Arbuckle but by junking his unreleased movies. It was question-

Fatty Arbuckle as the roly-poly comic.

able in any case whether those pictures could have been sold: exhibitors everywhere had marked the oversized star guilty long before the third jury had acquitted him.

Arbuckle changed his name to William Goodrich — somebody said he should have made it Will B. Good— and got some casual work as a director but eleven years passed before anyone let him act. Warner Brothers put him in some two-reel comedies in 1933, shooting in New York. He finished one on June 30 and said, "This is the happiest day of my life." In the morning he was dead—felled in his sleep by a heart attack. He was forty-six. Today you can see his old pie-in-the-face comedies on afternoon television programs aimed at the kiddie audience. The TV people figured, correctly, that the younger set couldn't possibly be contaminated by the pre-Rappe Arbuckle.

The Strange Death of William Desmond Taylor

"I loved him deeply..."
—MARY MILES MINTER

William Desmond Taylor, rather well-armed, in an acting role, before he turned director.

The movie magnates were still tearing their hair (what was left) over the Arbuckle scandal when somebody with a terrible sense of timing killed William Desmond Taylor, the Famous-Players Lasky Studio's $100,000-a-year Chief Director. This mystery melodrama would draw more headlines than *l'affaire* Arbuckle, for it brimmed with good names—Mary Miles Minter, Mary Pickford, Mabel Normand—and dark suspicions. It broke on February 2, 1922, while the third Arbuckle trial was pending. Taylor's hired man, Henry Peavey, found the handsome director dead in his bungalow when he reported in the morning. The body lay beside a desk in the study, a bullet in the heart.

The last person who saw Taylor alive the night before, apart from the murderer, appeared to be Miss Normand. She said she had dropped in around 7:05. She said they talked about her next starring vehicle, about good books and, finally, her French lessons. She said Taylor put her in her car at nine o'clock because she had an early studio call and, always thoughtful, lent her a book by Sigmund Freud when he observed some trashy magazines in her limousine.

Mary Pickford's name came into the case because her photo occupied a favored position in his bachelor quarters.

Real-life detectives, just like the movie kind, always question damsels in situations of this kind. Miss Pickford, of course, remained "America's Sweetheart" through the ordeal; she knew nothing about the murder.

Mary Miles Minter, the rage in a succession of Chaplin films, drew the major billing when a scented note on her monogrammed stationery fluttered out of one of Taylor's books while the police were ransacking the bungalow. The missive was brief but very warm. It was not the sort of thing movie fans imagined the demure screen heroine to be sending to a man twice her age. It follows:

"Dearest:
"I love you—I love you—I love you
"XXXXXXXXXXXXXXXXX
"Yours always,
"Mary."

The last X in the row of kisses was two inches high and punctuated by an exclamation point so "Dearest" would get the idea. Asked about her little composition, Miss Minter made her passion even clearer.

"I did love William Desmond Taylor," she said. "I loved him deeply, and tenderly, with all the admiration a young girl gives to a man with the poise and position of Mr. Taylor." For all her girlish ardor, the star said she and Taylor, an ex-British Army officer and a worldly fellow, were nothing more than good friends. The director had a garish funeral, with Miss Minter furnishing the big scene. She kissed the corpse on the lips, tenderly, and arose to report that her dreamboat had whispered something to her. She said it sounded like "I shall love you always, Mary." Naturally, the tabloids, not to mention the equally playful standard-size papers of the period, made much of the apparent traffic-unto-death between a movie star and her favorite director.

The scandal strung out like a cliff-

Mary Miles Minter and Mabel Normand found their careers shattered by the Taylor scandal.

hanging serial, producing words by the millions and theories by the square yard. There was talk about the varied amours of the deceased, talk about jealous females, talk about Taylor having thrashed a narcotics pusher for dealing junk to unnamed actresses, talk about blackmail, talk about a valet fired in a messy row not long before the slaying (and never found for questioning), talk about at least one initialed kimono found in the director's boudoir, talk about Miss Minter's mother having tried to keep her million-dollar baby away from the man. The script had more angles than the most fanciful screen writers had dared commit to paper.

The Hollywood purse-holders met in agonized all-night sessions as the presses turned. They didn't want the fortune invested in Miss Minter to go down the drain with the green stuff tied up in Arbuckle. They talked about the pure innocence of her twenty-two years and the unblemished name she

The dashing Mr. Taylor

had before that sizzling 18-X note turned up in William Desmond Taylor's library.

But in the end the girl went the Arbuckle way, into obscurity. Miss Minter, however, came out with some spending money. In 1956 she and her mother sued to draw more funds for investment out of a trust they had set up in 1924 and it was said to be worth a fortune. So the wolf never howled at their door.

Mabel Normand, shining brightly in the Mack Sennett comedy crown, could have survived her incidental role in the scandal even with the women's clubs clamoring to hang her scalp alongside Miss Minter's. But in 1924 she happened to be among those present when her chauffeur put a bullet into another gentleman, presumably in a battle over her favors, and then she turned up as a co-respondent in a third man's suit. Death spared her the long night, however. Only thirty-three, she was felled by TB in 1930.

HOLLYWOOD GOES MORAL

"Whatever will bring in the most money will happen."

—Elinor Glyn

Will Hays heard the magnates calling.

Cecil B. DeMille told the stars to behave.

Mrs. Glyn blamed the high life.

Will Hays, the Presbyterian elder newly drafted out of Warren Harding's Cabinet to clean up the Hollywood stables lest the box offices go to rot and ruin, pleaded with the masses not to judge hastily.

"The potentialities of motion pictures for moral influence and education are limitless," said the ex-Postmaster-General. "Therefore its integrity should be protected as we protect the integrity of our children and our churches, and its quality developed as we develop the quality of our schools . . . This industry must have toward that sacred thing, the mind of a child, toward that clean virgin thing, that unmarked slate, the same responsibility, the same care about the impressions made upon it, that the best clergyman or the most inspired teacher of youth would have."

Hays had a solid stake of his own in the matter. The studios' hurry-call to him during the Arbuckle mess carried a salary tag of $100,000 a year—quite a pile of money in 1922.

Mrs. Elinor Glyn, who wrote *Three Weeks* and found her exposition of the New Thought highly salable in Hollywood, offered *The New York Times* some much more candid observations than Will Hays was dispensing.

"The trouble with the movie industry," said Mrs. Glyn, a British import, "is that so many young people in it get rich suddenly. They are not taught control, and it is hard for them to resist temptation. A young girl acts with a handsome young star all day long in emotional scenes, and when she gets through she is apt to think that husband is an awful bore. But I think in a short time you will see a vast improvement and that the standard will come up to that of the stage."

The sudden-riches theme drew wide notice. "When people spring from poverty to affluence within a few weeks," said a *New York Journal* correspondent in Hollywood, "their mental equipment is not always equal to the strain. They have money, an unaccustomed toy, and

they spend it in bizarre ways. They may indulge in 'wild parties' or they may indulge in other forms of relaxation and excitement. Many of them spend all they make . . . Since Prohibition came in many of them who had no liquor stocks turned to other stimulants. The dealers in illicit drugs found a growing market." But the *Journal* man said these gray items applied only to a "relatively small group" in the movie mill.

Mrs. Glyn, for her part, pointed out that many stars contributed lavishly to charities rather than burn up their fat pay checks on the high life. Asked what should be done about the *other* kind of people in Hollywood, her answer was firm.

"If they are flagrantly immoral, hang them; do not show their pictures; suppress them; but do not make them all suffer for a few. This Arbuckle party was a beastly, disgusting thing and things like it should be stamped out. But I didn't see any such things in

Gloria Swanson was snapped in her favorite Lancia in her Beverly Hills driveway.

Ralph Forbes' Caddy, Vintage '27, had a built-in dressing table in the tonneau.

Pola Negri in her Cadillac—a rather unspectacular model for her flaming temperament.

MGM's Gertrude Olmstead poses on the running board of a Packard she designed herself.

Mae Murray liked the more formal Rolls Royce, complete with liveried chauffeur.

This 1923 model suited Ben Lyon nicely.

The big names of the silent screen took to the luxurious cars of the early twenties the way today's stars go for the low-slung, high-powered foreign sports models. When nothing quite suitable appeared in the showrooms, the free-spending New Rich in the movie colony ordered custom-built models—not solid gold but often running into five figures at a time when you could buy very pretentious standard models for $2000.

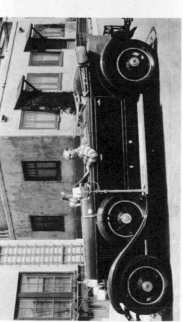

Western star Hoot Gibson had the Cadillac people build him a special sports model.

Olga Petrova liked her cars long and fast, so she favored this Packard touring sedan.

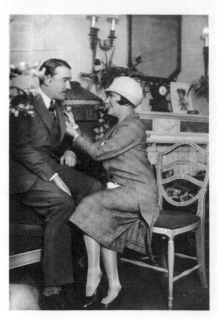

Jack Pickford and his first wife, Olive Thomas. Pickford went to the movies from the New York stage but was greatly overshadowed—as who wasn't in Hollywood in those days?—by his little sister. Olive Thomas—called "the most beautiful woman in the world" (above) by artist Harrison Fisher died of poisoning in 1920 while on a second honeymoon with Pickford in Paris following a rift in the marriage. The gendarmes said the actress took the lethal dose under the impression that it was a sleeping potion.

Gloria Swanson tried royalty, too. Here she's pinning a rose on her third husband, Marquis Henri de la Falaise. It was one of the world's most celebrated marriages, commanding reams of space, not only in the fan magazines but also in the general press.

Barbara LaMarr, one of the real beauties of the screen in the twenties. Drugs drove her to suicide.

Art Accord, horse opera movie star. It was drink that drove him to suicide.

Pola Negri and the White Russian nobleman she married in 1927, Prince Serge Mdivani of the Marrying Mdivanis.

Hollywood and if there are dope parties there, they must be very small."

The gentleman from *The Times* wanted to know what would happen in Hollywood in the wake of the Arbuckle and Taylor scandals.

"What ever will bring in the most money will happen," Mrs. Glyn replied.

The lady wasn't far off. The Hays Office issued a double proclamation: none but the most decorous and antiseptic movies could thenceforth pass the censors and everbody had to behave off-screen too. Quick like a flash, the studios inserted morals clauses in all contracts which in essence made

the male stars monks and the females akin to the Little Sisters of the Poor. Everybody had to take the vows or else.

William C. DeMille, brother of Cecil, cited the instance of a biblical epic in defense of the morals clause. "It would never do," he said, "to have

Norma Talmadge.

Hollywood's "Big Four" sits for a portrait in 1920 after forming United Artists: Fairbanks, Pickford, Chaplin and D. W. Griffith.

Theda Bara, "The Vampire."

"The Vampire" as Cleopatra.

The Marilyn Miller-Jack Pickford wedding in 1922 was a gala affair. Douglas Fairbanks and Mary Pickford are next to the bride—star of Ziegfeld's *Sally* — and the smiling man behind her right shoulder is Charlie Chaplin, then at his crest. Below, the newlyweds take tea and toast in rather lush surroundings.

the Virgin Mary getting a divorce, or St. John cutting up in a night club."

No, it would never do.

Not at that moment, anyway.

Lest a very large Hollywood name be taken in vain, let it be noted here that Cecil B. DeMille—even then a Colossus in the movie mills—did not introduce the Blue Law approach to Hollywood. Far from it. Before the Czar Hays swung his bludgeon, the Great Director had made movies under such provocative titles as *Don't Change Your Husband, Adam's Rib, Why Change Your Wife?, Forbidden Fruit, For Better or Worse,* and *The Golden Bed.* Indeed, DeMille wielded the first megaphone on many of the scenes that made the movie bedroom what it is to-day.

As Lloyd Morris put it in *Not So Long Ago,* "The DeMille boudoir became a chapel for the celebration of rites authorized by custom, but still accounted irregular by the law and the church." Morris also credited De-Mille with changing the meaning of the word "sleep," at least for the more attentive movie-goers. But De-Mille could go either way with the Hollywood winds. He made *The Ten Commandments* the year after the Arbuckle-Taylor scandals. He did as much as anyone to reduce the great sweat under Will Hays' high starched collar.

Wallace Reid at his peak in 1920.

"Nobody could do anything with Wally."
—FLORENCE REID

The Man in the Padded Room

Reid in 1923, on the road to doom.

The vast process of sweeping clean the Hollywood stables suffered during 1922 because there was no way to hide the sad rum- and morphine-wracked body of Wallace Reid. The immensely popular Wally—ex-artist, ex-writer, ex-jazz musician, ex-athlete, ex-very-big Box Office—was taking the cure as Hollywood's most dismal year came to a close. Will Hays didn't shed any tears over the pitiful, wasted 6-foot 3-inch hulk in the sanitarium. The film czar's Christmas message to the world outside the movie capital said that Reid "should be dealt with as a diseased person—not be censured, shunned." The star had in fact been shunned for the best part of two years before Hays' Yuletide greetings were issued. Indeed, the cure then in process may well have been for naught. Reid's name headed a roster of 117 persons deemed "unsafe" in a searching studio-sponsored shoo-fly survey into the private lives of Hollywood's working stiffs, big and small. There was a story that when the blacklist was shown to the producer who had Reid under contract, the man protested bitterly, saying:

"You should know that you are asking the impossible. Why, it would mean at least a two-million-dollar loss to us to do a thing like this in the case of this one man . . . a thing like that would simply be suicide."

Wally Reid solved the problem nicely for Will Hays, if not for the men who hoped someday to straighten him out again at the box office. He died on January 18, 1923, a victim of narcotics, and his passing came as something of a shot in the arm to another section of Hays' year-end pronouncement: "We are traveling the highway to better things in filmdom . . . soon there will be a model Hollywood . . . I have faith that unfortunate incidents will be things safely of the past . . ."

Reid's wife Florence, who had appeared in movies as Dorothy Davenport, blamed the tragedy on the wild life cited by Elinor Glyn in her dissection of the film colony. Mrs. Reid said the downfall started in 1920 when Reid went to New York to do a picture called *Forever.* She said he was hit on the head with a rock during the shooting and never seemed to be the same again. "Gradually, he got to drinking with his Bohemian friends," she went on, "and soon this wasn't a home. It was a roadhouse. Wally's friends would come in here by the scores, at any odd hour of the day or night. They came, they stayed, they drank. It was one wild party after another, each one worse than the last. Nobody could do anything with Wally. And then—morphine."

It was said that Reid suffered from insomnia and exhaustion as well as bootleg whiskey during the making of *Forever*—one of his best pictures—and had taken to morphine to shore up his energy so that he could go before the kleig lights day after day. The dread narcotic hooked the actor. Mrs. Reid laid his death to the unspeakable misery he suffered trying to break the habit. When the pathetic struggle was over, Mary Pickford uttered the kindest epitaph for Reid.

"His death is a very great tragedy," she said. "I know he would have lived down every mistake he made."

The Hays Office had no comment. The guardian of movie decency was too busy pre-digesting the product in the cans and making sure everything had a happy ending, preferably with a strong moral message. The producers, for their part, found that Hays' pious pronouncements didn't preclude a little passion on celluloid. Even while the nice-nelly talk was flowing forth, as Frederick Lewis Allen observed, there were movie ads heralding such items as "beautiful jazz babies, champagne baths, midnight revels, petting parties in the purple dawn" and "neckers, petters, white kisses, red kisses, pleasure-mad daughters, sensation-craving mothers . . . the truth—bold, naked, sensational." The pictures weren't quite as vivid as the ads said, of course, but neither were they ideal for Sunday evening socials, even with their happy endings. Hays undoubtedly knew it. He was a shrewd fellow. He kept the enemy at bay without driving the customers away.

TORCHLIGHTS AND G-MEN

"Workers of the world, unite!"
—The Communist Manifesto

Earl Browder (right) and William Z. Foster, long, long before the ins and outs of the line caused Browder's ouster from the Communist Party the summer of 1945.

In 1922 the Third International in Moscow announced in matter-of-fact tones that "the Class Struggle in almost every country of Europe and America is entering the phase of civil war." The statement was somewhat late, certainly as it referred to Uncle Sam's little piece of real estate. The fierce postwar battles between labor and capital now were over and so were the Great Red Raids; the jail doors had been opened for most of the small-fry political prisoners swept into the government dragnets when the hysteria was at its height. Even so, the Third International's American followers—a rather bare legion—elected to dissolve the underground Communist Party and come up into the sunlight to prepare for the new day hearkened by the typewriter generals in the USSR. For this purpose, a

secret meeting assembled in August in Bridgeman, Michigan. As a hush-hush affair, it was not notably successful. In little Bridgeman, Eugene Lyons noted, "the batches of mysterious city folk, many of them foreigners and outlandishly bearded, were as inconspicuous as a circus parade."

The revolutionaries did not meet in the town, but rather in the woods outside. And there the bright new future was mapped by the light of torches as its outlines issued from the lips of such men as William Z. Foster and Earl Browder. The convention then duly liquidated the CP and organized the Workers Party, which hoped to take in all the dissident political factions on the Left and prepare for the seizure of power under one happy United Front. When the rustic conclave was over,

government agents put the cuffs on seventeen of the delegates. It turned out that even then, as now, G-Men often sat in when the Left foregathered. As it happened, it didn't matter. The Workers Party enjoyed only a brief existence, for not even the best-laid plans could bring together the forces working either for a Soviet America or any variation on the theme. This was still true in the United States three decades later. You could never get any broad unanimity of thought on the ticklish issue of how—or sometimes *whether* —to overthrow the government. You couldn't even get any revolutionary harmony in the terrible depression of the thirties when the country of Washington and Jefferson was in the very worst possible condition. It is a nice note.

IT HAPPENED IN 1922...

James Branch Cabell's *Jurgen* bothered the self-appointed bluenoses on the literary beat.

Judge Charles C. Nott, Jr., of New York curled up one night with a copy of James Branch Cabell's *Jurgen, A Comedy of Justice*. The book, a fantasy set in the Middle Ages with a spot of sex here and there, had been under ban for two years because John S. Sumner's Society for the Suppression of Vice suspected it was obscene. "I have read the book," Judge Nott ruled, "and find nothing in it that is disgusting." The literati cheered wildly, including those who confessed they couldn't quite make the book out. The author pocketed the royalties and observed that there was a difference between pornography and literature. "Everybody enjoys the first," Cabell said, "while few care one way or another about the second."

Jurgen did not make the top of the best-seller lists, even with all the publicity John Sumner got it. A.S.M. Hutchinson's *If Winter Comes* was first. Booth Tarkington's *Julia* was close behind, and Zane Grey stayed in there with *To the Last Man*. Sinclair Lewis' *Babbitt* also sold well. In non-fiction, H. G. Wells' *The Outline of History,*

Hendrick Willem Van Loon's *The Story of Mankind*, and *The Americanization of Edward Bok* were the top three.

With our sex habits under attack—or at least under discussion—on a wide front, H. L. Mencken rose to the defense of American men in an essay called "The Libertine," in his book *In Defense of Women*. Mencken counseled each and every woman not to believe what she was hearing about her husband. He said the male partner, in the great majority of cases, was true to his wife. He said the man might not be "pure in heart," but the chances were that he was "pure in act, even in the face of temptation," for several reasons:

"One is that he lacks the courage. Another is that he lacks the money. Another is that he is fundamentally moral, and has a conscience. It takes more sinful initiative than he has to plunge into any affair save the most

The scandal-spiced marriage of Anne Stillman (above) and banker James A. Stillman drew headlines in the twenties. Stillman accused his wife of intimacies with Fred Beauvais, an Indian guide at their Canadian camp, and questioned the paternity of young Guy Stillman. Mrs. Stillman charged that her husband had sired an extramarital son by Florence Leeds, a chorus girl. The on-again, off-again marriage finally was dissolved in 1931.

Jeanne Eagels introduced the Sadie Thompson role in *Rain* on Broadway in 1922.

casual and sordid; it takes more ingenuity and intrepidity than he has to carry it off; it takes more money than he can conceal from his consort to finance it. A man may force his actual wife to share the direst poverty, but even the least vampirish woman of the third part demands to be courted in what, considering his station in life, is the grand manner, and the expenses of that grand manner scare off all save a small minority of specialists in deception . . .

"The moment a concrete Temptress rises before him, her nose talced, her lips scarlet, her eyelashes drooping provokingly — the moment such an abandoned wench has at him, and his lack of ready funds begins to conspire with his lack of courage to assault and wobble him—at that precise moment his conscience flares into function, and so finishes his business. First he sees difficulty, then he sees danger, then he sees wrong. The result? The result is that he slinks off in trepidation, and another vampire is baffled of her prey. It is, indeed, the secret scandal of

Christendom, at least in the Protestant region, that most men are faithful to their wives. You will travel a long way before you find a married man who will admit that *he* is, but the facts are the facts. For one American husband who maintains a chorus girl in levantine luxury around the corner, there are hundreds who are as true to their oaths, year in and year out, as so many convicts in the death house, and would be no more capable of any such loathsome malpractice even in the face of free opportunity, than they would be of cutting off the ears of their young."

Mencken added a footnote years later. He said nothing in the Kinsey report had changed his conclusions.

Maybe the men were as firmly bound by the vows as Mencken described. The women weren't, if *True Story* magazine was to be believed at the time. The Macfadden gazette ran such hair-raisers as these:

The Flapper-Wife
What Happened to a Girl Who
Wanted a Husband, Not a Home

———

"Thou Shalt
Not—"
'Tis Well to be off With
The Old Love Before You
Are on With the New

———

When Romance Paved Death's
Pathway
Life Stories of Women Who Have
Loved Too Well

———

The High Cost of Loving

Louis Wolheim as he appeared in Eugene O'Neill's *The Hairy Ape.*

New York City put a 2:00 A.M. curfew on dancing in cabarets and ordered the arrest of restaurant proprietors who let women smoke, but this edict lasted only one day . . . The Brooklyn Parents League set an evening curfew for teenage girls . . . Radio sermons became a daily feature on New York stations . . . Princeton University advised parents that students need not have autos, and Syracuse University banned dancing from May to December . . . The Pittsburgh *Observer,* a Catholic paper, noted "a change for the worse during the past year in feminine dress, dancing, manners, and general moral standards" and warned against any "failure to realize the serious ethical consequences of immodesty in girls' dress"

Barrymore played the tormented *Hamlet* and had New York at his feet.

. . . *The Southern Baptist Review and Expositor* complained that "the girls are actually tempting the boys more than the boys do the girls, by their dress and their conversation" . . . Yale football games drew $5,000,000 at the gate . . . The race tracks lured their biggest crowds and paid their highest purses . . . Tennis drew its biggest crowds . . .

President Harding said Prohibition had to be enforced . . . Two quarts of "ink" seized in a warehouse proved to be whiskey . . . The five-cent bread loaf appeared . . . John L. Lewis called out 500,000 miners in a wage fight . . . Harding assumed responsibility for the leasing of the Naval oil reserves to private interests . . . The Railway Labor Board, sitting in a shopmen's strike, ruled that

Will Rogers fights the inner man as a Ziegfeld Girl pursues him in the *Follies.*

any effort to relate wages to living costs would "wreck every railroad in the U.S. and if it extended to other industries would carry them into communistic ruin" . . . Ignace Paderewski, pianist and ex-Premier of Poland, returned to his first love and made a concert tour . . . Clemenceau of France said the trouble with America was that it grew faster than its ideas . . . Striking Illinois miners shot, hanged, or beat to death twenty-one strikebreakers in the Herrin Massacre . . . Henry Ford told his workers he would fire anyone caught on the job with liquor on his breath.

* * *

In the theater, Pauline Lord appeared in Eugene O'Neill's *Anna Christie,* Glenn Hunter scored a big hit in *Merton of the Movies,* and Helen Menken starred in *Seventh Heaven.* Out West, the film colony welcomed a distinguished foreign import. Strongheart, the police dog who served in the German Red Cross, came over to make pictures for First National.

The Washington Conference agreed to limit arms among the Big Five Powers (United States, Britain, Japan, France and Italy) and respect the territorial integrity of China.

The Rev. Edward Wheeler Hall and his choir leader, Mrs. James Mills, were murdered in a lover's lane in New Brunswick, N. J. Members of the pastor's family were suspected, but the Grand Jury refused to indict. The case would reappear in 1926 as one of the decade's great courtroom dramas.

"All the News That's Fit to Print."

The New York Times.

EXTRA 6 A. M.

THE WEATHER: Fair Today.

VOL. LXXII....No. 23,932. NEW YORK, FRIDAY, AUGUST 3, 1923. TWO CENTS In Greater New York | THREE CENTS Within 200 Miles

PRESIDENT HARDING DIES SUDDENLY; STROKE OF APOPLEXY AT 7:30 P. M.; CALVIN COOLIDGE IS PRESIDEN

COOLIDGE TAKES THE OATH OF OFFICE

His Father, Who Is a Notary Public, Administers It After Form Is Found By Him in His Library.

ANNOUNCES HE WILL FOLLOW THE HARDING POLICIES

Wants All Who Aided Harding to Remain in Office—Roused After Midnight to Be Told the News of the President's Death.

Statement by President Coolidge.

Special to The New York Times.

PLYMOUTH, Vt., Aug. 3.—President Calvin Coolidge issued the following statement early this morning:

"Reports have reached me, which I fear are correct, that President Harding is gone. The world has lost a great and good man. I mourn his loss. He was my chief and my friend.

It will be my purpose to carry out the policies which he has begun for the service of the American people and for meeting their responsibilities wherever they may arise.

For this purpose I shall seek the co-operation of all those who have been associated with the President during his term of office.

Those who have given their efforts to assist him I wish to remain in office that they may assist me. I have faith that God will direct the destinies of our nation.

It is my intention to remain here until I can secure the correct form for the oath of office, which will be administered to me by my father, who is a notary public, if that will meet the necessary requirement. I expect to leave for Washington during the day.

CALVIN COOLIDGE.

Takes the Oath of Office.

Special to The New York Times.

PLYMOUTH, Vt. (Friday), Aug. 3.—Calvin Coolidge took the oath of office as President of the United States at 2:47, Eastern Standard Time, this morning (3:47 New York time). The oath was administered by his father, John C. Coolidge, who found the text in a book in his library, after having expected to wait until it was received from Washington.

The taking of the oath was a simple and solmn scene. Those who gathered in the living room of the Coolidge rome at Plymouth Notch, besides the President and his father, were Mrs. Coolidge, L. L. Lane, President of the Railway Mail Association of New England; Congressman Porter H. Dale, of Vermont; Joseph H. Fountain, editor of the Springfield Reporter, and Erwin C. Geisser, Mr. Coolidge's Assistant Secretary.

As the elder Mr. Coolidge read the oath Mrs. Coolidge looked on with wet eyes. As the end was reached, President Coolidge, raising his right hand, said in a low, clear voice:

"I do, so help me God."

A moment later the group dissolved, and President and Mrs. Coolidge retired.

Special to The New York Times.

PLYMOUTH, Vt., Friday, Aug. 3.—Calvin Coolidge received the news of the death of President Harding and of his own elevation to the Presidency at ten minutes before 1 o'clock this morning, Daylight Saving Time.

Mr. Coolidge received the first news of President Harding's death from telegrams signed by George C. Christian, the late President's secretary, and from THE NEW YORK TIMES, whose telegram reached him at the same moment.

These telegrams were brought to the Coolidge home at Plymouth Notch by W. A. Perkins of Bridgewater, who owns the telephone line running from Bridgewater to Plymouth. About five minutes later the newspaper men arrived in Ludlow.

The following telegram was sent to Mrs. Harding:

Plymouth, Vt., Aug. 3, 1923.

Mrs. Warren G. Harding,
San Francisco, Cal.

We offer you our deepest sympathy. May God bless you and keep you.

CALVIN COOLIDGE.
GRACE COOLIDGE.

The following telegrams announcing the death of President Harding

Continued on Page Five.

CALVIN COOLIDGE
Thirtieth President of the United States by the Death of President Harding.

WARREN GAMALIEL HARDING
Twenty-ninth President of the United States, Who Died Yesterday in San Francisco.

Public Men Voice Tributes To Harding's Worth and Record

Hughes Says He Was a Brave and Strong Leader—Marshall Calls Him a Great Human American—Honored as Martyr to His Duty—Sympathy Goes Out to Mrs. Harding.

Special to The New York Times.

WASHINGTON, Friday, Aug. 3.—Politics was forgotten in comment by public men in Washington when informed of the death of President Harding. On account of the late hour at which the news was received it was difficult to reach officials.

Secretary Hughes, who came to his office in the State Department at an early hour this morning, was shaken by the news.

"No words can express," he said, "the grief into which we are plunged by this calamity. The nation has suffered an irreparable loss. A quiet, brave, strong leader has fallen, overborne by the burden he was carrying.

"He was not only an able and faithful public servant but one of nature's noblemen. A true hearted, generous spirit, he has left with the people he loved a rare example of gentleness in high office, and of the most conscientious and unselfish devotion to public duty."

Marshall Found Him High Minded.

Thomas R. Marshall, former Vice President of the United States, expressed the deepest sorrow and paid high tribute to the integrity and worth of Mr. Harding.

"The sad intelligence of the President's death has just been communicated to me," said Mr. Marshall. "These are times when all party considerations sink into insignificance. The right kind of a man thinks of the death of his President.

"This has been the death not only of my President but of a man who for many years in the Senate had been my friend of the personal and intimate kind. There is nothing that any man can say, on an occasion like this beyond bearing testimony that aside from political opinions he was a great human American who patriotically and honestly tried to serve his country.

"This is a tribute from a man who did not agree with his political principles, but it is not necessary to agree with his political principles in order to admire the integrity, patriotism and high-mindedness of a man. I think that as the years go by the people will realize that Mr. Harding tried to serve his country well."

Loss to the World, Says New.

Postmaster General New was at his home when the news of President Harding's death was flashed to him from San Francisco.

"I am simply overwhelmed," he said. "There are times when a man can not express his grief. This is one of them. The passing of President Harding is a loss to the world, the magnitude of which can not be overestimated."

Joseph P. Tumulty said:

"The new is a dreadful shock to me, as it must be to all who knew President Harding well. While at the White House I had many delightful associations with President Harding, who then was a member of the Senate. Like all men who came in contact with the President I knew him as a kindly gentleman and a true friend."

Says He Had People's Affection.

Senator Walsh of Massachusetts, Chairman of the Democratic Senatorial Campaign Committee, said:

"The President's death is a terrible shock, coming as it does so soon after it was believed that he was on the way to speedy recovery. His death will be mourned in every corner of the land by every class.

"Few Presidents have had a stronger grip upon the affections of our people. His dignity, simplicity, sincerity and graciousness won the hearts of all. His personality, however, did not alone account for his popularity. He has won a place in our history among the most worthy of those who have occupied the Presidency.

"His views were statesmanlike and the honor of our nation was safe and secure in his hands. The nation has lost a noble man, and a sound and safe leader."

Roosevelt Tells of Sacrifice.

Colonel Theodore Roosevelt, Acting Secretary of the Navy in the absence of Secretary Denby, said:

"Words cannot express my grief at the death of my chief, President Harding. It is idle to say that his death is a calamity for the United States, for every one knows it. He gave his life to the service of our country as truly as any one in our history."

Representative Stephen G. Porter of Pennsylvania, Chairman of the House Foreign Affairs Committee, a personal admirer as well as a friend of Mr. Harding said:

"I am simply overwhelmed. I hardly know what to say. He was so gentle, so kind, his every act was in the public interest. It is a terrible shock. I really can't understand it."

Mr. Porter returned recently from Europe, where he represented this country at the sessions of the commission of the League of Nations on the opium traffic. He was selected for the work by the President.

Senator Curtis of Kansas, Republican whip of the Senate, said:

"The entire world will be shocked at the death of President Harding. His passing at this time was very unfortunate. The extent of his loss cannot be expressed in words. The entire country

Continued on Page Four.

President's Death Shocks Capital, Which Had Expected Recovery

News Telephoned to Executive Clerk From San Francisco—Effort Made to Reach Coolidge in Vermont—Only Two Members of Cabinet in Washington.

Special to The New York Times.

WASHINGTON, Friday, Aug. 3.—News of the death of President Harding not only greatly shocked official and Washington but took the capital completely by surprise.

It was the sixth time in the history of the nation that the city had been brought face to face with the death of a President, but the shocking word was received under circumstances wholly different from those surrounding the death of any former President.

The only high officials of the Harding Administration in Washington are Secretary of State Hughes and Postmaster General New. All the other members of the Cabinet are out of the city, and two of them, Secretaries Mellon and Davis, are in Europe, while most of the others, with the exception of Secretaries Weeks and Denby, are in the Far West.

Calvin Coolidge, until last night Vice President, and who will immediately be sworn in as the next President of the United States, is likewise absent from Washington, but it has occurred several times in American annals that Vice Presidents have been absent from the capital on occasions of deaths of former Presidents.

When last heard from, Mr. Coolidge was at Plymouth, Vt. A message was sent direct from San Francisco notifying him of the death of Mr. Harding. From the Presidential party in San Francisco communications, the White House was advised late tonight, were sent direct to all other members of the Cabinet not now in San Francisco and to personal friends of the President.

Rudolph Forster, Executive Clerk at the White House, was communicated with direct from San Francisco shortly before midnight by long distance telephone. He talked with Mr. Smithers, the ranking member of the White House executive force in San Francisco in the absence of Mr. Christian who had gone to Los Angeles. Mr. Smithers confirmed the death of the President and informed Mr. Forster that messages were being sent to the Vice President and other Cabinet members.

Mr. Hughes is the ranking member of the Administration now in Washington, so that he will take such steps as are necessary in the present situation.

It will also be the duty of the Secretary of State to notify the members of the Diplomatic Corps, who will in turn officially cable their Governments that Mr. Harding is dead.

No plans have or can be made immediately for the swearing in of Mr. Coolidge as President. It is not necessary for him to take the oath from a member of the United States Supreme Court. Another Judge or other officer qualified to administer an oath can act in that capacity. Even a Justice of the Peace back in Vermont, where Mr. Coolidge was last known to be located, can administer the oath.

The first knowledge the White House had of the President's death came from the Rev. Dr. Freeman Anderson, assistant pastor of the Calvary Baptist Church, which President Harding attended. He telephoned to the Executive Mansion and the message was received by E. C. Goss, one of the White House police force, who was one of the few men on duty at that time of the night, as the President had been away since June 20.

In turn Patrolman Goss telephoned to Mr. Forster, who at once summoned the entire White House force. One of the first to arrive was Isaac Hoover for years chief usher at the mansion, and who has known many Presidents intimately, and Joseph Murphy, assistant chief of the Secret Service.

Pedestrians who passed the White House after the news of the President's death noticed that the iron gates on Pennsylvania Avenue were shut and locked, something which has been unknown since the advent of the Harding regime. It was explained, however, that the gates have been shut every night at 8 o'clock since the extensive repairs to the house and grounds have been going on.

Mr. Hoover, who has charge of the renovation of the White House, said at midnight that the mansion could be put in order in two days. In fact, preparations had been made to do this ever since the first news of the President's illness was received in Washington. At any time that notification was sent here that the President was to leave San Francisco the house could have been put in readiness for his reception. Workmen will begin at once this morning arranging the furniture and placing the draperies as usual.

Dancing Stops at the Hotels.

At the big hotels dancing was immediately stopped and a hush and gloom settled over the crowds who slowly began to leave. Extras were on the streets fairly early and residents ran out from their homes to call newsboys, and automobilists stopped their machines to buy the ink-wet sheets. Newsboys were crying extras in Executive Avenue and Pennsylvania Avenue, the two streets bounding the White House on the west and north at midnight, their cries [illegible] clearly into the Executive Offices.

When the news was communicated to William R. Heck, private secretary to the Secretary of State, at midnight, he started by automobile for the State Department and sent word to Mr. Hughes's

Continued on Page Six.

DEATH STROKE CAME WITHOUT WA

Mrs. Harding Was Reading to Husband When First Sign Appea —She Ran for Doctor

BUT NOTHING COULD BE DONE TO REVIVE PAT

News of Tragic End Shocks Everybody, Comi After Day Said to Have Been the Best Since His Illness Began a Week Ago.

Special to The New York Times.

SAN FRANCISCO, Aug. 2.—President Harding died at 7:3 tonight [11:30 o'clock New York time] of a stroke of apoplexy.

The end came suddenly while Mrs. Harding was reading to h the evening newspaper, and after what had been called the bes had had since the beginning of his illness exactly one week ago.

A shudder ran through the President's frame and he collapsed.

Mrs. Harding and the two nurses in the sick room knew the had come, and Mrs. Harding rushed out of the room and asked for Boone and the others to "come quick."

Dr. Boone and Brig. Gen. Sawyer reached the President befor passed away, but were not able to avert the inevitable.

This formal announcement following soon after told the st tragic end:

"The President died at 7:30 P. M. Mrs. Harding and the two nur Miss Ruth Powderly and Miss Sue Drusser, were in the room at the ti Mrs. Harding was reading to the President, when, utterly without wa ing, a slight shudder passed through his frame; he collapsed, and recognized that the end had come. A stroke of apoplexy was the caus his death.

"Within a few moments all of the President's official party h been summoned."

Shocking in Its Suddenness.

Nothing could have been a more shocking surprise. Shortly bef the President's sudden collapse General Sawyer had been telling news per men that Mr. Harding had had the best day since he became seriou ill. He said that the President had definitely entered upon the stage convalescence and that everything went to show that Mr. Harding w on the road to ultimate recovery.

The members of the official party had no warning that the Preside was in danger. They, like the newspaper men, had been assured tha fatal termination of the President's illness was a thing not likely a with good care he would be able to recover health and strength. M of the members of the official party were at dinner when the news ca George B. Christian Jr., secretary to the President and his devoted friend was in Los Angeles with Mrs. Christian. He had gone there at th President's solicitation to read at a gathering of the Knights Templ tonight an address which the President had prepared in the expectati that he would deliver it in person. Mr. Christian had declined to lea San Francisco until he was positively assured by the President's phy cians that there was no likelihood of any set-back in the President's c dition.

The newspaper men had an engagement with General Sawyer f o'clock. He was to tell them of how the President was progressing tow recovery. In view of what he had said on prior occasions during the d and statements in two official bulletins, the newspaper men had eve expectation that they would be able to record that Mr. Harding was o step nearer the goal of recovery.

"There will be a bulletin," said one of the White House messenge gathered in the corridor of the Presidential suite. In a few minut copies of the bulletin on thin white paper were handed to the waiting r porters. Instead of informing them that the President's condition co tinued to improve, it gave them the astounding information that h was dead.

Mrs. Harding Is Brave to the End.

First reports that Mrs. Harding had collapsed were denied. The offi cial version indicates that she was calm throughout her husband's last illness. She has been extremely courageous and by her manner and words helped him when he was suffering intensely and was apprehensive of a fatal termination. The official account says:

"Mrs. Harding, who from the beginning of the President's illness had expressed confidence in his recovery, did not break down. On the other hand, she continued, as from the beginning, the bravest member of the group.

"When it was realized that the President had [...] she turned to those in the room, whose concern h[...] 'I am not going to break down.'"

Mrs. Harding was seated by [...] President suddenly collapsed. H[...] since the illness overtook him, [...] leaving the two nurses to take w[...] ran to the door of the Presidenti[...]

"Dr. Boone!" she called, as [...] corridor. A Secret Service oper[...] the hall. She hurriedly told the S[...] had a sudden and severe relapse [...] Dr. Boone or any of the other ph[...]

The Secret Service man took [...]

Mr. Coolidge Prays

On a lonely kerosene-lit Vermont farm a President is sworn into office.

Calvin Coolidge, without peer as a sleeper, in or out of high office, went to bed at 9:00 P.M. on August 2, 1923, in the family farmhouse in Vermont. Mr. Harding lay ill on the West Coast but the Vice President felt no need to keep a hand close to the throttle. Plymouth was delightfully cool and Washington was hot and muggy and there was nothing to worry about. The President's doctors had said that his Alaskan goodwill journey had caused some weariness, compounded first by ptomaine poisoning from tainted crabs and then by a touch of bronchial pneumonia, but he was resting comfortably in the Palace Hotel in San Francisco. And just before Coolidge retired, someone called from the general store in the village and relayed a fresh bulletin from the medical men saying the fifty-eight-year-old President definitely was recovering.

Mr. Harding died of apoplexy at 10:30 P.M. But four hours passed before the news made its way east to Vermont. So it was 2:30 A.M. when

John Coolidge trudged up to the bedroom to tell his son he was President.

"My wife and I dressed at once," Coolidge said in his autobiography. "Before leaving the room I knelt down and, with the prayer with which I have since approached the altar of the church, asked God to bless the American people and give me power to serve them."

The elder Coolidge, a notary public, administered the oath by the light of two kerosene lamps in the sitting room of the old wooden house at 3:57 A.M. When daylight came, the new President went alone to his mother's grave. "It had been a comfort to me during my boyhood when I was troubled to be near her resting place, even in the dead of night," he said. "Some way, that morning, she seemed very near to me."

1923

Mrs. Coolidge had died when he was twelve but her Puritan teachings stayed with him all the way from the farm to the one-room stone schoolhouse, to the academy at Ludlow, to Amherst College, to the law school at Northampton and a succession of local offices in the town, to the lower House and a dollar-a-day room in Boston, to the State Senate, to the lieutenant-governorship and governorship, to the Vice Presidency and now the Presidency.

No, Calvin Coolidge never forgot anything his mother told him, whether he was doing the simplest farm chores or running the State of Massachusetts or the whole U.S.A. He did all the right things, according to the New England copybooks. He was frugal, honest, God-fearing, free of vices. He would have no trouble getting nominated to serve a full four-year term. He was just the man to carry on the Harding dictum—"not nostrums but normalcy"—and he himself would add a dandy expression to the language: "Coolidge Prosperity."

BLOODSHED ON THE COMMON

"A policeman's lot is not a happy one."

—Pirates of Penzance

On a pleasant evening in June, 1920, Governor Coolidge took his usual stroll along the Boston Common from the Executive Mansion to his two-room, $27.50-a-month flat in the Old Adams House. Mrs. Coolidge waited for him there, but he had scarcely said "Good evening" before the telephone rang—long distance from Chicago. When the Governor hung up, as Grace Coolidge told it to Mark Sullivan years later, this conversation took place:

COOLIDGE: I have been nominated for Vice President.

MRS. COOLIDGE: You are not going to accept it, are you?

COOLIDGE: I suppose I shall have to.

It was as simple as that. Calvin Coolidge was not the emotional kind. The nation's second highest office came to him like the rain that falleth from the heavens. He accepted it that way. It was nothing to have a lot of chatter about. If his party wanted him to run with Ohio's Harding to balance the ticket with some earth-bound Yankee simplicity, he would run. He never asked them; they asked him. He hadn't even set up headquarters in Chicago to stalk the backrooms in the pursuit of the nomination. He was happy on the Common.

To understand how Calvin Coolidge enjoyed such national eminence in 1920, you have to go back a year to the Boston Police Strike and the worst lawlessness any American city witnessed in the twentieth century. Since the bread-and-butter argument between the police and the Massachusetts capital was a local matter, the Governor stood aloof from it. While Commission-er Edwin U. Curtis was refusing to see his men or arbitrate their grievances, and the walkout approached, Coolidge left town for the week end. Neither did he act when most of the force—1117 men out of 1534—struck on Tuesday. But when rioting and pillage swept the capital, the Governor shook the peace and quiet of the State House with decisive action indeed. He sent AFL President Samuel Gompers the 16-word wire that made him famous—"There is no right to strike against the public safety by anybody, anywhere, at any time"—and called out the 6000-man State Guard. It was strong stuff, but the mob was out of hand by then.

The cavalry had to ride down the hoodlums running wild on the sidewalks. As the looting went on in South Boston, the infantry opened fire, killing two men and wounding nine. In the Scollay Square section, 15,000 rioters defied the Governor's troops. The mob had been ravaging the stores for days and wanted one more fling. It took a six-hour battle to close the Square. The *Boston Globe* likened the scene to something out of "some ferocious pageant."

In the mood of the day, the typewriter strategists assailed the strike and its effects as evidence that the revolution was just around the corner. Some papers compared the street mobs to the "mad minority" that overthrew the Kerensky government in Russia. President Wilson called the strike "a crime against civilization." What everyone overlooked was that the police had gone into the American Federation of Labor because they couldn't feed their families on $1,100 per year — twenty-two dollars a week, minus what their uniforms cost them. In the eventual settlement, police pay rose to $1,400 and the city bought the uniforms.

Coolidge came out the big winner. He drew plaudits everywhere for crushing a strike in one swoop while the entire nation was plagued by industrial warfare. The Republicans remembered this when it came time to pick up a man to run with Warren Harding in 1920. Coolidge's name couldn't hurt. It was an even better name four years later, backed by a little practical experience in the White House.

Coolidge inspects State Guardsmen he called out during the Boston police strike.

KEEP COOL
WITH COOLIDGE

*"When more and more
people are thrown out of
work, unemployment re-
sults."*

—CALVIN COOLIDGE

There was one very sour note for the Republicans in the 1924 Presidential campaign. The unfolding Teapot Dome scandal had begun to demonstrate that the Ohio Gang's two-year-and-five-month visit in Washington very likely had set an all-time record for thievery and corruption in the national government. This was the story:

Three months after taking office President Harding signed an executive order turning over to his Interior Department the custody of the government oil fields at Elk Hills and Buena Vista, California, and Teapot Dome, Wyoming. The reserves since 1909 had reposed under the Navy's jurisdiction as a gigantic defense store. Harding's Secretary of the Interior, Albert M. Fall, had many dear friends among the private oil interests and in 1922 he leased the Teapot Dome Reserve to Harry F. Sinclair's Mammoth Oil Company and the Elks Hills Reserve to Edward F. Doheny's Pan-American

Company. The leases were made in secret. Capitol Hill never knew the war reserves were in private hands until a Wyoming oilman wrote to his congressman and wanted to know how come Harry Sinclair had been able to lease Teapot Dome without competitive bidding. The resulting senatorial inquiry, under the tireless Tom Walsh of Montana, produced astonishing revelations.

It turned out that Fall had received $260,000 in Liberty bonds as "loans" from Sinclair and $100,000 in cash from Doheny. The immensely wealthy Doheny told the investigators that he had sent his son over with the money, nesting in a little black satchel, because his old friend Fall wanted to buy a new ranch in New Mexico and needed a stake. He said it was "a mere bagatelle" to him and he saw nothing improper in lending money to the Secretary of the Interior who was about to lease the nation's oil reserves to him for his personal profit.

In the eventual trials, Fall drew a year's jail sentence for accepting a bribe from Doheny but Doheny, in a separate trial, was found not guilty of paying any bribe to Fall. Sinclair beat the case against him but was jailed years later on two counts: contempt of the Senate and contempt of court for having a Burns detective shadow the jury in one of his trials.

There was an embarrassing sidelight in the oil scandal having to do with Sinclair's financial relations with the Republican National Committee. It turned out that the promoter had helped pay off the costs of the Harding campaign with a gift of $75,000 and a "loan" of $185,000 for which he had taken only $100,000 in repayment. The Republican chairman at the time happened to be Will Hays, later borrowed by Hollywood as the ideal man to police movie morals.

On another front, in 1927, the long arm of scandal fell heavily on Harry

Vice-President Coolidge at the 1922 Army-Navy football game.

Mr Coolidge close-up.

H. L. Mencken, an acid-penned observer of the government under Silent Cal, sits for a portrait by Nikol Schattenstein.

The 1924 Democratic Convention in New York was deadlocked so long over Al Smith and William G. McAdoo that it finally picked a virtual unknown—John W. Davis—to run against Calvin Coolidge.

The Teapot Dome scandal: Albert Fall, Harding's Secretary of the Interior, (left) poses outside court with oilman Harry F.

Sinclair after their arraignment on charges of conspiring to defraud the government.

ballot only after the long deadlock between Alfred E. Smith and William G. McAdoo and the blistering July heat in New York had wilted the convention delegates.

Thus, as the campaign proceeded, *Time* magazine was able to report week after week that while Davis rolled through the whistle-stops "Cal Coolidge sat tight and kept his peace." Why not? The Republican slogan was "Keep Cool With Coolidge"; why get into needlesss debates on the issues? Why debate the Harding record? He was dead. Why debate the recurrent Davis cry that the Republicans were the party of Big Business and wouldn't do anything for the little man? "This is a business country," Coolidge said in his one radio speech, with the United States Chamber of Commerce as his host, "it wants a business government." He must have been right. He drew 15,725,016 votes against 8,386,503 for Davis (third in thirteen states) and 4,822,856 for LaFollette.

In the next four years Coolidge demonstrated, if nothing else, that he was the most relaxed Chief Executive the nation ever had. Irwin (Ike) Hoover, the White House's Chief Usher, said the President usually found time for a two- to four-hour afternoon nap. When he didn't, he might rock on the porch for a while, watching the Model T's going by on Pennsylvania Avenue, feasting on the good expanse of lawn,

Daugherty. The former Attorney General had to stand trial after the Harding Administration's Alien Property Custodian, Thomas W. Miller, was sent to jail because $50,000 stuck to his hands in a curious transaction in which the American Metal Company—originally deemed to be owned by a German bank—managed to recover $6,000,000 in war-seized assets. The company paid out a total of $441,000 for various services in the process of getting its money back, and another party who picked up $50,000 was Jess Smith, Daugherty's roommate and lifetime buddy. Smith took his own life long before this item came out, but Daugherty was hauled into court because circumstantial evidence placed him somewhere in the lush Metal Company deal; however, a jury acquitted him after deliberating for 66 hours.

In the 1924 campaign, as it happened, the Republicans had an antidote for such of the Harding scandals as were already in the public record. Their candidate was Calvin Coolidge

and he himself had ushered out of the Cabinet not only Albert Fall, but also Secretary of the Navy Edwin L. Denby, in bad repute for maintaining too much silence when the nation's oil reserves were wrested from his hands and handed over to Fall. So the candidate's own halo of primitive Yankee honesty was secure; it would never tilt. Indeed, if anyone were needed to clean up the oil-smeared Potomac reservation, the man from Vermont fitted the role perfectly. There would be no fast-buck guys around the White House while he had the key. Beyond this happy circumstance, there appeared to be enough prosperity in the happy air to override Teapot Dome and any disclosures to come.

And, better still, Senator Robert M. LaFollette had entered the presidential sweepstakes on the Progressive ticket. His vote figured to dissipate whatever long-shot chance the badly split Democrats might have had with their compromise candidate, John W. Davis, picked on a record one-hundred-third

Charles R. Forbes handled the Veterans' Bureau for Harding during a period when something like $200,000,000 in graft was changing hands. He went to jail.

or perhaps dwelling idly on the great abundance that lay over the land. Will Rogers asked him how he kept fit, and he said, "By avoiding the big problems."

Coolidge avoided all manner of problems, big and little. He steered clear of the Prohibition mess, simply issuing an occasional manifesto saying the law really should be obeyed; unlike his predecessor, he could honestly claim that he for one wasn't helping the bootleggers by using their stuff. He didn't get too deep into foreign affairs, letting far-away Europe sweat out its own reconstruction problems. On the broader domestic scene, he kept an eye peeled to see that no new-fangled ideas crept into government; things were all right the way they were. He put the lid on suggestions that Washington do something about the frenzied speculation in Wall Street; the financial community knew what it was doing.

Years later, when the notion was put forth that Coolidge had spurned another term because he foresaw the depression, H. L. Mencken entered a strong dissent in the *Baltimore Sun.* "He showed not the slightest sign that he smelt black clouds ahead," Mencken said. "On the contrary, he talked and lived only sunshine. There was a volcano boiling under him, but he did not know it . . . Here, indeed, was his one really notable talent. He slept more than any other President, whether by day or night. Nero fiddled, but Coolidge only snored." Irving Stone, in an essay called "A Study in Inertia," noted that the passive country squire in the White House "believed that the least government was the best government; he aspired to become the least President the country ever had; he attained his desire." The Beards were more genteel in their judgment of New England's favorite son. "Never in all his career," said the historians, "had he shocked his neighbors by advocating strange things prematurely; neither had he been the last of the faithful to appear on the scene in appropriate armor. Conciliation and prudence had been his watchwords; patience and simplicity his symbols of life."

The man himself made no large claims about his horizons. "There is only one form of political strategy in which I have any confidence," his autobiography said, "and that is to try to do the right thing and sometimes succed."

Warren Harding's trust in the man who made him, Harry M. Daugherty (above), opened the door to the vast corruption in Washington from 1920 to 1923. The ex-Attorney General himself had to stand trial in a strange multimillion-dollar alien property swindle. He beat the charges but had been thoroughly discredited long before that particular case hit the headlines.

Jess Smith shared a room and a fat bank account or two with Harry Daugherty but killed himself just as the party ended for the freebooters from Ohio.

The Yankee President did succeed. He managed five years and seven months in the White House without getting into any kind of trouble. He went out of office—"I do not choose to run for President in 1928," he said—wearing

Gaston B. Means, an Ohio Gang henchman and quite a highbinder on his own, produced a book—*The Strange Death of President Harding*—broadly hinting that Flossie Harding poisoned her husband because (A) she found out about his affair with Nan Britton and (B) she wanted to spare him from the gathering revelations of sin-in-government. But Means' story was never substantiated.

Edwin N. Denby, Secretary of the Navy, walked the plank for letting the nation's oil reserves pass from his guardianship to the sticky fingers of Albert Fall.

all kinds of garlands, and there would be no surgical examination of his reign until after the Great Crash of 1929. Not till then would the post mortems cast some doubt on the record and much-heralded wisdom of Calvin Coolidge.

Big Boom in the West

"...The hardest thing about prizefighting is pickin' up yer teeth with a boxin' glove on."

— KIN HUBBARD

Shelby, Montana, July 4, 1923—a day nobody wanted to remember.

Way out in the Montana cowboy suburb of Shelby, a bunch of the boys were whooping it up one night in 1923 in an all-night saloon (Prohibition hadn't reached into this distant oasis). An oil strike had boomed the town's populace from 500 to 10,000, and the leading citizens were gathered around some Red Eye to discuss the filthy rich vistas that lay ahead. Somebody said why not *really* put Shelby on the map? Why not get Jack Dempsey to come out and defend his world's heavyweight title against someone like Tom Neil Gibbons? Everybody liked the idea but Dempsey didn't even answer the first few wires. Neither did Gibbons, an aging light-heavy from St. Paul. But the Chamber of Commerce spirit in Shelby wouldn't down and soon the champion's manager, Doc Kearns, began to smell money in the great outdoors. He said he would bring his boy out for a guarantee of, say, $300,000 plus 50 per cent of the gate in excess of that sum. High-riding Shelby's leading citizens took a deep breath, and maybe some more Red Eye, and started prospecting for investors.

Montana turned out to be crawling with believers-in-the-future. Dirt farmers, sheepherders, cowhands, bankers and the new oil barons put out money in stacks. In no time at all, Shelby had a $200,000 bundle ready for Kearns as evidence of its good intentions. In another twenty days, willing hands threw up a clapboard arena for 40,000—all on owings. The fight was staged July 4, 1923, and it turned out to be the blackest day in Montana's history. The expected migration from the sports-loving neighboring states simply failed to occur. Came the broiling noonday sun, there were but 1,500 paying customers sitting under ten-gallon hats in the rickety stands, while a scant 10,000 lounged outside wondering whether a fist fight between Jack Dempsey and Tom Gibbons could possibly be worth a $20 to $50 scale. Some 6,000 eventually dug into their jeans, but another 4,000 took the more thifty way and crashed the jerry-built arena even as Internal Revenue agents—on hand to put the lock on Uncle Sam's share of the gate—fired pistols over their heads.

The battle in the ring didn't help.

Tommy Gibbons—not much fight and not much money.

Dempsey, inactive except for his stage labors since his 1921 defense against Georges Carpentier, toiled through fifteen dreary rounds to a decision. Then he had to be spirited aboard a train for Great Falls because there were hotheads in Shelby who thought he hadn't put out enough muscle and sweat.

Kearns, a fastidious gentleman in money matters, tarried long enough to sweep up $80,000 out of the $201,000 in receipts. It was about all he could carry, what with so many silver dollars in the haul. The wily manager hid out in the cellar of the town barbershop before slipping into the caboose of an east-bound choo-choo under nightfall's merciful cover; his popularity had suffered even more than the champion's. In the wake of Shelby's debacle, mortgage holders seized the lumber from the arena to satisfy unpaid bills, the principal investors went broke, three banks collapsed and the town fell back into its former obscurity; even the oil ceased to flow. John Lardner called the incident "The Sack of Shelby"—a suitable epitaph. It couldn't have happened, of course, in any other time than the Lawless Decade. There would never again be a scramble for gold so frantic that the rankest amateurs would undertake to get in with the city slickers and promote a heavyweight title bout. Not in our time, certainly.

DEMPSEY AND THE WILD BULL

"There could be no honor in a sure success, but much might be wrested from a sure defeat."

—THOMAS EDWARD LAWRENCE

Mr. Firpo

The thing to do after the Dempsey-Gibbons fiasco was to rebuild the Manassa Mauler's injured name. The best possible party of the second part in this undertaking appeared to be Luis Angel Firpo, the heavyweight champion of South America, who was an inch and a half taller than Dempsey at six-foot-three, substantially wider and heavier and at least as ferocious. Everyone said that a meeting between these two prehistoric specimens would be a throwback to the days when men fought with clubs. So the fight drew 80,000 curious customers—some in mink—to the Polo Grounds in New York on September 14, 1923. The fans paid $1,188,603 (ringside seats selling for $27.50), and went home or back to the speakeasies with no sense of having been cheated. The gladiators only used up three minutes and fifty-seven seconds but put on the most savage prize fight in recorded history. Both men emerged covered with blood and glory.

Firpo, 216½ pounds on the hoof, and justly called the Wild Bull of the Pampas, landed the first blows. A left to the head and a right to the body caused Dempsey's knees to wobble and touch the canvas. This was the wrong way to play with the sensitive champion, of course. He got so angry he knocked Firpo down seven times. Dempsey used all the known combinations, and between knockdowns, instead of going to the prescribed neutral corner, stood over the Argentinian to hit him again as he got up. But for all this awful punishment the hairy Good Neighbor retained enough strength in that round to summon up a fierce right that knocked his tormentor clear out of the ring. Willing hands working in the press delegation pushed the champion back through the ropes at the count of nine, saving his title. In the second, Dempsey quickly floored Firpo with a series of pile-driving short hooks, but the challenger kept coming. "He did not rise like a beaten man," said W. O. McGeehan in the *New York Herald.* "The blood gushed from the battered lips, but the eyes behind the narrow lids were gleaming like the points of white-hot needles. His stout heart was still full of fight." It didn't help. A left and right to the jaw put the Wild Bull down again and it was over.

To this day the Argentine's proud partisans continue to ask the delicate question: Was it fair for those guys in the press row to push Dempsey back into the ring? Well, it was unfair, unsporting and also illegal. At the time, Firpo didn't linger to cry over spilled champions. He went home to buy some ranches with his new-found wealth and found plenty of fresh trouble the next year when he came back to fight Harry Wills. It turned out that his entourage on the steamer included a curvy Latin beauty who was listed as the gladiator's stenographer but really possessed no skill in the secretarial arts. This rather personal item formed the basis of a battle by Canon William Sheafe Chase of Brooklyn to get Firpo arrested for perjury, banished from our shores for moral turpitude and jailed for violation of the Mann Act, among other bad things.

The Argentine giant either had excellent presence of mind or good legal counsel. He shipped the lovely evidence—the Señorita, that is—down to Havana just as the Canon and a small army of recruits was closing the net around him. The Clean-Living forces couldn't even stop the Wills fight, although they were joined by eager morals crusaders in New Jersey, where the bout had to be held because lil' old New York didn't want a mixed prize fight. Wills, by the way, slapped Firpo around for the full twelve rounds, beating him badly. There may be a lesson in that, but this author is loath to draw it.

Willing hands help a fallen champion rise to fight some more.

John Barleycorn: Outlaw

"May you be in heaven half an hour before The Devil knows you're dead...."

—OLD IRISH TOAST

A Coast Guard destroyer on the Rum Row beat. The Coast Guard did the best it could, and brought in many captives. But with such a long coast to guard and such a small force for it, the patrol was only partly effective. The amateurs and smaller operators were likely to be caught. The big professionals, highly organized, generally ran the blockade successfully.

Worn out by his strenuous labors on the Broadway boards in *Clair de Lune*, John Barrymore (not to be confused with the man in the title of this chapter) betook himself to Europe for his version of some rest. Somebody over there asked the Great Profile what he thought of Prohibition.

"Fortunately," Barrymore replied, with vast disdain, "I don't think of it."

This was true of millions of otherwise true-blue Americans.

It was true of Americans who had never broken any other law and wouldn't even dream of exceeding the fifteen-mile speed limit on the city streets.

It was true of Americans who said grace before meals and went to church every Sunday and sometimes twice a week.

It was true of Americans who could take the hard stuff or leave it before the nation went Dry by fiat. Whiskey acquired a brand new taste in the twenties. It was forbidden fruit.

Nobody who wanted to savor that fruit paid any attention to the law. "The business of evading it and making a mock of it," H. L. Mencken observed,

For this purpose, the old-fashioned below-the-knee skirt was more appropriate.

"has ceased to wear any aspects of crime, and has become a sort of national sport." Polly Adler, the celebrated New York madam whose occupation took her into intimate contact with all manner of life during the bad old days, had an equally cynical view of Prohibition. "They might as well have been trying to dry up the Atlantic with a post-office blotter," she said. Her point was that as long as people wanted to drink and pay the price there would be limitless amounts to go around. Polly Adler found it that way in her own field.

As it happened, nothing in the Eighteenth Amendment took dead aim on the thirsty citizen. The government, in its half-hearted way, sought out the man who made whiskey or ran it through our wafer-thin land and sea blockades or sold it over the bar. Uncle Sam wanted the purveyor of bottled fun, not the fellow foolhardy enough to drink when so much rotgut was in circulation.

Bootleggers load beer and whiskey on the Canadian side for the quick run to the wet American shore.

The U.S. Coast Guard cutter *Lexington* brings in four rum boats caught in the government net.

Connecticut State Police grab a $100,000 liquor haul off their shores on a lucky strike.

The Detroit shore abounded in the cup that cheers. Note the beer barrels on the dock.

In full flight from the Coast Guard, a rumrunner dumps the evidence.

The forces of Dry law 'n' order haul a sinner in off the Atlantic Coast.

William Vincent (Big Bill) Dwyer was only a stevedore on the New York docks when Prohibition arrived. He moved into the lush bootlegging trade, dealing in home brew as well as the Rum Row imports, and quickly became an associate of Owney Madden and George (Big Frenchy) DeMange. In time his varied interests, shady or otherwise, put him in the upper brackets. Apart from pure racket operations, he had a large hand in the New York night clubs during the Lawless Decade and eventually turned up with William J. (Big Bill) Duffy as the man behind Primo Carnera's strange emergence as heavyweight boxing champion. The clumsy Italian giant barely got off with coffee-and-cake money after Dwyer, Duffy and other helping hands split his title earnings.

The Rose-Colored Glass

"We regard voluntary total abstinence from all intoxicants as the obligation of the citizen..."
—The doctrines and discipline of the Methodist Episcopal Church, II, 1932

The Drys went through their thirteen-year moment in the sun bravely piling up statistics to show that Prohibition was a huge success. Professor Irving Fisher of Yale, the bluenoses' intellectual battering ram, said that the Volstead Act cut deaths, poverty, disease, divorce and industrial accidents and made cash registers jingle like sleighbells in groceries, candy shops, shoe stores, restaurants, hardware stores, jewelry shops and clothing stores.

Deets Pickett, secretary of the Methodist Episcopal Church's Board of Temperance, Prohibition, and Public Morals, said the Dry law had done more for our health than anything since

medical science put the finger on bacteria. Pickett called the Lawless Decade the "astounding twenties" and saw it as a time of "unprecedented confidence, of record-breaking business achievement," even of achievement in the world of athletics which had been hitherto unknown. "We learned to drink milk as never before," he said, "and our tables were loaded with fresh vegetables and fruits . . . and the young people became taller and healthier and more vigorous." Pickett also noted that more men bought life insurance, presumably because they got more serious once the laughing water ran out. He credited Prohibition with the fact that bank deposits rose from fifteen billion dollars in 1920 to just under twenty-

Time for a refill.

nine billion in 1929, while deposits in savings and loan associations went up from two to seven billion dollars.

Roy A. Haynes, an early Prohibition Commissioner, said the law cut drunk arrests in half (for women, 80 per cent), cut deaths from alcohol, cut the population of prisons and almshouses and cut juvenile delinquency and offenses against chastity. Dr. Louis Henry Smith, president of Washington & Lee University, called the law "the longest and most effective step forward in the uplift of the human race ever taken by any civilized nation." And all the Drys said all the happy workers were doing a better job, now that their eyes were clear, and thus were making more money.

Other authorities, digging even deeper, cited "surveys" to show that profanity had decreased by 80 per cent and prostitution by 97 per cent, while some said that even the slums had disappeared from the big cities.

The Wets went to the other extreme, naturally. They gave Prohibition credit for nothing more than the biggest sick headache in history. Wherever the Drys threw out a figure involving the purse, such as the nation's higher purchasing power or the boom in savings and salaries, the Wets reminded people about our vast economic prosperity. It was something like a murder case based on an insanity plea: each side had a set of separate facts and a set of separate experts to support them. In the case of Prohibition, there was so much passion on both sides that the truth couldn't possibly be known, then or now.

What'll you have?

"Prohibition only drives drunkenness behind doors and into dark places, and does not cure or even diminish it."
—Mark Twain

Was there any way to enforce Prohibition?

Was there any way to seal off our borders?

Was there any way to flush the moonshiners out of all the hills or go into all the basements and kitchens where

Vannie Higgins, a hoodlum lieutenant of Dwyer's and Rum Row entrepreneur on his own, was well connected in high places. Once he flew his private plane upstate to take dinner with the warden at Comstock Prison, Joseph H. Wilson. Governor Franklin Delano Roosevelt got angry about it, so Wilson candidly explained that Vannie was an old friend. A spot-killing erased Higgins from the New York scene in 1932.

Americans were cooking their own alcohol during the twenties?

The record won't show. Congress never put out enough money to do anything more than make an occasional lame swipe at the illicit liquor trade and grab off some headlines. And in the White House three successive Administrations gave nothing but lip

New York State Troopers put the arm on this ship-to-shore wagonload before it could reach the wholesale marts.

Crude, but from this came a thing people called liquor in those days.

service (wet lips, in Harding's case) to the Dry cause.

But consider the situation realistically.

Our Canadian border is 3,986 miles long. An army would have a hard time policing it. Liquor flowed into the United States by land and sea from this giant spigot so freely that the supply always exceeded the demand; too many bootleggers elected to peddle inferior homemade brands under Canadian labels and make a killing on the price. They only bought what they had to buy in the overland trade, or from the boats plying the Lake Erie ports, or from the sleds that ran the stuff when the waterways froze over.

Our vast Atlantic seaboard similarly defied policing, so the Rum Row flotilla plied almost at will between New York and such points as Nassau ("The Isle of Rum") and St. Pierre of the Miquelons ("The Isle of Champagne") and the other ports of supply. The Prohibition people, of course, publicly proclaimed the doom of the rumrunners every time a pinch was made at sea, just as they always talked of the Canadian traffic as a mere trickle that would be under control any day—or sooner.

Now consider the moonshiners, flourishing in the most unlikely places. An abandoned church in Iowa had a $50,000 rig in its sub-cellar. A Virginia farmer sliced his dugout right into the green hills. An Omaha still trailed out of a barn through a sixty-five-foot concrete tunnel. A Colorado moonshiner set up in a cave under heavy brush and buried dead animals nearby so the stench would counteract the mash and whiskey fumes. A Mississippi man with the same idea had a huge manure pile over his underground still.

Even if it wanted to—and there was never more than a handful of "revenooers" beating the bushes—how could the government put a dent in this thriving, resourceful and highly profitable industry? The pastoral bootlegger hummed along nicely before, during, and after Prohibition. He is doing business today at the same stand, although understandably on a much smaller scale.

Beyond the Canadian supply, beyond the freebooters on the Atlantic and beyond the moonshiners lay the legion of alky cookers in the cities. It would have taken nothing short of a federal census—preferably in simultaneous night raids—to get a count on that industry's output. The tenements simply ran with alcohol. How could you stop that flow?

And, again, did anybody want to? The courts dealt out nothing but small fines to the offenders who got caught. For that matter, jail sentences for Prohibition violators would have filled the prisons to overflowing, just as today there wouldn't be room enough behind bars to hold the traffic violators if the courts got tough with them. Or the income tax corner-cutters, for that matter.

One of the stock pictures of the Prohibition Era, but not a common sight, nevertheless, even for those zany days.

The border patrol. Officers on the El Paso-Hueco Tanks Road intercept a smuggler and capture his liquor. The Mexican border, less publicized than the Canadian, was more easily crossed by illicit importers.

"THE BROKEN BUTTERFLY"

"A moth, too close to the flame ..."

—Alvin Davis

Dot King, who died so young.

money and got nothing but beatings in return. But the grieving Señor was able to show that he was on the speakeasy rounds all night and never came near the girl.

The variety of love letters found in the apartment from an assortment of admirers turned up only one that seemed fruitful. "Darling Dottie," it began. "Only two days before I will be with you. I want to see you, O so much! And to kiss your pretty pink toes . . ." This burst of passion was traced to J. Kearsley Mitchell, wealthy son-in-law of the late Edward (Uncle Ned) Stotesbury, celebrated in his time as the sole dictator of Philadelphia's Four Hundred. Mitchell conceded that the purple prose *and* the yellow pajamas fit his style. He liked Dot King and sometimes tucked $1,000 bills under her pillow to prove it. He said that he and his attorney spent the day of March 14 with the playgirl, separately in the boudoir and together in the town's flossier resorts, and bid her good night at 2:30 A.M., some time before the murder. So the red-faced society man was permitted to go home to Philadelphia's even redder-faced Main Line.

The investigation withered.

The tabloid writers who used to call Dot King the Broadway Butterfly changed it to the Broken Butterfly and let it go at that. To this day it is one of the more intriguing chapters in the history of sinful New York.

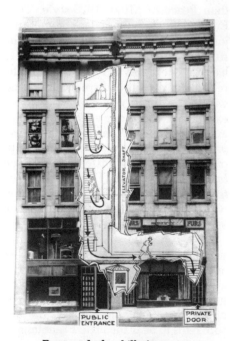

Route of the killer's escape.

Dot King came out of the *Ziegfeld Follies* chorus. She had a doll's face and an hour-glass body. She had nighttime New York at her feet. She had her choice of men: sugar daddies, playboys, top-hatted stage-door Johnnies bearing red roses, and at least one Just Plain Gigolo. She had diamonds and furs and a plush bachelor-girl apartment five minutes from the Great White Way. In her way, she had everything.

Billie Bradford, Dot King's maid, found her sprawled lifeless across her bed on the morning of March 15, 1923. Billie grabbed up a pair of yellow silk men's pajamas from a chair near the bed, stuffed them under a cushion on the living room couch, and went for a policeman. The intern who answered the routine ambulance call said it looked like suicide to him, but Dr. Charles Norris, the Chief Medical Examiner,

put it down as murder. He detected signs of a struggle in the grotesque way the ex-Follies girl's right arm was twisted behind her back. He thought the killer probably had snuffed out her life with chloroform while trying to subdue her during a robbery; there was an empty chloroform bottle in the room.

The slain twenty-seven-year-old beauty's missing baubles included a $15,000 ruby necklace, two diamond bracelets, a diamond and emerald studded wrist watch and other trifles, all adding up to about $30,000 worth.

Mrs. Anna Keenan, Dot King's mother, leaned to the murder theory, with or without the robbery motive. She even named the man—Alberto Santos Guimares, a Latin Man-About-Manhattan, complete with sideburns and mustache. She said Dot loved Alberto intensely, furnished all his spending

IT HAPPENED IN 1923 . . .

Emile Coué (right) peddling his brand of do-it-yourself contentment.

It was the best of times but everybody wanted something even better. The welcome mat was out not only for the super-salesmen in the Get-Rich-Quick marts but even for the sweet-talker who was peddling nothing more than Peace of Mind, 1923-style. Thus Emil Coué was hailed as something just short of the Messiah when he stepped off the boat from France. He had an idea and his advance public relations platoons had spread it far and wide. The thing was simplicity itself, except for the clumsy name it bore: autosuggestion. What M. Coué prescribed for total, true and lasting happiness was twelve little words—"*Day by day in every way I am getting better and better.*" M. Coué said it would work on any man—or even any woman —who kept repeating it.

We go a little deeper in our time, what with the big boom in couches and psychiatrists, but in the New Era a man like M. Coué could live pretty good on a simple phrase with a touch of yoga in it. People jammed the lecture halls to hear the little Frenchman's magic formula in person. Others rushed to newly-organized Coué Institutes to make sure they had the twelve words right. But like anything else, Americans being such fickle lovers, Couéism didn't last. After a while people were making jokes about it, such as the one about the woman who went to M. Coué with a problem:

> WOMAN: My husband thinks he's sick. He's always complaining.
> M. COUÉ: Simple. You just tell him that day by day in every way he is getting better and better.
> WOMAN (a few days later): I'm sorry but I have even worse trouble now.
> M. COUÉ: What is it, my dear lady?
> WOMAN: Now my husband thinks he's dead.

It was all in fun, of course. But M. Coué went home after a while.

New York's Great White Way rejoiced in 1923 because Police Commissioner Richard E. Enright took his standing guards out of the cafés, cabarets and restaurants and also extended the dancing curfew from 1:00 A.M. to 2:00 A.M. . . The dance marathon, an import from Europe, began to sweep the country. One contest set a record of ninety hours and ten minutes. A high-stepper in Tonawanda, New York, dropped dead on his eighty-seventh hour. Chicago in 1930 would stage a marathon that would go on—and on and on—for 3,327 hours . . . Greta Gustafsson made a movie in Sweden; in American movies she would be Greta Garbo . . . Portable radios for cars, set in clumsy wooden cases, made their bow . . . President Coolidge freed the last of the political prisoners . . . Nicola Sacco went on a thirty-one-day hunger strike in a Massachusetts prison . . . Sarah Bernhardt died in Paris at seventy-eight . . . A. Conan Doyle, creator of Sherlock Holmes, came to the States with a photograph supposedly showing the faces of the war dead peeking in on a memorial service in London. Sir Arthur had strong connections in the spirit world . . . Britain barred boys and girls under eighteen from drinking in the pubs.

The first transatlantic radio news dispatches were broadcast to England from New Jersey . . . In Columbia, Missouri, fifty women attended the hanging of a Negro accused of assaulting a fourteen-year-old girl . . . The Senate voted a $5,000 annual pension to President Harding's widow . . . Henry Ford said no, he would not run against Calvin Coolidge for President . . . Thomas E. Dewey was graduated from the University of Michigan . . . Bad liquor killed fourteen persons during the New Year's celebration in New York . . . Dr. Ales Hrdlicka, a leading anthropologist, said that man did not descend directly from the ape we knew then but had his origin 400,000 years ago in Europe . . . Clarence Darrow and William Jennings Bryan debated fundamentalism vs. evolution in the *Chicago Tribune* . . . U. S. Steel abolished the twelve-hour day and came down to ten . . . A federal judge ruled that the Prohibition Law did not limit the number of liquor prescriptions doctors could write . . . Navy Lieutenant Alford I. Williams, a former Giant pitcher, flew a Curtiss monoplane 243.67 miles per hour—a new world's speed record . . . Ex-President Wilson charged that our isolation from the Allies was "cowardly and dishonorable."

This trio put golf into the big money: Bobby Jones, Walter Hagen (center), and Gene Sarazen, shown with his wife.

In New York the feud between the murderous gangs of Nathan (Kid Dropper) Kaplan and Jacob (Little Augie) Orgen boiled over. Police Captain Cornelius W. Willemse hauled Dropper and some of his troops into Essex Market Court on an assortment of charges and got him to agree to depart the city forever. As the Captain escorted the Kid to a taxi outside the courthouse, an undersized immigrant boy named Louis Cohen poked a revolver through the rear window of the cab and pumped three bullets into the gang leader. The boy, 17, had slipped through a cordon of eighty detectives to carry out the deed. He said the Little Augie gang got him hopped up on liquor and cocaine and told him he'd be the biggest man in New York if he "croaked" Kid Dropper. With the help of an eloquent lawyer named James J. Walker, later Mayor, the boy beat the chair.

* * *

Robert Tyre Jones, Jr., called Bobby, won the National Open golf championship. The stocky Atlanta boy was only twenty-one but he had been on the golf circuit seven years, knocking on the door all the time. To win the big one, he had to beat defending champion Gene Sarazen, Walter Hagen, Bobby Cruikshank and Jock Hutchinson. He won it on the eighteenth hole after coming up to it tied with the other Bobby at 296 strokes each. He would reign on the links all through the Golden Age of Sports and past it . . . In baseball, Henry Lou Gehrig, a local boy from Commerce High School and Columbia University, played first base for the New York Yankees in a few games and was shipped to Hartford, in the minors. Manager Miller Huggins said he needed a little more seasoning. . . . In tennis, a 17-year-old named Helen Wills, called Little Miss Poker Face by the sports writers, won the Women's National Singles title from Molla Mallory.

The non-fiction best-seller of 1923 was Emily Post's *Etiquette,* followed by Giovanni Papini's *Life of Christ* . . . *The Mind in the Making,* by James Harvey Robinson, also sold well . . .

Fiction was topped by Gertrude Atherton's *Black Oxen* . . . Sinclair Lewis' *Babbitt* and Rafael Sabatini's *The Sea Hawk* were on the list . . . On the silent screen, adventure and the spine-chillers were big: Lon Chaney in *The Hunchback of Notre Dame,* Ramon Novarro in *Scaramouche,* Clara Bow in *Down to the Sea in Ships* and Douglas Fairbanks in *Robin Hood.* In the theater, Broadway had Jane Cowl in *Romeo and Juliet,* Walter Hampden in *Cyrano de Bergerac,* Winifred Lenihan in Shaw's *Saint Joan,* Irene Bordoni in *Little Miss Bluebeard,* and W. C. Fields in *Poppy* . . . The great Duse died in Pittsburgh on her farewell American tour.

Little Augie

Captain Willemse

Murder for fun

"Everybody is a potential murderer..."
—CLARENCE DARROW

One afternoon in the spring of 1924, two youths drew up in front of the Harvard School for Boys in the Chicago suburb of South Side Kenwood. They had been plotting the "perfect murder" for seven months. They had no particular victim in mind until little Bobby Franks, a neighbor of theirs, came by. He seemed an excellent candidate. Would Bobby like a ride home? The boy eagerly said yes. He held Dickie Loeb and Nathan Leopold in awe. Loeb, eighteen, the University of Michigan's youngest graduate, was doing postgraduate work at the University of Chicago. Leopold, nineteen, Phi Beta Kappa, had a B.S. from Chicago and was taking a law course there now. They were *cum laude* all the way. Bobby Franks was always flattered when they talked to him. He hopped into the car.

It was the beginning of the big horror saga of the Lawless Decade. It would turn the nation's insides.

Loeb and Leopold took their fourteen-year-old admirer within a few blocks of his home in Hyde Park and then stuffed a gag into his mouth and crashed a heavy cold chisel against his skull four times. Then they drove idly over to the marshy wasteland near Hegewisch and carried the still-warm body into a culvert alongside the Pennsylvania Railroad tracks. They held the head under swamp water for a while to make sure all life had fled. Then they poured hydrochloric acid on the face to make identification hard. Then they wedged the body, all but the feet, into a drain pipe obscured by shrubbery and weeds. After that, they drove to a restaurant and got some sandwiches. Their labors, however casual and unhurried, had made them hungry.

That night the two intellectual prodigies sipped liquor and played cards at Leopold's home until midnight, but took time to call Jacob Franks and inform him that his son had been kidnaped. They told Franks, a wealthy retired pawnbroker, that he would receive mailed instructions as to how to get the boy back—and for how much.

Franks notified the police.

Detectives called him back at noon the next day—May 22. Two workmen taking a shortcut through a culvert had found the body of a boy; the police wanted Franks to come and look at it. Franks said no, he had heard from the kidnapers. Bobby was fine and was about to be returned for $10,000—$2,000 in "old twenties" and $8,000 in "old fifties." But later, tortured by anxiety, Franks sent his brother-in-law to the Hegewisch Morgue and heard the horrible truth.

There was no shortage of clues in the "perfect murder."

Leopold, son of a millionaire lake transport executive, had dropped his glasses during the burial scene without bothering to recover them. It took the police eight days, but they found the oculist who made them. Leopold denied the glasses were his but the empty case betrayed him. Then he said he must have lost them in the culvert weeks ago, while studying bird life there. But it had rained hard for days before the murder and the glasses were spotless.

That didn't shake Leopold. "He was a nice little boy," he said airily. "What motive did I have for killing him? I didn't need the money; my father is rich. Whenever I want money all I have to do is ask him for it. And I earn money myself teaching ornithology." Besides, he had an alibi for May 21. He said he and Dickie Loeb were out in his car all afternoon. He said they got a bottle of gin and picked up two girls—"May" and "Edna"—and went joy-riding. Loeb, son of a vice-president of Sears, Roebuck & Co., told the same story. But the Leopold chauffeur said Nathan's Willys-Knight never left the garage on May 21. And while all this was going on two cub reporters on the *Chicago Daily News*, Jim Mulroy and Al Goldstein, were checking sam-

Richard Loeb

Nathan Leopold

1924

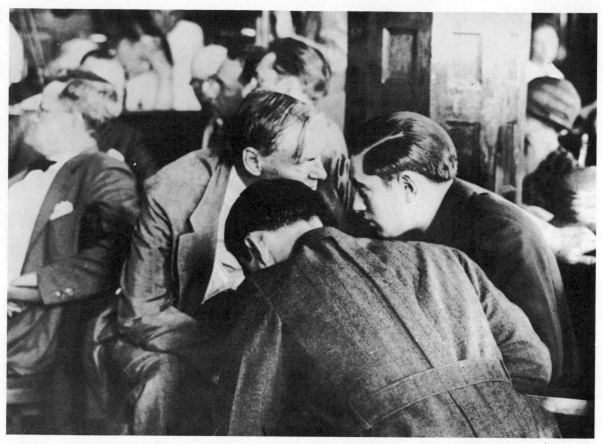

Clarence Darrow in a huddled courtroom conversation with Loeb and Leopold (right).

ples of Leopold's typing against a ransom note Bobby Franks' father had received. The type seemed to match; Leopold's Underwood portable, found in a lagoon later, would bear this out.

The handsome, well-mannered Loeb, a self-styled amateur criminologist, cracked first. He had offered detectives some theories on the murder early in the investigation, before his arrest; now he told them all about it. It was only a lark, really; he and Babe wanted to see what turmoil a "perfect murder" would create in a city like Chicago. Lord knows they didn't dislike Bobby Franks; he seemed like a nice kid. But Loeb was critical of Leopold, whom he called "Babe." He said he never approved of Babe's perverted sex habits.

Leopold, a small, round-shouldered boy with bulging eyes, said Loeb was a Superman type and had made him his slave. He said Dickie planned the murder.

The families sent for Clarence Darrow. He was sixty-eight and very tired, but he didn't like capital punish-

Darrow for the Defense
"A man who lives, not by what he loves but what he hates, is a sick man."
—Archibald MacLeish

ment. He had saved 104 men from the death penalty. He would save two boys now and then quit.

There was no need to prove anything against the twisted killers of Bobby Franks, but the State of Illinois put each and every gruesome fact into the record in endless array as the newspapers screamed the eye-for-an-eye theme. Clarence Darrow countered with a small battalion of alienists, psychiatrists and neurologists, and for thirty-three days the nation heard all about the wondrous, inexplicable ways of the billion-cell labyrinth we call the brain. Darrow's best witness wasn't even in the courtroom during those hot summer days; his real star was Freud. Darrow did not argue that the honor students before the bar didn't know right from wrong; he argued that they didn't know what they were doing because they were sick in their brilliant

heads. But Darrow didn't plead insanity. He pleaded mental illness.

It was something new in courtroom spectacles, another trail-blazer for the New Era. The human brain was on trial in Chicago and some fancy words got in the papers. Darrow offered evidence that Leopold was a paranoiac with a severe manic drive, and Loeb a dangerous schizophrenic. The lawyer made much of the fact that a governess forcibly introduced Leopold to sex when he was fourteen and a chauffeur performed the same disservice for Loeb. He noted that they had supernormal intelligences, but emotionally weren't past the age of seven. He noted that Loeb existed in a world of fantasy, alternately imagining himself a frontiersman in pioneer days or the master criminal of our times. He said the boys didn't make sense: just for kicks, they cheated at bridge, broke automobile windows, fired an abandoned building, and looted fraternity houses when they had all the money they could use.

Darrow talked for two days. He

talked about fathers and sons. He quoted from Housman's "A Shropshire Lad":

The night my father got me
his mind was not on me;
He did not play his fancy
to muse if it should be
the son you see.

"No one knows what will be the fate of the child he begets," Darrow told the court. "This weary world goes on begetting . . . and all of it is blind from beginning to end. I don't know what it was that made these boys do this mad act, but I know there is no reason for it. I know they did not beget themselves . . . We are all helpless . . . But when you are pitying the father and the mother of poor Bobby Franks, what about the fathers and mothers of all the boys and all the girls who tread a dangerous maze in darkness from birth to death? . . . I am sorry for all fathers and all mothers. The mother who looks into the blue eyes of her little baby cannot help musing of the end of the child, whether it will be crowned with the greatest promises that mind can imagine—or whether he will meet death upon the scaffold. All she can do is to rear him with love and with care, to watch over him tenderly, and to meet life with hope and trust and confidence, and to leave the rest with fate."

Darrow argued that the scaffold was not the answer to the ills that beset Loeb and Leopold or the others like them in all the cities and towns everywhere.

"Do you think you can cure the hatreds and the maladjustments of the world by hanging them?" he asked. "You simply show your ignorance and your hate when you say it. You may heal and cure hatred with love and understanding, but you can only add fuel to the flames with cruelty and hating."

Here Darrow wept.

The defendants had sat impassively through the horror of the State's presentation and through the moving rhetoric of the masterful advocate pleading for their lives. At times they had seemed bored, but now Darrow got to them. He said he could think of a scene even more macabre than the one in the culvert—"I can think of taking two boys . . . irresponsible, weak, diseased . . . penning them in a cell, checking off the days, the hours and the minutes, until they be taken out and hanged."

Dickie Loeb shuddered. Babe Leopold got hysterical and had to be taken out of the courtroom. When the boy came back Darrow returned to his theme:

"Wouldn't it be a glorious day for Chicago, wouldn't it be a glorious triumph for the State's Attorney, wouldn't it be a glorious triumph for justice in this land, wouldn't it be a glorious illustration of Christianity, and kindness and charity? I can picture them awakened in the gray light of morning, furnished a suit of clothes by the State, led to the scaffold, and fitting tight, black caps down over their heads, stood on a trap door, the hangman

Bobby Franks

pressing a spring, so that it gives way under them; I can see them fall through space—and—stopped by rope around their necks."

John R. Caverly, Chief Justice of the Criminal Court of Cook County, had a hard decision to make. He had heard the case himself, without a jury. He had heard the murder of Bobby Franks described as the most heinous in Illinois' history. He had heard the Battle of the Head Shrinkers—a most puzzling thing because the State's witnesses, equally qualified, countered every point made by the defense's learned experts. He knew the agony of the parents on both sides. He knew what passions had boiled up; his bailiffs had to break up near-riots outside the courtroom as the people battled for seats. He could sense what they were there for. Should he call for the hangman?

The sentence came in two parts:

For the murder of Bobby Franks, life.

For kidnapping the boy, ninety-nine years.

Darrow had won.

Darrow pleads the cause of Loeb and Leopold before Judge John R. Caverly.

Brute Force: Red Grange

"The football season is the only time of year when girls whistle at men in sweaters."
—Robert Q. Lewis

Harold Grange, son of a sheriff's deputy in Wheaton, Illinois, went out for the high school football team because the uniform was attractive. "The sight of it was too much to resist," he said. He averaged five touchdowns a game that season, and two years later he was playing for Bob Zuppke at the University of Illinois. He was a good back and a good learner. He made All America, quite a trick for a green kid.

The lightning struck in the next season, 1924, in the Michigan game in the Illinois Memorial Stadium at Urbana. Harold Grange, who carried ice in the summer to put muscle on his five-foot, eleven-inch frame, took the opening kick-off and ran it 95 yards for a touchdown. Then he went 66, 55 and 40 yards for three more TDs, leaning against the Michigan goal post for a

moment between times to store up some wind. It all happened within 12 minutes and when Zuppke took the boy out to rest him the crowd of 67,000 set off a demonstration that delayed the second quarter for five minutes. It was the greatest ovation in the whole history of football, and it could have rattled Zuppke's *wunderkind*. He made only one more touchdown that afternoon, passing for another as Illinois won, 39-14. In the dressing room, Grange gave the coach all the credit. "Zuppke's plays were designed to shake me loose," he said. "It has all been a combination of circumstances."

Circumstances would continue to be favorable for the kid in the yellow helmet. Red Grange, No. 77, made Jack Dempsey move over. He put college football ahead of boxing as the Golden

Age picked up momentum. He also made some of the ball yards obsolete; they couldn't handle the crowds. He made people buy more radios: how could you wait until Sunday morning to find out what deeds Red Grange had performed on Saturday? He was "The Galloping Ghost" and he made the sports historians torture their portables without mercy. "What a football player —this man Red Grange," Damon Runyon wrote: "He is melody and symphony . . . He is crashing sound. He is poetry. He is brute force." Someone else likened the speedy back to "young Lochinvar come out of the West," but assured his readers that "Red Grange is human. He is not a myth." Another borrowed from Kipling: "East is East and Grange is Grange."

PLAY FOR PAY

"I do not like football well enough to play it for nothing."

—RED GRANGE

C. C. Pyle managed Grange in the Gold and Glory leagues.

It was a time for superlatives in words, in deeds and in money.

Red Grange turned and twisted and shook off the enemy along thousands of yards of turf for a third year at Illinois, and the undergraduates carried him two miles in a great victory procession. His fellow students wanted him to run for Congress and write the nation's laws now that he had rewritten all its football records. Hollywood wanted him to come out and make pictures. A real estate firm offered him $125,000 a year, experience unnecessary. The New York Football Giants offered him $40,000 for three games. College officials and the holier-than-thou types in amateur sports begged him to shun these blandishments and finish his education. But Grange had his own view.

"A couple of years from now," he said, "the same fellows who advised me not to play professional wouldn't lend me a dollar if I were broke. In this world I figure it is every man for himself."

No. 77 turned pro.

On December 8 he was granted an audience with President Coolidge. The interview, in full:

COOLIDGE: Howdy. Where do you live?

GRANGE: Wheaton, Illinois.

COOLIDGE: Well, young man, I wish you luck.

Red Grange didn't need luck. He was box office. He proceeded to work some magic for the professional game. The Chicago Bears paid him $15,000 to pack their park for one Sunday outing and the Giants paid him $35,000 for the same service. He picked up $50,000 in endorsements under the shrewd handling of his new-found manager, C. C. Pyle, the Bunion Derby man. He got $300,000 from Arrow Studios for a movie. "I don't want to play a sheik part," he said. "This business of lollygagging around with a girl most of the time, as movie actors usually do in all the pictures I've seen, is not in my line. I can do all the rough work on the gridiron, but I want to do very little in the parlor." The people at Arrow put him in something called *One Minute to Play*. It was a football epic, to be sure, but the script did call for some "lollygagging" with girls.

Back on the playing field, Grange's labors earned him about $1,000 a minute and he had an answer for the envious few who professed to view this form of inflation with alarm. "I do not like football well enough to play it for nothing," said the policeman's boy from Illinois. His earnings ran into a million in the first three years, dropping thereafter with the inevitable decline of his talents. He stayed in the game thirteen years as player, coach, and promoter. Later he managed a night club in Hollywood, functioned as sales manager for a bottling company and sold insurance. Now he is back in public view as a between-halves television commentator on the football beat. And his old jersey—No. 77—reposes in a frame at the University of Illinois. No one ever carried that number again.

Carrying the ball for the Chicago Bears, Red Grange loses his helmet as he scores against Los Angeles in 1926.

THE FLORIDA BUBBLE

In the early twenties the vision of riches—wonderful, sudden boundless riches—turned south. For there lay Florida, nested under a powder-blue sky, baked by the soft sun, caressed by tropical breezes wafted in from the West Indies. There she lay, an American Paradise, right off the paved road, there for the taking. No, not just a place to thrive on low-cost land and low-cost year-round sunshine (no heating bills), but also a place to grab off a fortune. If you moved fast, you could buy a piece of land for a few hundred or so and sell it for fifty times that much as soon as the promoters arrived, bearing blueprints for a dream village.

The papers were full of stories like that. Coolidge Prosperity was fanning out from the stock market to the sticks: you could make it even faster in Florida. And there was room for everybody. You could take your life savings into Miami ("The Fair White Goddess of Cities"), Coral Gables, Boca Raton, St. Petersburg, Orlando, Hollywood-By-The-Sea. Name it. They all had the same climate and they were all close to wherever you were—New York, Cleveland, Fort Wayne, any place. If you were a peculiar sort and didn't want to speculate, why not just pull up stakes and go down there and build yourself a house for, say, eight or ten thousand dollars. The same house would cost you twenty to twenty-five thousand in the Northeast, what with the high cost of labor and land.

The people went.

All roads—paved, as noted—led to the booming, bustling Florida-on-the-Sea. Somebody compared it to the opening of the Cherokee Strip in frontier days, but the Florida land run was more orderly. You didn't need a Winchester. Wherever you were going, there was a man waiting with the deed; you staked your claim with Mr. Waterman's pen and some money. It was

Opening of the $300,000 Swimming Pool and Casino at Hollywood, 1925.

This was a gag photo but it contained painful truths for thousands of gullible investors who took a bath in Florida real estate.

Palm Beach while the boom was on.

legal and clean from start to finish. After that the decision was all yours. You could settle down and suck in the dream climate (no winter clothes to buy) or you could sell to the guy who was snapping up lots to build a bigger and better community for tomorrow's arrivals.

For the late-starting American who needed a little more salesmanship Florida had some live walking and talking exhibits. The developer of Coral Gables—"America's Most Beautiful Suburb"—had none other than William Jennings Bryan, in person, lecturing the masses on the climate. If you needed even more persuasion, once the pearly tones of the Great Orator subsided, there was a dance by Gilda Gray. Other ballyhoo carnivals of the same nature, tent-show style, were put on across the state.

Naturally, there were some catches in the balmy Florida story.

By 1924 the Get-Rich-Quick legion had begun to suffer some casualties. Some long-distance buyers found that

they had bought swamps or palmetto groves, not land to build on or resell; you couldn't give it away. Some found that their lots "outside of Miami Beach" were seventy miles from any community. Some found their little piece of the dandy future tucked away

Paul Whiteman midst the sheltering palms.

in deserts where there would be no water or electricity—or anything else—for years to come.

But Americans gave up slowly in the New Era.

The boom ran through 1925 and values continued to soar. It wasn't until the next year that the bubble burst. By then, the Everglades State had hopelessly oversold itself and values dipped. The two great hurricanes of September and October of 1926 didn't help, either; hundreds of investments were wafted away in the suddenly-angry tropical breeze. In another year, the boom was a forlorn memory, not just for the little men who had rushed to the seaside El Dorado with their life savings, but also for some of the shrewd and experienced operators who had taken millions of dollars into Florida.

But that was 1927.

There was still the stock market. Nothing wrong with that if you wanted to turn a fast dollar. The stock market went only one way—UP.

ðion O'Banion:

ALTAR BOY

GONE WRONG

The O'Banion

"... and he never left home without telling me where he was going or kissing me good-bye."
—Viola O'Banion, *the wife*

"We're businessmen without high hats," Dion O'Banion used to say, and it was sort of true. He had a flower shop in Chicago and he could furnish wreaths and garlands in any quantity. If the floral pieces were for a funeral and you were shy a corpse, he could furnish that, too, if he was so minded. That's how diverse his business was, and flowers and cadavers were only a sideline. Dion O'Banion also ran the bootleg liquor and manned the gambling traps for the Gold Coast and the slums north of the Loop; he wouldn't dream of limiting his public services to the carriage trade when the other side of the tracks teemed with decent, honest, hard-working citizens equally in need of diversion. He was poor himself before he went wrong. The elder O'Banion, a plasterer, had a time scraping together the few dollars for the lad's surplice and cassock back at the turn of the century when he was in the choir at the Holy Name Cathedral.

Nobody could say how bright little Dion—called Dean or Deanie and sometimes "Gimpy" because an accident had left him with a limp—got off the straight and narrow. Maybe it was because he grew so fast. Even in his teens he had enough brawn to take a job in McGovern's Saloon in the Little Hell section, running beer and sentimental ballads to some very tough customers. Before long, he was an apprentice stick-up man and safe-blower, and a muscleman in the Chicago newspapers' early circulation wars. He did time in Bridewell for burglary in 1909 and for assault in 1911. He was caught tampering with somebody else's vault in the Postal Telegraph building once but beat that rap. He got into the trade in stamp-free liquor fairly early, using hijacked supplies because his capital was low. Come Prohibition's golden flow, he was a fairly well-established tradesman and his firm abounded in such true and trusted chums of his

young manhood as Hymie (The Polack) Weiss, George (Bugs) Moran, Vincent (Schemer) Drucci, Louis (Three-Gun) Alterie, and assorted PFC's. Once this happy-go-lucky set was caught borrowing 1,750 barrels' worth of prewar bonded Kentucky bourbon from a warehouse, but the proprietors and even the police guard appeared to be helping them with the million-dollar haul, so that case never got to the annoying courtroom stage.

When Johnny Torrio inherited Big Jim Colosimo's throne, he summoned O'Banion. Deanie was not above heisting an occasional truckload of his liquor, so Torrio explained to him that this form of poaching would be frowned on in the new and more formal organization of the underworld empire. He said O'Banion and his playmates could have the whole North Side preserve for their very own exploitation, plus some brewery interests, but they would (A) have to cease all hijacking and (B) observe the territorial rights of their underworld neighbors. Otherwise, trouble. O'Banion got in line and, while he lived, it proved to be a good idea.

The ex-choir boy tied up the loose ends in the retail liquor outlets in his barony, not overlooking the drugstores, and tightened his grip on the varied gambling activity. He passed up the prostitution industry, having a decided aversion to the love-for-sale bit. Even without this lush sideline, O'Banion got so rich that he shed his former coloring as a hoodlum and brawler. He dressed better—but conservatively—and got his nails manicured. He married Viola Kaniff, a nice girl with some book learning, and had her dress up their Pine Grove Avenue love nest with good paintings. He put in a $14,000 player piano and a console radio. He had some tuxedos made (with special pockets for artillery). He went to Mass regularly. He made pilgrimages to his boyhood streets in Little Hell and spread odd sums among the needy. ("I am a swell fellow," Dean might say, "a very swell fellow.") And he acquired half a touch of respectability by buying a half interest in William F. Schofield's flower shop on North State Street, right by the Holy Name Cathedral. He loved flowers. He would spend lots of time in the shop.

Trouble in Paradise

"Good men must not obey the laws too well."

—RALPH WALDO EMERSON

For all his outward Peace of Mind, Dion O'Banion, Baron of the North Side, had a king-sized assortment of headaches, tabled below:

I—He talked vaguely about retreating from Chicago to more genteel environs and got Johnny Torrio to buy his $500,000 interest in the giant Sieben brewery. Then Reform Mayor William E. Dever ordered a police drive on illegal beer operations, and both O'Banion and Torrio were arrested when the raiding forces got around to Sieben's. Torrio didn't mind the pinch so much but couldn't shake the nagging feeling that Deanie—always well-connected in official circles— knew the crackdown was coming before he sold his piece. This sort of dark suspicion in the racket empire's throne room wasn't calculated to do O'Banion any good.

Hymie Weiss

Frankie Yale: Did he kill O'Banion?

II—He took to feudin' with the Genna Brothers, also known as The Terrible Gennas. He said they were selling their corn-sugar alcohol—home-cooked in hundreds of friendly tenements—in his bailiwick for three dollars per gallon, while his had a six dollar to nine dollar price tag. The Gennas, so affluent that they had five police captains and four hundred patrolmen on their payroll, drawing $350,000 a month in "ice," charged in turn that O'Banion had fallen into his old habits and was hijacking liquor out of their West Side domain. Hymie Weiss suggested to O'Banion that the Gennas were most excitable fellows and might get violent. Deanie cast off his new-found respectability for a moment. "Aw," he said, "to hell with them Sicilians." It was not a nice way to talk in Chicago in 1924.

III—He got into an inter-mob squabble over a matter of $30,000 in IOU's spread around the syndicate's Cicero gambling casino, The Ship, by Angelo Genna. Al Capone wanted to write off Genna's losses as trifling, but Deanie insisted that a man should pay his debts. O'Banion paid no mind to Capone, The Ship's skipper-of-record, and told Genna to get up the thirty Big Ones or else. Again, no way to talk to people named Genna.

IV—He touched off a noisy municipal scandal, quite innocently, by filling the Guest of Honor's chair at a testimonial dinner and accepting a $2,000 platinum wrist watch set in diamonds and a smattering of rubies. Mayor Dever raised the City Hall roof the next day because the highest police brass had attended the affair, breaking bread with such celebrated O'Banion associates as Schemer Drucci, Hymie Weiss, Bugs Moran and Three-Gun Alterie. The storm didn't quiet down until Chief-of-Detectives Michael Hughes turned in his badge and gun, all the while protesting that he left the affair "almost at once" when he learned to his dismay that it was a memorial to the living O'Banion.

Flowers and Bullets

"We usually meet all of our relatives only at funerals where somebody always observes: 'Too bad we can't get together more often.'"

—SAM LEVENSON

Mike Merlo, first president of the Unione Siciliana, passed away in Chicago on November 8, 1924. He died of natural causes, an unusual avenue of exit for the society in which he dwelt. It was a nice thing, in a way, because it meant there would be no recriminations in the underworld, no petty finger-pointing, no hard feelings. Everyone could get together to give Mike Merlo a funeral befitting his exalted station. Thus, the next day, orders for floral tributes poured into the O'Banion-Schofield flower emporium in unprecedented quantities. John Torrio selected a $10,000 display. Al Capone picked out an $8,000 item. Someone else told O'Banion to rustle up a floral effigy of the departed Merlo—life-size, of course. That night another party ordered an elaborate spray and said he would send around for it at noon. O'Banion said he would attend to that one himself and he was out front, clipping some chrysanthemums, when three men came in at the appointed hour.

O'Banion limped toward them—he evidently knew the trio—and extended his right hand. The man in the middle took the proffered handshake and held tight. The other two drew revolvers and pumped fire into O'Banion until he slumped to the floor. Then the trio hurried to an undertaker's limousine waiting at the curb. When the police arrived to inspect the remains, they found that the executioners had held their guns so close that there were powder burns among the six gaping holes ripped into the husky gangster's head and torso. The shop's porter, who was on the premises during O'Banion's demise, had no idea what the three messengers of death looked like. Nor could anyone in the noonday crowd outside throw any light on this point. With O'Banion's own hard lips and blue eyes forever closed, the usual fruitless investigation followed. The police called in everybody, more or less, and let them all out again. Torrio and Capone were invited downtown, along with Mike Genna, Albert Anselmi and John Scalisi. The latter two, the most accomplished torpedo men in The Terrible Gennas' troop, were widely credited with the deed. Others said that Frankie Yale, nee Uale, a citizen of Brooklyn but a dear friend of Torrio's, was in on the job. In any case, nobody was held long enough to delay the funeral—and Dion O'Banion, departing at 32, got a $100,000 send-off that made the Mike Merlo obsequies look like the services for any Skid Row bum.

The carcass lay in state at the Sbarbo Funeral Home in a $10,000 bronze casket, with solid gold candlesticks and silver angels at either end. Forty thousand persons filed past the bier in three days and the funeral itself, ablaze in flowers and regal trappings, drew 20,-000. The mourners included Torrio—"From Johnny," his floral tribute said —and Capone, and Angelo Genna, newly installed as president of the Unione Siciliana. O'Banion's forlorn lieutenants stood on the other side of the grave, weeping real tears in copious amounts. The choir boy gone bad was denied Catholic rites but the Rev. Patrick Malloy came out to Mount Carmel Cemetery without his priestly vestments and said three Hail Mary's and the Lord's Prayer. Father Malloy had grown up with Deanie in Little

Dion O'Banion, much mourned, departs in style.

Hell; he wouldn't abandon him at the end.

O'Banion's last resting place lay only forty feet from a granite mausoleum where a Bishop and two Archbishops reposed, so when Viola O'Banion built a tall shaft over his grave with the inscription "My Sweetheart," George Cardinal Mundelein asked her to take it down in favor of a less ostentatious headstone. Viola did that, but she paid the deceased—linked to twenty-five unsolved killings but never once arrested in such unpleasant circumstances—the ultimate tribute. "Dean loved his home and spent most of his evenings in it, fooling with his radio, singing a song, listening to the player piano. He was not a man to run around nights with women. I was his only sweetheart. . . . He never left home without telling

me where he was going and kissing me good-by."

For such a homebody, the O'Banion slaying had the most curious repercussions, starting right after the funeral, when Louis Alterie publicly challenged the assassins to a pistol duel. He said he would meet the enemy at State and Madison Streets at any time, including high noon. Alterie's bold declaration horrified Bill Dever. "I am staggered," the Mayor said. "Are we living by the code of the Dark Ages or is Chicago part of an American commonwealth?"

The answer would come very fast—in the high-level gunfire that marked 1925 as one of the Lawless Decade's more interesting years, in that department, anyway. Deanie O'Banion was a likeable fellow. His playmates stood loyal not only unto death but unto the next round of bloodletting as well.

THE BLACKFACE BLUES

Frank Tinney, the great blackface comedian of the postwar years, is shown strolling with his wife, Edna Davenport, in a rare moment of domestic tranquility. Miss Davenport, a musical comedy star in her own right, gave up her career to make a home for Tinney and stood by him even when his flaming, free-swinging romance with Imogene Wilson made fat headlines for the papers. The blonde Miss Wilson, often described as the most

dazzling flower in the Ziegfeld hot-house, had the $2,500-a-week funnyman arrested in 1924 on the allegation that he had beat and kicked her once too often—and too hard. (Tinney is shown in court to face the charges.) Mrs. Tinney took a most charitable and sophisticated view of the unfolding scandal. "I think the love between Frank and this girl is really beautiful—if it is sincere," the betrayed wife said. "She tells me she really loves him."

Flo Ziegfeld took a more severe view and fired the battered Miss Wilson from the *Follies*. Tinney's brilliant career, all but destroyed, came to a complete halt two years later when he collapsed on a Detroit stage and wound up in a hospital for 18 months, much of it in total blankness. He came out a wreck.

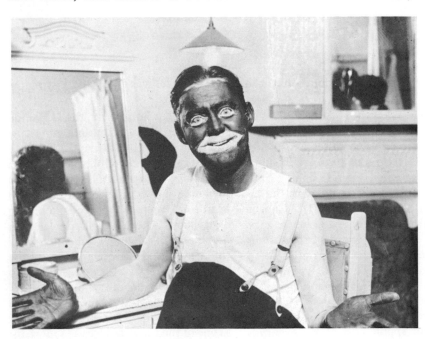

Frank Tinney gets set to go on in Earl Carroll's *Vanities*. He was the comedy rage of Broadway before his off-stage frolics led to his downfall.

Ousted from the *Follies* because of her over-publicized romance with the long-married Frank Tinney, Imogene Wilson went on to Hollywood and appeared in films under the name of Mary Nolan.

IT HAPPENED IN 1924...

Barbara LaMarr, the beautiful screen star, sat for an interview with a journalist from the *Metropolitan Magazine*. Miss LaMarr authorized this quote: "Any woman who prefers a lap dog to a baby is unnatural."

* * *

The WCTU celebrated its golden anniversary . . . William Z. Foster and Benjamin Gitlow ran for President and Vice President on the Communist ticket, polling 33,361 votes . . . Lou Gehrig led the minor leagues in batting . . . Charles H. Levermore of Brooklyn won $50,000 in a contest for the best essay on how to prevent war . . . Lenin died . . . The clothing Abe Lincoln had on when he was assassinated was sold at auction for $6,500 . . . The Committee of Fourteen said it was worried about all the secret vice in New York . . . Woodrow Wilson died . . . Prohibition agents and bootleggers fought a pistol battle in the capital and Senator Frank L. Greene of Vermont was seriously wounded by a stray bullet . . .

The Lutherans voted to drop the word "Hell" from the Apostle's Creed

Edward, Prince of Wales, paid us a visit.

and use the word "Hades" . . . A Negro farm laborer was whipped to death in Marshall, Texas, for swearing at his employer . . . The Presbyterian Church in the United States (Southern) declared that it could not believe in evolution . . . Edward S. Cooney and his wife Celia, "the bobbed-hair bandit," drew ten to twenty years in prison . . . Peggy Hopkins Joyce took a fourth husband, Count Gosta Morner of Sweden.

President Coolidge denounced the Senate's inquiry into the tax returns of corporations in which Secretary of the Treasury Mellon had a financial interest . . . The Prince of Wales, visiting the States, played squash and joined in a fox hunt on Long Island . . . William H. Anderson, former superintendent of the Anti-Saloon League in

New York, lost his appeal from a forgery conviction . . . An American automobile crossed the Sinai desert between the Gulf of Suez and the Gulf of Aqaba in four hours. It took the Israelites forty years to cover the same 130 miles in their Exodus from Egypt . . .

Al Jolson and Raymond Hitchcock had breakfast with the President at the White House and made him laugh . . . Mrs. Harding died . . . RCA sent the first news pictures across the Atlantic by wireless . . . Jimmy O'Connell and Cozy Dolan, outfielder and coach on the Giants, offered Philadelphia shortstop Heinie Sand $500 to throw the game the Giants needed to clinch the pennant. Commissioner Landis found them guilty of the bribe attempt. The Giants won the game . . . Victor Herbert died . . . The Methodist Episcopal General Conference lifted the church's ban on dancing and theater-going . . . Ford made his ten millionth car and paid an income tax of $2,467,946 . . . Lew Dockstader, the Minstrel Man, died at sixty-eight . . . Americans in East Coast cities heard the first broadcast from the British Isles . . . The

Cozy Dolan (above) and Jimmy O'Connell: more trouble on the baseball beat.

The Marx Brothers

Chaplin married Lita Grey, age sixteen.

heavy turnover in stocks—18,000,000 shares in the ten days after Calvin Coolidge's election — worried some Wall Street observers . . .

The *New York Evening Graphic* advised its male readers, "Don't Try to Reform a Gold Digger" (*"If you have fallen in love with her, you have truly sunk far below the depths to which Lucifer sank"*) . . . The *Graphic's* love-lorn column advised an inquiring reader to spurn an adventurer bearing pretty baubles. "Of all the gifts that can be offered to a woman," the *Graphic* said, "love is the most precious."

* * *

In the theater, Judith Anderson appeared in *The Cobra* . . . Lady Diana Manners played the Madonna and Rosamond Pinchot the nun in *The Miracle* . . . The Marx Brothers starred in *I'll Say She Is*, Alfred Lunt, Leslie Howard and Margalo Gilmore in *Outward Bound* and Helen Hayes was in *Dancing Mothers* . . . Fred Astaire and his sister Adele danced to George Gershwin's music in *Lady, Be Good.*

On the silent screen, the box-office names included Rod La Rocque, Jack Holt, Hoot Gibson, Thomas Meighan, Agnes Ayres, the Bennett sisters, Richard Dix, Harry Carey, Gloria Swanson, Ben Lyon, and George O'Brien.

* * *

Ernest Hemingway's *In Our Time*, a book of short stories, came out, but the people were descending on the stores for such items as Edna Ferber's *So Big*, Zane Grey's *The Call of the Canyon*, Percy Marks' *The Plastic Age* and Rafael Sabatini's *Mistress Wilding*. In non-fiction, the best-seller was Lulu Hunt Peters' *Diet and Health* (yes, even then). It was followed by Fannie Farmer's cook book and, still up there, Emily Post's bible of etiquette. The crossword puzzle books swept the land that year, too, putting Simon & Schuster on the publishing map and straining American eyes and dictionaries almost beyond endurance.

William Boyd (with garrison cap) played Sergeant Quirt to Louis Wolheim's Captain Flagg in the Maxwell Anderson war play, *What Price Glory?*

Ethel Barrymore appeared on Broadway in *The Second Mrs. Tanqueray.*

Mr. Torrio,

Chairman of the Board

Johnny Torrio in 1949.

Johnny Torrio and his missus went shopping in the better stores on Michigan Avenue in Chicago on January 24, 1925, and drove back to their apartment on Clyde Avenue. Mrs. Torrio went upstairs. Mr. Torrio said he would gather up the packages and join her but as he started for the house two gunmen bore down on him from across the street and opened fire. Torrio sank to the pavement with garlic-tipped bullets in his chest, abdomen, jaw and arm. Doctors at Jackson Park Hospital didn't give the racket emperor much chance to live, but ten days later he was well enough to look over suspects hustled in by the police. Nothing came of this process, of course. "No use bringing anyone in here," the wounded millionaire told the detectives. "I won't rap any of them. I wouldn't lay the finger on . . . I know the man who shot me."

He knew the five slugs in him had come from the vengeance-bent North Side heirs of the late Dion O'Banion. He had just got careless. It wouldn't happen again. Torrio had the streets outside the hospital patrolled by his own guard, led by Al Capone, lest the O'Banions come back to finish the bungled job. And he went from his bed of pain direct to the Lake County jail; it seemed a good time to serve the nine-month sentence he drew when he got caught in the Sieben brewery raid which he believed O'Banion engineered. The jail proved a very snug haven. Torrio's cell had a bed instead

of a cot, a dresser, easy chairs for approved guests, a rug on the cold stone floor and bullet-proof steel-mesh blinds. The racket king also enjoyed the additional security of extra round-the-clock deputies to patrol the corridor, paid out of his own ample purse.

The North Side gang didn't let its shooting irons go rusty while its prime target hid behind the state's concrete-and-steel curtain. Three of the Terrible Gennas—Angelo, Michael, and Anthony (also called Tony the Gentleman)—were rubbed out from May to July. The Sicilian brotherhood, close to Torrio and similarly on the outs with O'Banion when he was assassinated, stood high on the drop-dead list drawn up by Hymie Weiss, Deanie's successor. Nobody on that roster was safe now, Weiss being such a dedicated type. Torrio was so convinced of this that he turned the baton over to Al Capone when his time in the homey jail was up. "It's all yours, Al," said the

dandy little organizer. "Me, I'm quittin'. It's Europe for me." If it was an outright gift, it was a healthy one. The gangland Empire then was grossing some $70,000,000 a year from bootleg booze, gambling and girls.

Torrio was going to Italy. He had bought his mother a luxurious seaside villa on her native Neapolitan soil a few years back. There, three thousand miles away from Hymie the Polack and the blood-letting due to wet down Chicago right through 1926, he could reflect on some pretty good old days. He started out as Big Jim Colosimo's bodyguard around 1910. He became overseer of Big Jim's flesh-peddling operations, running such Chicago landmarks as the House of All Nations and the low-cost Bedbug Row joints. He took over everything after Big Jim went on the spot marked X. He called in the warring gangs—O'Banion and the Gennas, Frankie Lake and Terry Druggan, Klondike O'Donnell, Polack Joe Saltis, and the little ones. He organized The Syndicate and cut down all the senseless gunfire just in time for the big clean-up on Prohibition. He made the move into the outlying gold mines—Cicero, Chicago Heights, Burn-

1925

Johnny Torrio: Please, no gunfire.

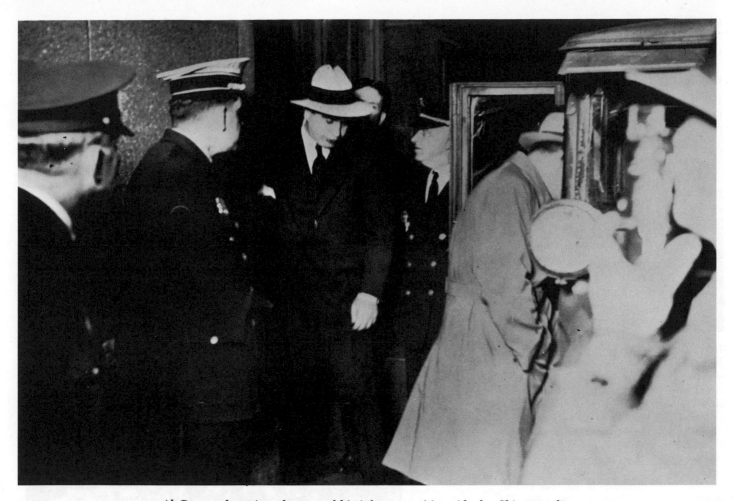

Al Capone departing after one of his infrequent visits with the Chicago police.

Fifteen years after he supposedly shed his criminal ways forever, Johnny Torrio was linked to the nationwide death-for-sale cartel known as Murder Inc. The torrential confessions of killer Abe (Kid Twist) Reles listed (left to right) Torrio, Ciro Terranova, Little Augie Pisano, and Joe Adonis among the many racket guys with a voting interest in the murder bund. None but Adonis ever came close to achieving the eminence Torrio knew in his Chicago days, and the debonair gangster paid heavily for his success: the government deported him to his native Italy in 1956. Terranova reigned for two decades as New York's Artichoke King, levying tribute on vegetables brought into the city. Pisano, whose real name was Anthony Carfano, branched out from strong-arm stuff and beer-running into the labor and industrial rackets, and was still around—and thriving—in the fifties.

William Hale (Big Bill) Thompson, the on-again off-again Republican Mayor of Chicago in the Lawless Decade, originally was elected on a "reform" platform. "Vote for Big Bill the Builder," said his campaign posters. "He cannot be bought, bossed or bluffed." But once in office, the barrel-bellied Mayor demonstrated a remarkable faculty for getting along with the Windy City's rampant racketeers. John Torrio never had occasion to utter a harsh word about the live-and-let-live Mayor and Al Capone kept a picture of the congenial giant on his office wall. It figured, because all the vices flourished best, and bootleg beer and liquor always flowed most freely, when Big Bill was the man in City Hall. Here he is shown celebrating his re-election in 1927.

The O'Donnell Mob on the South Side paid dearly for resisting the march of progress when the orderly-minded Mr. Torrio decided to organize all the Chicago gangs under his blood-stained standard. Five of the six O'Donnells and any number of their hired hands were shot down before the surviving brother, Edward, affectionately called Spike (above), saw the light and made peace with the new underworld order. Spike rose high in the combine and prospered. In his quieter moments he talked about turning actor. He wanted to play Robin Hood. While he had a satisfactory background for it, there were no takers in Hollywood, so Spike stayed in his own very real world.

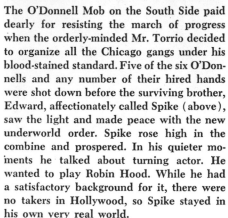

Angelo Genna, Torrio-installed boss of the Unione Siciliana, was rubbed out in 1926 because the late Dion O'Banion's playmates couldn't shake the notion that he had something to do with the assassination of their leader. Befitting his exalted station, Genna was honored with one of the Lawless Decade's gaudier gangster funerals. Note that the pallbearers wore tuxedos for the ritual. In the lower societies of Chicago and New York in those days, men dressed for going-away parties of this kind.

ham, Calumet City, and the other suburbs. He blazed the dirty trail in the 932 square miles of corruption known as Cook County. He kept the cops in line—"I own the police force," he said once. He made the high-up political connections, even carrying a card in the William Hale Thompson Republican Club (named for the flamboyant and tolerant Mayor who always ran on an "Open-City" platform). He made

the brewery connections and kept the beer coming. He was The Brain, The Supreme Court, The Chairman of the Board. He made the rackets Big Business. He brought civilization to the gangland jungle. He kept the peace. In Italy, he might reflect that everything could still have been that way except for the trouble with Deanie O'Banion.

Maybe it was all for the best. He

would never want for money; no one would ever know how much he carried out of Chicago or shipped out ahead of him. Now he was a young man of thirty-nine, untainted by bad booze or other temptations. He could sit by the Blue Mediterranean or go back to his boyhood Brooklyn and settle on middle-class Shore Road and take his ease. Johnny Torrio needed no pity and no handouts.

F. Scott Fitzgerald

PARADISE
AND
ZELDA

"...I can only cry out that I have lost my splendid mirage. Come back, come back, O glittering and white."
—F. SCOTT FITZGERALD, 1932

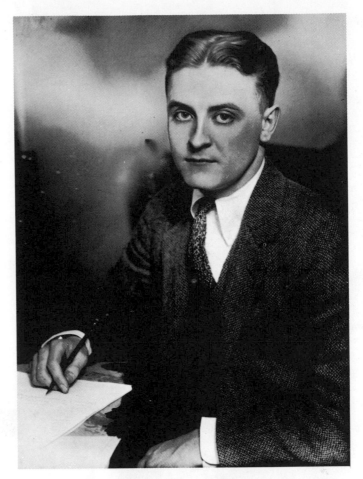

F. Scott Fitzgerald—Poet of the Jazz Age.

Francis Scott Key Fitzgerald came to Princeton bright and shining out of a little prep school in St. Paul, Minnesota. He was a fine-looking boy with yellow hair and green eyes. He did well in the Triangle Club and on the undergraduate paper, *The Tiger;* he had a flair for writing. But he only lasted one day on the freshman eleven —too light—and that hurt him. He went into uniform (cut by Brooks Brothers) as a second lieutenant in October '17 but they kept him Stateside, and that hurt, too. When he got out he took a job doing slogans for an advertising agency, for ninety dollars a month. He moved into a one-room apartment on Claremont Parkway in the Bronx. He was going to write short stories in his spare hours, but he spent the time around the plush Manhattan bars. When he did write, the stories didn't sell.

He drank too much and he brooded about Zelda Sayre, the pretty Alabama teenager he fell in love with when he was stationed at Camp Montgomery during the war. Would she wait for him? "As I hovered ghost-like in the Plaza Red Room of a Saturday afternoon, or went to lush and liquid garden parties in the East Sixties or tippled with Princetonians in the Biltmore Bar," he wrote later, "I was haunted always by my other life—my drab room in the Bronx, my square foot of the subway, my fixation upon the day's letter from Alabama—would it come and what would it say?—my shabby suits, my poverty, and love . . . I was a failure—mediocre at advertising work and unable to get started as a writer. Hating the city, I got roaring, weeping drunk on my last penny and went home."

In St. Paul, he locked himself in his old room and wrote *This Side of Paradise,* the story of Amory Blaine and all the fast girls he knew. It was not just another novel, but an eyewitness report on the New Freedom. "Oh, she's average," a girl in the book says of another flapper, "smokes sometimes, drinks punch, frequently kissed—Oh, yes—common knowledge—one of the effects of the war, you know." It was a surgical survey of the times. The bar-and-boudoir scenes weren't such as to lure .book-buyers away from the outdoor dramas of Zane Grey, Peter B. Kyne, or James Oliver Curwood in 1920, or to compete with the blazing desert passion in "The Sheik" in 1921, but Fitzgerald was off and running.

He brought Zelda to New York and married her at St. Patrick's, and if there was anything in "Paradise" that seemed improbable, Fitzgerald and his vivacious Southern beauty proceeded to put it in the record. They passed out on strangers' divans at fancy parties, rode down Fifth Avenue atop a taxi on a hot Sunday night, waded in the Pulitzer Fountain outside the Plaza. Scott started to shed his clothes at the *Scandals* and got thrown out of the theater. Zelda danced on tables and livened up dinner gatherings where the hootch wasn't flowing fast enough. They bought a Marmon and Zelda hung it on a fire hydrant.

Three months after the whirl began, Fitzgerald didn't have the price of his hotel bill. When he came out of the bank with the horrible facts, Zelda asked why he looked so unhappy.

"We haven't got any money," he said.

"Well, let's go to the movies," Zelda replied.

There would always be more advances from the publisher; more royalties, more advances, and fat checks from the magazines for short stories. They took a house in Westport to get away from the high life in Manhattan

Fitzgerald on the decade of his own triumph and tragedy: "It was an age of miracles, it was an age of art, it was an age of excess, and it was an age of satire."

but their drinking companions found their way to Connecticut. A fresh reckoning came in December, 1920. They had used up $18,000 in three months. They were broke again, Zelda was pregnant, and they didn't want to bring a baby into what Fitzgerald called "the glamor and loneliness" of their existence. So they retreated to the family homestead in St. Paul. The novelist was gloomy there.

"I should like to sit down with ½ a dozen chosen companions and drink myself to death but I am sick of life, liquor and literature," the author wrote Max Perkins at Scribners. ". . . I'm sick of the flabby semi-intellectual softness in which I flounder with my generation." But he dug in and finished *The Beautiful and The Damned.* (Zelda wrote a review of it and asked everyone to buy it because, she said, she wanted a $300 cloth of gold dress, a platinum ring, and a new coat.) Then they came back East with their daughter and took a $300-a-month house on Long Island, complete with a secondhand Rolls Royce. The welcome sign went up again and the parties got longer. Another stock-taking in 1924 showed that the happy couple had run through $113,000 in four years, so Fitzgerald wrote an article for the *Saturday Evening Post* called "How to Live on $36,000 a Year." In it he repeated a remark he made to Zelda once when they were discussing the recurrent shortage of ready cash in the family: "We're too poor to economize. Economy is a luxury . . . Our only salvation is in extravagance." He had no regrets. "We had spent $36,000," he said of the semester under examination, "and purchased for one year the right to be members of the newly rich class. What more can money buy?"

Somewhere along the way Fitzgerald wrote *The Great Gatsby,* a novel of the Manhattan-Long Island speakeasy set with a bootlegger as its central character. It was generally hailed as his best book and seemed to some critics to mark Fitzgerald's flowering as a novelist, but by the time it appeared in 1925 the young author was heading over the hill. He was wandering around Europe with Zelda, savoring Paris—"a thousand parties and no work," he said—and the lush Riviera resorts. Back in America, broke, Fitzgerald tried script-writing in Hollywood but it was an unhappy experience. In time, Fitzgerald

Virtually a commuter between New York and Paris as long as his books made money, Fitzgerald is shown on shipboard in 1928 with his daughter, Frances.

Christmas in Paris, 1925: Scott, Zelda and the baby.

looked back glumly on his Jazz Age.

"It was an age of miracles, it was an age of art, it was an age of excess, and it was an age of satire," he wrote in *The Crack-Up* "... This was the generation whose girls dramatized themselves as flappers, the generation that corrupted its elders and eventually overreached itself less through lack of morals than lack of taste. May one offer in exhibit the year 1922! That was the peak of the younger generation, for though the Jazz Age continued, it became less and less an affair of youth.

"The sequel was like a children's party taken over by the elders, leaving the children puzzled and rather neglected and rather taken aback. By 1923 their elders, tired of watching the carnival with ill-concealed envy, had discovered that young liquor will take the place of young blood, and with a whoop the orgy began. The younger generation was starred no longer."

He didn't blame it on Prohibition. He didn't blame it on anything. He fell into despair. "In the real dark night of

Judging a beauty contest in 1929, Fitzgerald is shown with Cornelius Vanderbilt, Jr.

the soul it is always three o'clock in the morning," he wrote, and in 1936, in *The Crack-Up*, he talked about "too much anger and too many tears." In that year he was in a sanitarium, trying to dry out and perhaps find himself again. "A series of things happened to papa," he told Michel Mok, a reporter for the *New York Post*. "So papa got depressed, and started to drink a little." What happened? "One blow after another," Fitzgerald said, "and something snapped."

Something had snapped with Zelda too. She had a series of mental breakdowns, beginning in Paris in 1929, and never completely recovered. She died in 1948 when fire swept a sanitarium in Asheville, North Carolina, where she was a patient. Fitzgerald, forty-four, died of a heart attack eight years earlier in Hollywood. There was only a handful of people at the services for the poet-prophet of the Jazz Age but he left a mark on his generation. The pity was that his own dark tragedy exceeded anything he put on paper on the good days when he locked himself away and played with words.

"In the real dark night of the soul," Fitzgerald wrote, "it is always three o'clock in the morning."

TWO DRY CLOWNS—IZZY AND MOE

Another still bites the dust at the hands of Moe Smith and Izzy Einstein.

Tne "Dry" Congress put out only enough money to hire 1,500 Prohibition agents to keep strong beverages off the lips of 125,000,000 Americans, give or take the children or the unborn. The 1,500 shoo-flies drew salaries of forty dollars a week and were expected to shrug off all the bribe money and other temptations then in vogue. They were also expected to fan out over the broad landscape, into each and every hamlet, and put the cork on all the bottles. It was a rather large order, to put it mildly, but two New York agents gave it a good substantial try. Izzy Einstein and Moe Smith cut a hole in the wet world—without drying it up, of course.

Izzy and Moe were made to order for the snooper's trade because they didn't look the part. The 225-pound Izzy, a former post-office clerk, was five feet high and almost as wide, and Moe, an ex-cigar salesman, out-weighed him only with the help of some added height. Izzy had more disguises than Lon Chaney, knew more roles, and stayed up later. Moe was the perfect straight man. Some speakeasy proprietors hung up the pair's pictures after a while so that the bar help would recognize them, but the agents had a selection of false whiskers and rubber noses to counteract that sort of cowardice.

Izzy put on a football uniform—not an improbable sight, considering how coaches go for great heft in their lines—and knocked over a place dealing the hard stuff to athletes grown thirsty on

the green fields of Van Cortlandt Park in the Bronx. He carried a violin to get into an oasis catering to longhair musicians. He wore blackface on the Harlem beat, and overalls to take the neighborhood places catering to working men. He made his way into a tuxedo for raiding excursions to the more flossy Manhattan resorts. He wore a frock coat to get the welcome nod at a downtown Brooklyn place frequented by lawyers and jurists. The Dry twins did not lack sympathy for their victims. "Dere's sad news," they would announce while producing their badges and pouring the contents of their shot glasses into tiny funnels strapped inside their vests.

Izzy once was privileged to meet Professor Albert Einstein, so he asked him what he did for a living. "I discover stars in the sky," the scientist said. "I'm a discoverer too," Izzy replied, "only I discover in the basements." The combined discoveries of Izzy and Moe over a five-year period resulted in 4,392 arrests, accompanied by the confiscation of an estimated 5,000,000 bottles of bootleg liquor and enough beer to float the Navy. Their fame was such that bureaus in other cities often borrowed them when it was deemed necessary to knock off particularly stubborn joints.

But something happened in 1925. Izzy and Moe were fired. The Prohibition Bureau simply said it was "for the good of the service." Others said the elaborate newspaper space the pair was drawing finally had irritated their superiors. Izzy and Moe, out of character, said nothing. Later Izzy produced an autobiography, *Prohibition Agent Number 1*, but only 575 copies were sold. The people, it appeared, only had a passing interest in the reminiscences of a man whose job was to pour whiskey down drains.

The Word, the Book and Mr. Bryan

"With flying banners and beating drums we are marching backward to the glorious age of the sixteenth century, when bigots lighted fagots to burn the men who dared to bring any intelligence and enlightenment and culture to the human mind."
—CLARENCE DARROW,
on the Monkey Trial

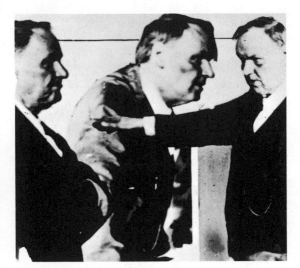

Five views of . . .

William Jennings Bryan at Dayton

. . . Clarence Darrow

Freckled-faced John T. Scopes, 24, taught science (and a little football on the side) in the drowsy Tennessee town of Dayton. One day in 1925 he read his class this sentence from Hunter's *Civic Biology:* "We have now learned that animal forms may be arranged so as to begin with the simple one-celled forms and culminate with a group which includes man himself." Scopes knew he would get arrested. He had talked to three lawyers about it over some soda pop in Robinson's Drugstore on Main Street. Tennessee had a brand new law—first in the nation—making it a crime to "teach any theory that denies the story of the Divine creation of man as taught in the Bible." So a Special Grand Jury quickly indicted the upstart teacher for his assault on the beliefs and dignity of the state.

William Jennings Bryan, three-time candidate for the presidency, one-time Secretary of State and long-time Defender of the Word, laid aside his ventures in Florida real estate and hastened to the Volunteer State as the volunteer prosecutor in the case.

When old Clarence Darrow heard this, he made tracks for the Cumberland Country too, bringing along two other eminent Counsels-for-the-Defense, Dudley Field Malone and Arthur Garfield Hays. Protestant Dayton, population 1,500, rallied to stand four-square against the arriving infidel horde. The town blossomed out with signs that summer:

READ YOUR BIBLE DAILY
SWEETHEART, COME TO JESUS

BE SURE YOUR SINS
WILL FIND YOU OUT

YOU NEED GOD IN YOUR
BUSINESS

PREPARE TO MEET THY MAKER
GOD IS LOVE

WHERE WILL YOU SPEND
ETERNITY?

Beneath these banners, strung across the narrow streets near Judge John T. Raulston's musty old courthouse, evangelists and hot-dog vendors competed with Bible salesmen and purveyors of "ice-cold" lemonade (you could get corn likker too, if you knew the right vendor). By wagon, mule, horse or foot, the oldest settlers and the Holy Rollers came down from the hills. An atmosphere of carnival, weighted with serious things, overtook the town. So many reporters flocked in that twenty-

The "infidel" who started it all: John T. Scopes.

Where the crime occurred: the Dayton High School.

Where the plot was hatched: Robinson's Drug Store.

two telegraph operators had to be imported to send out their frontline dispatches in the Battle of Fundamentalism vs. Evolution.

Judge Raulston, six feet of solid Bible-taught stock, and self-introduced as "jist a reg'lar mountaineer jedge," set himself up with a strong supply of chewing gum and two flunkies to wield fans over his ample dome. He had a spittoon by his feet and a ten-foot banner hung behind his head, facing the jury. It said, READ YOUR BIBLE!

The aging Bryan, bald and paunchy and visibly suffering in the fetid Dayton heat after his pleasant and profitable sojourn in the Florida lagoons, appeared coatless in a pleated white shirt with a starched front. He carried his own palm leaf fan and a three-gallon graniteware jug for water. Darrow shed his coat, too, exposing wide lavender suspenders over a blue summer shirt. When the heat got him he would make his way into the line of the electric fans; the Tennessee-financed breezes were being wafted in directions away from the defense table.

The Judge opened court with a prayer and announced that counsel would be addressed by honorary titles —"general" for prosecution lawyers and "colonel" for the defenders of John Thomas Scopes. Darrow let that pass, but not the form of the opening. "I object to the turning of this court into a meetinghouse," he said. Overruled, he observed later that in forty years he had never before "heard God called in to referee a court trial."

The state put on Howard Morgan, fourteen, a pupil of the defendant, to lay bare the nature of the crime. It was plain that the boy liked his teacher but he had to tell the whole truth and nothing but.

"He said that the earth was once a hot, molten mass, too hot for plant or animal life to exist upon it; in the sea the earth cooled off; there was a little germ of one-celled organism formed, and this organism kept on evolving and from this was man."

When Darrow asked Howard whether he thought this intelligence had damaged him in any way, the boy said, "Oh, no sir."

The Judge sent the jurors out, listened to defense references to such items as the Paleozoic era, the Heidelberg Man and the Cro-Magnons and said no, he couldn't see the purpose of

Two views of Clarence Darrow: In 1900, when he was forty-three years old and quite celebrated for his defense of Gene Debs in the Pullman Strike six years earlier, and (right) towards the end of his career. In the days when William Jennings Bryan was the Democratic Party's "prairie radical," Darrow backed him for President. When a

stroke killed Bryan after the Scopes trial, Darrow issued the usual formal expression of pain and sympathy, noting in particular his deceased adversary's devotion to conviction—right or wrong. Then, according to his biographer, Charles Yale Harrison, Darrow turned to a friend and said: "Now, wasn't that man a god-damned fool?"

any evidence by a bunch of imported scientists. Darrow argued that testimony tracing the human specimen back to his beginnings, maybe 600,000 years ago, was indeed pertinent. The Judge said no, everybody knew, or should know, that God created man 6,000 years ago; it was in the Bible. The exchange grew rather heated—

RAULSTON: I hope that counsel intends no reflection upon this court.

DARROW: Your Honor, of course, is entitled to hope.

That cost Darrow a citation for contempt but he got off with an apology, the "Jedge" observing that the Book taught him that "it was godly to forgive." With his learned witnesses declared null, void and irrelevant, "Colonel" Darrow surprised everyone and called William Jennings Bryan for the defense, as an expert on the Bible. Now the stage was set for high drama. The courtroom could not safely hold the throng that wanted to see the Plumed Knight of Fundamentalism take up the sword against the Infidel Darrow, so the judge moved the trial to the lawn. There, on a platform built under the maple trees, the fetid July heat wouldn't go over 100 degrees—

except under the Bryan collar—on July 20, 1925.

The Drama on the Lawn
"The Bible states it. It must be ·so."
—WILLIAM JENNINGS BRYAN

On the lawn at Dayton, with the whole world watching, Clarence Darrow and William Jennings Bryan acted out the classic Science vs. Religion conflict of the century. The timing was right; everything else was going under the microscope for open examination in the twenties, why not the Bible? The casting was perfect; the principals were men of formidable convictions, each in his own way. The record would tell:

DARROW: Do you claim that everything in the Bible should be literally interpreted?

BRYAN: I believe everything in the Bible should be accepted as it is given there.

DARROW: Now, you say, the big fish swallowed Jonah, and he remained there how long—three days —and then he spewed him upon the land . . . Do you believe that He made them—that He made such a fish and that it was big enough to swallow Jonah?

BRYAN: Yes, sir. Let me add: One miracle is just as easy to believe as another.

DARROW: Do you believe Joshua made the sun stand still?

BRYAN: I believe what the Bible says.

DARROW: Now, Mr. Bryan, have you ever pondered what would have happened to the earth if it had stood still?

BRYAN: No, the God I believe in could have taken care of that, Mr. Darrow.

DARROW: You believe the story of the flood to be a literal interpretation.

BRYAN: Yes, sir.

Attorney General E. T. Stewart protested when Darrow tried to get the witness to fix the date of the flood. Bryan broke in: "These gentlemen . . . did not come here to try this case. They came here to try revealed religion. I am here to defend it, and they can ask me any question they please." There was loud applause and when Darrow remarked on it Bryan accused him of insulting the people of Tennessee. Darrow in turn accused Bryan of insulting "every man of science and learning in

Darrow addresses the Monkey Trial jury.

the world because he does not believe in your fool religion."

The examination went on. Did Bryan know there were ancient civilizations and ancient religions going back long before Biblical times? "I have never felt it necessary to look up competing religions," the witness said. Did Bryan believe God confused the tongues of the men building the Tower of Babel because he was afraid they were reaching unto heaven? "Something like that . . ." the witness said. The Attorney General wanted to know the purpose of this line of questioning but Bryan, not Darrow, answered him.

BRYAN: The purpose is to cast ridicule on everybody who believes in the Bible, and I am perfectly willing that the world shall know that these gentlemen have no other purpose than ridiculing every Christian who believes in the Bible.

DARROW: We have the purpose of preventing bigots and ignoramuses from controlling the education of the United States, and you know it, and that is all.

Bryan said he was "simply trying to protect the word of God against the greatest atheist or agnostic in the States." The gallery, more like a campmeeting, cheered again.

The questioning turned to the Garden of Eden.

DARROW: Mr. Bryan, do you believe that the first woman was Eve?

BRYAN: Yes.

DARROW: Do you believe she was literally made out of Adam's rib?

BRYAN: I do.

DARROW: Do you believe that after Eve ate the apple, or gave it to Adam, whichever way it was, that God cursed Eve, and at that time decreed that all womankind thenceforth and forever should suffer the pains of childbirth in the reproduction of the earth?

This led to the most vehement clash of the day, Darrow and Bryan shaking their fists at each other before the examination could proceed. It didn't matter. In essence one answer of Bryan's stood for all: "The Bible states it; it must be so." When Darrow talked about geology, he got this answer: "I am more interested in the Rock of Ages than in the age of rocks." When he talked about the manifold discoveries of science over the years, shedding light on our beginnings, Bryan stood on "the Word as it is written."

DARROW: You don't care how old the earth is, how old man is, and how long the animals have been here?

BRYAN: I am not much interested in that.

DARROW: You have never made an investigation to find out.

BRYAN: No, sir, I have never.

Judge Raulston ordered court opened with a prayer. Here Darrow waits for it to end be- fore registering a strong objection. The Judge, Bible-bred, overruled him.

John Scopes (bow tie) hears the price he must pay for teaching the forbidden doctrine of evolution to Dayton's children. The fine was $100, later revoked on a technicality without a high court test of the real issues. Right, Dudley Field Malone, of defense counsel.

Judge Raulston mercifully called a halt to the unequal encounter the next morning. He said no purpose was being served by it because all the jury had to decide was whether man was made by God or descended from "a lower order of animals." And "General" Bryan, wearied by his last-ditch defense of the True Faith against "the greatest infidel of his age," did not pursue a threat he had made to put Darrow on the stand. It hardly mattered. There could only be one verdict and the shirt-sleeved hillbilly jury didn't tarry over it. The boy over there in the bow tie, the pagan Scopes, was guilty as charged. Genesis had triumphed over Darwin in Dayton, Tennessee. The monkey was on the run.

The Aftermath

"He came into life a hero, a Galahad, in bright and shining armor. He was passing out a poor mountebank."
—H. L. MENCKEN, on Bryan

Judge John T. Raulston robbed the Monkey Trial of one element of suspense present in all trials. He told the jury in advance that if it found for the State he would fine John T. Scopes one hundred dollars—"our practice in whiskey cases." This assessment, of course, failed to bring home the desired lesson to the defendant. "Your Honor," Scopes said, "I feel that I have been convicted for violation of an unjust statute. I will continue to oppose this law in any way I can. Any other action would be a violation of my ideal of academic freedom."

Darrow went up into the Big Smoky Mountains in search of some fresh air.

The victor, Bryan, sixty-five and tired, retired to a friend's home in Dayton to read his clippings. What he read could not have cheered him. He found even his pearly tones under attack. "The corrosion of nearly three decades became apparent at once," W. O. McGeehan had wired the *New York Herald*

from the courtroom. "Once the voice had in it the qualities of brazen trumpets, but the resonance had gone from the brass." And that was Sunday School-mild alongside what H. L. Mencken had filed to the *Baltimore Sun*:

"The old boy grows more and more pathetic. He has aged greatly during the past few years and begins to look elderly and enfeebled . . . Once he had one leg in the White House and the nation trembled under his roars. Now he is a tinpot pope in the Coca-Cola belt and a brother to the forlorn pastors who belabor half-wits in the galvanized iron tabernacles behind the railroad yards."

Bryan could expect that from such a notorious non-believer as Mencken. He knew Mencken. What he could not expect was the nationwide scorn heaped on the Monkey Trial outside of the Bible Belt. The drama at Dayton

John J. Raulston: "Jist a reg'lar mountaineer jedge," he said.

William Jennings Bryan: The end was near.

had come out as a farce instead of a holy thing. In the Year of Our Lord 1925, it had to; the clock couldn't be turned back, not even for William Jennings Bryan. Tennessee, of course, did stand firm for the Word. While it threw out the Scopes conviction because the "Jedge" erred in setting the sentence instead of letting the jury do it, the State Supreme Court did uphold the evolution law itself.

But by then it was too late for Bryan to savor his victory. He was dead. He died of apoplexy on July 26, five days after the trial, six days after his ordeal on the stand against the wily Darrow. He was buried in Arlington National Cemetery with the nation's best.

THE HERO DOG...

*"One morning the world woke up
and there was no news."*
—OSCAR WILLIAMS

For sustained, paper-selling interest, only two stories used up more space during 1925 than the Scopes trial. One had to do with a half-breed malamute dog named Balto, previously unknown to fame, and the other recorded the demise of Floyd Collins, who liked to poke around in caves.

Balto came first. He starred in an epic drama of the frozen North touched off when an Eskimo in ice-bound Nome caught diphtheria. The nearest railhead was 655 miles away in Nenana, and the way was lined with blizzard (80 miles an hour), snow (blinding) and cold (50 below). All kinds of weather-bitten denizens of that icy hell started out for Nome with life-saving serum for the anonymous Eskimo but the team that mushed it all the way was led by the indomitable Balto. Gunnar Kaasen, the man behind the reins, was all but forgotten as the story unfolded. Indeed, Kaasen confessed that he had run out of steam as the perilous journey neared its end. He said Balto made the final push without any encouragement. He wanted Balto to have all the glory. And Balto did; his star hung so high in the heavens that it made Rin Tin Tin and Strongheart look like movie dogs, which they were. The more elementary question—why didn't somebody just drop some antitoxin into Nome by plane?—got buried in the avalanche of editorials hailing the canine hero.

...AND THE MAN IN THE CAVE

The Kentucky explorer was photographed in another cave not long before tragedy struck.

Floyd Collins: The nation prayed for him.

Floyd Collins had to get stuck underground to push Balto off Page One. A rock fall pinned the Kentuckian 125 feet down in a sand cave near Cave City, Kentucky, on January 30. His cries were heard by passing hillmen the next morning but he was eight hundred feet from the tunnel entrance and there appeared to be no way to get to him. William B. (Skeets) Miller, a skinny reporter for the *Louisville Courier-Journal*, wriggled into the treacherous hole and interviewed Collins, and pretty soon newspapers everywhere were rushing correspondents to the scene. Then, while the wires hummed, an assortment of experts squabbled outside the cave over a means of rescue. They never did quite agree, and Collins' ordeal went on. On the eighteenth day, a rescue worker made his way to the unlucky man and found him dead. The body was left in the rocky mausoleum and there's a marker over it today.

Why did the plight of Floyd Collins draw such big headlines at a time when mine disasters involving scores of men often got stuck away on back pages? The answer was simple. In terms of human interest, it was a better story than an everyday explosion or dirt slide in a mine. It was one man's fight against Mother Nature. It was better than fiction and better than a movie script.

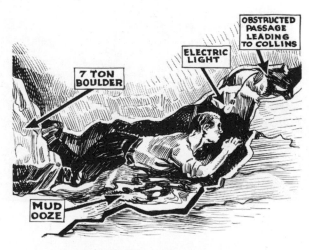

A typical diagram to illustrate news stories.

The monument marks the spot.

KIP RHINELANDER AND THE JONES GIRL

"Husbands, love your wives, and be not bitter against them."
—COLOSSIANS III, 19

The girl is Alice Beatrice Jones, shown with her parents. The youth in the other photo is Leonard (Kip) Rhinelander. Kip wooed and won Alice in a four-year teen-age courtship over violent objections from the very social Rhinelanders. He was heir to a $100,000,000 Manhattan real estate fortune and she was the daughter of a struggling cab driver who happened to be a Negro. They were married late in 1924 and Kip proceeded to furnish the tabloids with one of the more lurid domestic sensations of the scandal-ridden twenties. He sued for an annulment on the allegation that his dark-haired bride had concealed her half-Negro ancestry from him. In the trial, spiced with erotic letters that had passed between the principals in better days, Rhinelander's case suffered fatal reverses. Among other things, it turned out that he had dwelt in the humble Jones home in New Rochelle before the nuptials, so any question of fraud on the bride's part went down the legal drain. The annulment was denied. Later Kip got a Nevada divorce after agreeing to pay Alice $31,500 in cash and $300 a month for life.

IT HAPPENED IN 1925...

Bruce Barton wrote a book called *The Man Nobody Knows* and it put Jesus Christ squarely into the current business scene in 1925. In the Barton parable, Christ became the Great Executive and the Great Advertiser, come to bear witness to the American way as it was practiced under Calvin Coolidge. Barton, an advertising man himself, wasn't alone. Ministers in pulpits everywhere were busily citing the Bible to drive home the notion that man could indeed worship God and Mammon without losing his pass to the pearly gates.

Barton found in the story of Jesus the ideal of service, the ideal of honest toil, the ideal of brevity, the ideal of success, and the ideal of advertising. He found where the "real significance of Jesus' life" lay. "It was not to preach that He came into the world; nor to teach; nor to heal," Barton wrote. "These are all departments of His Father's business, but the business itself is far larger, more inclusive. For if human life has any significance it is this—that God has set going here an experiment to which all His resources are committed. He seeks to develop perfect human beings, superior to circumstance, victorious over Fate. No single kind of human talent or effort can be spared if the experiment is to succeed. The race must be fed and clothed and housed and transported, as well as preached to, and taught and healed. Thus *all* business is His Father's business. All work is worship; all useful service prayer." Barton found in the parables "crisp, graphic language and a message so clear that even the dullest can not escape it." He quoted the line, "Ten virgins . . . went forth to meet the bridegroom," and noted what a "striking picture and what a striking headline" it made and how there were no wasted words under it, either. He said

Battling Siki came out of Senegal, in French West Africa, and fought and lived with such abandon that reams of newspaper space were devoted to him. Siki knocked out Georges Carpentier in Paris the year after Jack Dempsey flattened the beautiful Frenchman, but the barriers of color and his own dissipations kept him from the heights. In 1925 a mysterious assailant shot him to death in Hell's Kitchen in New York, possibly after a barroom brawl.

Gertrude Ederle worked hard at swimming because her father said she could bob her hair if she made good. She tried to swim the English Channel in 1925 but had to turn back.

that Christ, "the founder of modern business," would have been a national advertiser in 1925 because He had purpose and *know-how*. Beyond that, Barton's point simply was that the American businessman, selling, selling, selling, was only carrying on along the path blazed by the super-salesman Christ.

The Man Nobody Knows outstripped all other non-fiction not just in 1925, but also in 1926.

Barton had said something everyone wanted to hear in the time of Coolidge prosperity.

* * *

The House of Bishops of the Protestant Episcopal Church dropped from the wedding ritual the word "obey" and the phrase that followed it, "with all my wordly goods I thee endow" . . . A Grand Jury in Philadelphia refused to vote any more indictments in liquor cases. The court denounced the jurors and sent them home . . . Miller Huggins suspended Babe Ruth for misconduct, fined him five thousand dollars and sent him home from St. Louis in the middle of a road trip . . . The Methodist Board of Temperance, Prohibition and Public Morals charged that in New York even vaudeville acts and comic strips were being used to dispense Wet propaganda. The Board called New York "a foreign city, run by foreigners for foreigners and according to foreign ideas"

Benny Leonard, stylish lightweight from Manhattan's slums, wrote a great record in the early twenties and retired with the title. But he made the mistake of coming back.

. . . President Coolidge got himself a mechanical hobby horse to take exercise in the White House . . . The Government extended the "war" on rumrunners all the way to the Gulf and Pacific Coasts and the Canadian border . . .

The estate of Charles F. Murphy, departed leader of New York's Tammany Hall, came to $2,170,761 . . . The Internal Revenue Bureau revoked all permits allowing people to make two hundred gallons of tax-free wines in their homes . . . Senator Robert M.

The silver-tongued Jimmy Walker, who loved the high life more than the infinite detail of running the world's richest city, was sworn in as Mayor of New York.

LaFollette died . . . Theodore Dreiser's *An American Tragedy* and John Dos Passos' *Manhattan Transfer* came out but neither made number one on the bestseller lists . . . The Ford roadster sold for $260 . . . Bryn Mawr canceled a twenty-eight-year-old ban and let its students smoke on the college grounds . . . Bernard Macfadden's *True Story*, two years old, achieved a sale of 1,500,-000 a month. A new Macfadden magazine, *True Experiences*, carried "The adventures of a man who was caught, unwillingly, in the boisterous whirl of the younger fast set—a crowd that went in for sin and jollity and the pace that sometimes kills!"

Benjamin (Benny Leonard) Leiner of New York's East Side, possibly the greatest lightweight of all time, always called himself "the original Mama's

It was the year in which Harold Ross founded the *New Yorker* with a prospectus proclaiming that it was "not for the old lady from Dubuque." This was not to suggest that the magazine meant to deal in salacious themes but only that it would record the passing scene in realistic, post-Victorian terms. In a word, it would deal with S-E-X (if that was the topic) in cartoon and prose, good prose, as a commodity very much on display in postwar America. This simple, sophisticated approach made Harold Ross a reasonably wealthy citizen.

boy." In 1925 his mother asked him to quit the ring before he got hurt, so he retired—the undefeated champion. He lost $800,000 in the Wall Street crash in 1929 and put the gloves on again. He came back as a welterweight but was knocked out by Jimmy McLarnin. He died in a ring in 1947 while refereeing a fight.

On Broadway, you could see Josephine Hull in *Craig's Wife*, Lunt and Fontanne in *Arms and the Man*, Fay Bainter in *The Enemy*, Ina Claire in *The Last of Mrs. Cheney*, Noel Coward in *The Vortex*, George Jessel in *The Jazz Singer*, Jane Cowl in *Easy Virtue*, Peggy Wood in *Candida*, Lionel Barrymore in *The Piker*, Basil Rathbone in *The Duchess and the Waiter*, Marilyn Miller in *Sunny*, Al Jolson in *Puzzles of 1925*, Dennis King in *The Vagabond King*, and Ethel Barrymore and Walter Hampden in *The Merchant of Venice*. Humphrey Bogart had a part in *The Cradle Snatchers* with Raymond Hackett, Mary Boland and Edna May Oliver.

Clara Bow

"You either have it or you don't."

—Elinor Glyn

Miss Bow: "We did as we pleased. . . ."

Clara Bow was born in 1905 on a rotten side street in the Bay Ridge section of Brooklyn, New York. Her father made a bare existence as a carpenter. "I never had a doll when I was a kid," she recalled years later. She had more searing memories, too. "No one wanted me," she said. "My folks didn't want me because two babies had died before me and when I came along they were afraid it would kill mother. My mother never knew a moment free from illness. I've never forgotten how she suffered. I can remember yet how white she looked as she stood over the tub scrubbing out an old red-checkered tablecloth."

Mrs. Bow had a nervous disease and Clara remembered that she sometimes went into a "trance." She said she awoke one night and found her mother pressing a kitchen knife to her throat. The child swung wildly, knocked the knife to the floor and ran screaming from the room.

In 1922 the girl in the dingy Bay Ridge flat sent two photos of herself to a fan magazine looking for "The Most Beautiful Girl in the World." She was seventeen and had flaming red hair and a lovely round face and a body to match it. She won the contest and got a part in a movie but her scenes perished in the cutting room. Then she got into *Down to the Sea in Ships,* a whaling epic shot in New Bedford, Massachu-

setts, and her playing caught the eye of producer B. P. Schulberg. He brought her to Hollywood—salary, fifty dollars a week—and Paramount Studios soon signed them both. The newcomer did well in such films as *Ladies of the Mob, The Fleet's In* and *Three Weekends.*

The big break came in 1926. Elinor Glyn dreamed up two magic words to Clara Bow's measurements: "It Girl." What did it mean? "It is an indefinable sort of sex appeal," Mrs. Glyn said. "There are few people in the world who possess it. The only ones in Hollywood who do are Rex, the wild stallion; actor Tony Moreno, the Ambassador Hotel doorman and Clara Bow." But it

really wasn't indefinable at all. It went back to the discarding of the ankle-length skirt and the high-buttoned shoe and the burlap-bag undergarment. Now it was better advertised and not a sin but a virtue. Now it marked the woman's total emancipation; the shackles were off. The "It Girl" had the same sex appeal as before but more of it was showing, and it was also a little more available. That was the point. The "It Girl" was the next step—or the next step-in—from the Flapper to Flaming Youth. Anybody who didn't get the idea needed to do no more than catch Clara Bow in the movie of the same name as she soared to Hollywood's dizziest heights. "It" didn't need any words.

For herself, Miss Bow came to look back on the time with a sense of regret. "In my era," she said in 1951, "We had individuality. We did as we pleased. We stayed up late. We dressed the way we wanted. I'd whiz down Sunset Boulevard in my open Kissel (flaming

1926

133

Clara Bow—from the Hollywood heights to the depths of despair.

Gary Cooper, on view here as a tenderfoot in *The Winning of Barbara Worth*, made in 1926, was one of Clara Bow's early flames.

Miss Bow in an early South Sea epic.

Harry Richman, the singer, was another swain on the Bow roster. Later he married a showgirl, Hazel Forbes, shown with him.

Gilbert Roland also was an early passion. He is shown with Miss Bow in a movie scene.

Came the revolution—talking pictures. This was the scene outside the Warner Theater on Broadway on October 6, 1927, when *The Jazz Singer* opened with Al Jolson.

Gloria Swanson (left) and Pola Negri saw their stars dim as sound was ushered in.

red, of course) with seven red chow dogs to match my hair. Today they're sensible and end up with better health —but we had more fun."

In Clara Bow's case, the fun took all manner of turns. She could carry on blazing off-screen romances with Gary Cooper, Harry Richman ("Other men did not understand her as I did. They petted her too much"), Gilbert Roland, or Director Victor Fleming. Or she could have the University of Southern California's famed "Thundering Herd" in for brawling backyard parties; football players fascinated her. Or she could sit up all night playing poker with the maid, cook, and chauffeur. Or break out some beer for the cops on the Beverly Hills night patrol. Or go roller skating on the block. Or put on a pair of slacks and go to a party. But nothing would help. Clara Bow felt lonely and unwanted even when there were crowds around.

The merry-go-round slowed down pretty fast. The movies began to talk— and sing, too—in 1927. Warner Brothers blazed the trail with Al Jolson in *The Jazz Singer*, adding a dimension to the film art. The casualties would be great: John Gilbert's piping tones, very bad for the talkies, ruined his career. Greta Garbo didn't like the new order well enough to stay ("Ay tank I go home"). Other imported stars— Pola Negri, Emil Jannings, Conrad Veidt—had to go into limbo until they could master English. Gloria Swanson and Norma Shearer had to step down from their pinnacles.

Clara Bow compounded her troubles with some touches of scandal. A "Love Balm" suit brought by the wife of Dr. William Earl Pearson cost her $30,000 and some even more costly publicity. A legal battle with her ex-secretary, Daisy De Voe, involved scandalous charges on both sides, spiced with juicy tales out of the star's love-and-liquor department. Daisy De Voe went to jail for pilfering from the "It Girl's" five thousand-dollar-a-week pay check but the winner paid the bigger price. Her

Emil Jannings (beaming alongside his new Model A Ford) and Norma Talmadge were among the silent stars shelved by the talkies.

136

Clara Bow front and back.

The 1930 court battle between Clara Bow and her ex-secretary, Daisy De Voe, heard conflicting testimony about the manner in which the It Girl's heavy income got used up so fast. Miss De Voe maintained that the star lavished expensive jewels on a succession of boy friends, kept the bootleggers in the money, and even squandered some play-ing poker in the kitchen with the household help. Miss Bow charged that Miss De Voe (above), lifted large amounts from their joint bank account to line her own purse. The secretary was found guilty but the lurid head-lines damaged Miss Bow's reputation beyond repair.

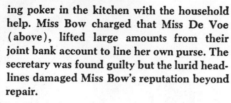

Rex Bell: "The emotional strain . . . was too much . . ."

Paramount contract was terminated by the usual "mutual consent" in 1931. She married cowboy star Rex Bell that year, saying she was looking for some-thing "you cannot obtain with money." She tried a comeback in 1932 and 1933, but failed. She brought up two sons. Somewhere along the line she began to crack up. She suffered periodic breakdowns and wound up in a sani-tarium in the Hollywood hills. Bell, now Lieutanant Governor of Nevada, blames it all on the ex-movie queen's career. "If she had been Minnie Zilch instead of Clara Bow," Bell said in 1956, "perhaps this never would have happened to her. But the emotional strain of her early years was just too much for her nervous system. Its like training horses. Sometimes when you're starting thoroughbreds, you break 'em in too early, while you take a saddle-horse and bring him along easy."

In the sanitarium Clara Bow has trouble sleeping. She paces her room much of the time. She paints in oils. She reads the movie magazines. She watches television and writes fan let-ters to TV players. She has one conso-lation: the sick, workworn mother who was afraid to bring her into her world never knew the good and can't know the bad in her girl's eventful journey. Mrs. Bow died before the name flashed across the nation's conscience in the twenties.

THE GREAT LOVER

"The lover is the husband's instrument of revenge."
—BALZAC

Valentino as The Sheik.

Rodolpho Alfonzo Raffaeli Pierre Filibert di Valentina d'Antonguolla had an Italian father and a French mother. His father was the town veterinarian in Castellaneta in the South of Italy. The boy left there in 1913 to seek a career in the United States. He stated his occupation as "agriculturist" and hired out as a gardener on Long Island. Later he worked as a bus boy and a waiter and started to learn the barber's trade. He knew some hardships; between jobs there were times when he slept on a bench in New York's Central Park. But he was a strikingly handsome and virile teenager and a splendid dancer. A friend got him a job at Maxim's as a dancing partner, also called gigolo in those

days, and after a while he went into a touring musical show. The company broke up out West and Rudolph crashed the movies as an extra.

June Mathis, one of Hollywood's top scenario writers, saw him in a small role and got him tested for *The Four Horsemen of the Apocalypse* when she drew the continuity job on the Ibáñez adventure story. A fast runthrough in the projection room sold him to Rex Ingram, the director, and Rudolph Valentino was on the glory road. *The Four Horsemen* was a smash hit in 1921 and others followed in a rush, including the role of Armand opposite Nazimova's Camille. Then came *The Sheik*, the lusty hot-sands role which capped Valentino's rocket-like

rise to the heights. The Latin collar-ad with the classic features and the bedroom eyes had so much appeal that he utterly enslaved the female moviegoers and had the green-eyed males growing sideburns and greasing their hair down in a frantic effort to steal some of his enchantment. For the girls, no other celluloid hero, before or after, would match Valentino's boundless magnetism. He became the Flapper's dreamboat just as Clara Bow, right on his heels, became the vicarious soulmate of Lord knows how many otherwise normal men and boys.

Valentino thought he had an answer for his own success with the ticket-buying fair sex. "Women," he said, "do not become infatuated with Rudolph

Valentino. They do not love him. They are infatuated with what he stands for. They love the man they imagine he represents. They are in love with love."

Valentino's private life failed to match the smooth perfection written into his scripts. Thus his divorce from actress Jean Acker in 1922 had its embarrassing moments. Miss Acker alleged that the Great Lover, perish the thought, had struck her during a household quarrel. Valentino in turn said his wife had deserted his bed and board, an item which must have made some American women wonder more about him than her. Natacha Rambova, ex-ballet dancer, art director for Nazimova and step-daughter of the millionaire cosmetics man, Richard Hudnut, became the dashing film hero's next bride. There was some trouble about that, too. The groom was accused of bigamy for slipping down to Mexico and tying a second knot before Miss Acker's one-year interlocutory decree became final. Valentino explained that he didn't really mean to set up housekeeping with Miss Rambova until his divorce came of age, so a kindly judge let him off.

Miss Rambova had strong ideas about her husband's work before the cameras and was not above demanding changes in script, lighting or costumes on his pictures. He called her "The Boss," but the studio evidently had another name for the lady, and eventually Valentino agreed to a contract with a proviso which barred her from the set. Miss Rambova packed up and left presently, letting it be known that the Great Lover got on her nerves. She went to Paris for a divorce while Valentino consoled himself with the sultry Pola Negri and some high-powered cars.

That same summer—it was 1926, Valentino's last—a new unpleasantness arose. An editorial writer for the *Chicago Tribune*, dismayed to find pink talcum powder in a hotel washroom, charged that the American male was going positively effeminate under the Valentino influence. It was a light-hearted piece but the fiery Latin, passing through the City of Capone after finishing *The Son of the Sheik*, angrily challenged the *Tribune* man to a duel (name your weapons) or even a fist fight. In turn, Valentino was accused of lusting after publicity, but it wasn't so. The incident hurt him deeply.

Three contrasting views of Valentino. Top, he presents a cup to a beauty contest winner, Norma Niblock of Toronto. Center, he is adorned by two movie colony glamor girls, Nita Naldi (left) and his second wife, Natacha Rambova. Bottom, a moment of repose; note the pointed sideburns.

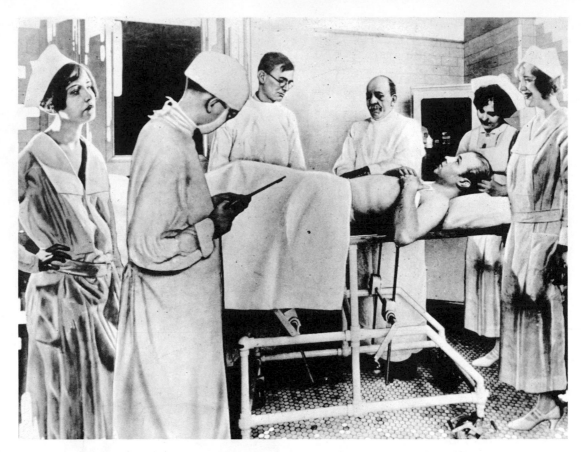

These two composite photographs were dreamed up by Harry Grogin of the *New York Evening Graphic* during the hysteria over Rudolph Valentino. One shows what The Great Lover *might* have looked like on the operating table. The other, inspired by a medium, shows the Great Lover in Heaven, no less, with Enrico Caruso. The medium told the *Graphic* that the actor and the tenor had become very good friends upstairs.

The Big Funeral

"We wish to announce that normal decorum and dignity now prevail at the Frank E. Campbell Funeral Church."
—Ad in the New York papers after the services for Rudolph Valentino

In New York in mid-August, 1926, Rudolph Valentino became violently ill. Doctors operating to remove an inflamed appendix found two perforated gastric ulcers and in time pleurisy, pneumonia, and peritonitis developed. For days the nation hung on every bedside bulletin, the fans alternating between hope and despair. Then the star died, on August 23, and the city was treated to the gaudiest display of sopping-wet mass emotion in its history.

The body was hardly cold before the enterprising inside men on Bernarr Macfadden's *Evening Graphic* concocted a most ghoulish idea. The paper sent two photographers to Frank E. Campbell's Funeral Church on Broadway—one to make pictures and the other to pose in an empty casket. A head-shot of Valentino was superimposed on the photo—this was the *Graphic's* "composograph" technique —and the tabloid hit the streets an hour later with a ghastly front page portrait of the Great Lover "lying in state" *before* the cadaver reached the undertaking parlor. The *Graphic* had to run its presses all night to meet the demand

for the grisly fake photo, and by morning the situation at Campbell's also was out of hand.

More than 30,000 people, men as well as women, descended on Broadway for a final in-person look at the departed idol. More than one hundred were injured as mounted police staged repeated charges to keep the frenzied mob from overrunning the chapel. Foot police swung their clubs freely in the near-riots which followed. When order was restored, the line waiting to file past the catafalque in Campbell's Gold Room extended for eleven blocks. The "Funeral King" had a highly-skilled press agent, Harry C. Klemfuss, beating the drums for the Broadway spectacle, and Hollywood had a solid-gold stake in the publicity avalanche because it had unreleased Valentino pictures in the cans. The crafty Klemfuss left no angles unturned. He had armed Black Shirt guards (supposedly genuine Fascisti) guarding the coffin and among the wreaths he had one labeled "From Benito." This started a lively political argument to fill whatever empty spaces were left in the papers. Mussolini, as it happened, wouldn't buy the gag. He cabled a denial that he had (A) authorized the Black Shirts or (B) sent the flowers.

Why, he didn't even know the guy!

Pola Negri rushed in from California and wept real tears, in cascades, at the station, on the plush red carpet beneath the candle-lit bier, at her hotel and at all stops in between. The grief-stricken brunette withheld her giant sobs only long enough to announce that she was Rudolph's one true love and that nothing but the hand of death, and death alone, could have stayed them from the altar. (Ziegfeld's Marion Kay Brenda put in an immediate demurrer, saying Valentino really meant to marry *her*). As a sideline for the historians, a separate communique revealed that Miss Negri's mourning weeds, all specially tailored, had cost no less than $3,000. In the Actor's Chapel at St. Malachy's Church, where the services were held, Mary Pickford also wept for Valentino but there too Miss Negri stole the show; she became hysterical.

The boy from Castellaneta, an able gardener and expert tango dancer and a pretty good actor, too, was shipped West for burial in Hollywood Memorial Park. But as Mark Hellinger remarked, "Even in death there is no peace for Rudolph Valentino." Before he was in the grave Tin Pan Alley produced a song called "There's a New Star in Heaven Tonight," with his picture on the cover. The composer said it was a simple sentimental tune and could be played with two fingers. A critic went further: he said it could be played with two thumbs.

This is surely one of the more depressing pictures of the decade. It shows the wildly curious throng on Broadway waiting to get into Campbell's for a two-second view of the dead Valentino. A high-pressure behind-the-scenes press-agent operation helped whip up the gruesome carnival. The funeral parlor feasted on the results but the greater immediate return went to the movie magnates. Re-issues of the screen idol's films earned $2,000,000 within a month after the frenzied New York demonstration. Sordid as it was, it furnished a last payday for "The Sheik." A free spender, he died heavily in debt but the fresh box-office money straightened out his estate.

THE MURDERS IN LOVERS LANE

"Everybody is a potential murderer. I've never killed anyone, but I frequently get satisfaction reading the obituary notices."

—CLARENCE DARROW

The Rev. Mr. Hall: "Darling Wonder Heart . . ."

Eleanor Mills: "My heart is his . . ."

The *New York Daily Mirror* broke out on July 17, 1926, with a front page that was lively and also exclusive:

Hall-Mills Murder Mystery Bared

To get the full flavor of it you had to reassemble the cast of characters in the four-year-old crime.

First the dead:

The Rev. Mr. Edward Wheeler Hall, forty-one, stubby and balding, rector of the Protestant Episcopal Church of St. John the Evangelist in New Brunswick, New Jersey.

Mrs. Eleanor Mills, thirty-four, petite, pretty and vivacious, mother of two children, soloist in the Rev. Mr. Hall's choir.

They had been slain under a crabapple tree in De Russey's Lane on the old Phillips Farm, near their homes, on Friday night, September 16, 1922. A .32 calibre slug had passed through the rector's brain. The killer or killers had shot the blond choir singer three times

and then slashed her throat. The deed done, somebody arranged the bodies in a position of decorous intimacy and scattered over them selections from the burning love missiles of Eleanor Mills to her "true heart," Edward Hall.

And now the living:

Mrs. Frances Stevens Hall, dumpy, plain, severe-looking wife of the pastor, seven years his senior.

Willie and *Henry Stevens*, her devoted brothers.

Henry de la Bruyere Carpender, her cousin, member of the New York Stock Exchange.

James Mills, husband of the slain woman, eleven years older, janitor in the school and sexton of St. John's, raising a family on thirty-five dollars a week.

Jane Gibson, "The Pig Woman," chief witness in the rather casual 1922 investigation and due to serve as the State's prime weapon in the new case.

Mrs. Hall and her brothers and cousin were indicted in the double murder because of the *Mirror* story. The newspaper charged that they had

bribed police and witnesses and sweet-talked the local prosecutor to escape prosecution in 1922.

The trial in November and December turned the eyes of the nation to the white-marble courthouse at Somerville, New Jersey. The newspapers sent three hundred reporters, augmented by a small army of "experts"—Mary Roberts Rinehart, Billy Sunday, Peggy Hopkins Joyce, and Eleanor Mills' husband James, himself, and his flapper daughter, Charlotte, to mention a few. The sixty leased wires set up in the basement spewed out words in a torrent—5,000,000 in the first eleven days, 9,000,000 in the full eighteen trial days, 12,000,000 in the twenty-four days in which the spectacle stayed on the front pages. Even *The New York Times* had four stenographers on the scene, so that not a single word-fit-to-print would get away.

The Hall-Mills story, an orgy of murder, intrigue, and purple passion without equal in the Lawless Decade, owed much of its celebrity to the fact that the departed had committed their

The unsuspecting Frances Hall had the kindliest feelings toward her husband's favorite choir singer, shown with her in this photo. The wealthy New Jersey matron paid Mrs. Mills' hospital bill after an operation and often had her join the Reverend and herself on family outings.

James Mills, husband of the slain woman. In 1922, he sold the newspapers his wife's passion-stained letters to the minister who died with her. In 1926, he hired out to one of the tabloids as a guest observer at the trial of Frances Hall and her brothers.

emotions to paper so freely. "Sweetheart, my true heart," Eleanor Mills had written, "I could crush you—oh, I am so happy tonight! I'm not pretty. I know there are girls with more shapely bodies, but I'm not caring what they have. I have the greatest part of all blessings, a noble man's deep, true, eternal love, and my heart is his, my life is his; poor as my body is, scrawny as my skin may be; but I am his forever. How impatient I am and will be! I want to look up into your dear face for hours as you touch my body close."

Hall's letters, a smoking cache sold to the newspapers by the widower Mills for five hundred dollars, made it plain that the little soprano's ardor was well matched. "Darling Wonder Heart," the pastor had written, "I just want to crush you for two hours. I want to see you Friday night alone by our road; where we can let out, unrestrained, that universe of joy and happiness that will be ours." He called Mrs. Mills his "Gypsy Queen" and signed himself "D.T.L.," the German *Deiner Treuer Lieber*, translated Thy True Lover. The sexton's wife called the rector by the shorter, more explicit "Babykins."

The special prosecutor, State Senator Alexander Simpson, offered the jury this thesis: when the struggling pastor married Frances Hall, "he got position, wealth, and refinement" but "he found he was in a chill, cold household" and took up with the gay and zestful Eleanor. Mrs. Hall came upon some of the pastor's passionate incoming mail, overheard the rendezvous made by phone that ghastly night, assembled her kin and stage-managed the execution of the sinners. Simpson had eighty-four witnesses to expand on this story but his case hinged on one person alone—Mrs. Jane Gibson.

The Pig Woman, fifty-six and dying of cancer, had to testify from an iron hospital bed. She was attended by a nurse and doctor and as she croaked out her story the smell of iodoform and formaldehyde suffused a trial chamber made for 280 people and packed with 500. The witness, who raised Poland China pigs, said that on the fatal night she was riding her mule Jenny down De Russey's Lane on a kind of patrol because thieves had rustled two rows of corn from her farm. She said the moon was "shinin' bright and pretty" and she saw Mrs. Hall and Willie Stevens get out of an auto and go into the orchard, so she tied up

Jenny and went "peeking and peeking and peeking." She said she heard many voices—"the men were talking and a woman said very quick, 'explain those letters.'"

Q—(by Simpson) What did you hear the men say? A—They were saying "God damn it" and everything else. All that kind of stuff.

Q—Did you hear more than one man say anything? A—Someone was hitting, hitting, hitting. I could hear somebody's wind going out, and somebody said, "Ugh." Then somebody said, "God damn it, let go." A man hollered . . . then somebody threw a flash toward where they were hollering . . . I see something glitter and I see a man and I see another man like they were wrestling together. [The witness paused while the nurse applied cold cream to her parched lips.] I heard a shot . . . then I heard something fall heavy. Then I run for the mule . . .

Q—Did you hear a woman's voice after you heard the shot? A—One said, "Oh, Henry," easy, very easy; and the other began to scream, scream, scream so loud, "Oh my, oh my, oh my," so terrible loud.

The Pig Woman said she heard three more shots and then mounted Jenny and hurried away from the ghastly tableau under the apple tree.

Neither Mrs. Hall nor her brothers showed any emotion during this recital, but the Pig Woman's own mother showed plenty. The aged crone sat in a front row muttering, "She's a liar, she's a liar, she's a liar," as the grisly story unfolded. The seven-man "million-dollar" defense battery addressed itself to that point at once by bringing out discrepancies in the Gibson story of 1922, as told to a Grand Jury, and the 1926 testimony. Then came damaging items bearing on the witness's vaunted memory for detail. She couldn't remember where she had married, whether she had been divorced, whether she had remarried or whether she had ever known certain gentlemen named by the defense. The point could not have escaped the jury: if Jane Gibson couldn't remember the men in her life, husbands or otherwise, how could she retain after four years every detail of that horror-filled night in De Russey's Lane?

Then Senator Clarence E. Case, handling the cross-examination, returned to the murder scene. He wanted to know why Mrs. Gibson hadn't thought of getting help when she heard

De Russey's Lane, scene of the double murder. Today it is the center of a real estate development.

The spot near the crabapple tree where the bodies were found.

a woman screeching in the Lane. He got a curious answer from the ashen-gray witness on the bed. She said she thought she detected a Negro among the men in the clearing and she figured that the screaming woman there had got into trouble by going out with the Negro. "When I see a white woman with a colored man," she said, "it serves them right."

There were only a few more questions. As the Pig Woman was lifted from the bed to a stretcher to go back to the hospital, she shook her finger at Frances Hall and gasped: "I've told the truth, so help me God, and you know it, you know it!" Then she fell back in a sweat.

The Iron Widow

"Mrs. Hall is not an emotionless woman, she is a pent-up woman."
—DUDLEY NICHOLS, *New York World*

Some of the newspapers had a name for Frances Hall, the rich and dignified matron of New Brunswick. They called her The Iron Widow. She made the headline label stand up. She took the Trial of the Century in stride. What went on inside was her affair; her emotions were her own. On the outside, she betrayed nothing. She heard her husband's torrid letters to Eleanor Mills read in court; she sat impassive. She heard a dozen witnesses say that *everybody* knew about the affair between the pastor and the choir singer for oh, a year or two; she never winced. She heard that someone saw Eleanor Mills sitting on the rector's lap in the vestry at St. John's; she heard that the rector used to slip into the dingy Mills apartment when James Mills was working in the church and the children were in school; she betrayed nothing. She heard a grim recital of the events of September 16, 1922. How she couldn't sleep because the Reverend Hall didn't come home; how she went to the church to look for him; how she called the police at 6:00 A.M. and asked if any "casualties" had been reported; how she met James Mills in the morning and asked him if his wife was home . . . She heard Jane Gibson and looked her straight in the eye. She heard them all; her steel reserve never cracked.

And now she heard Henry Stevens' testimony only as another spectator in the packed courtroom; her big brother could take care of himself. He said he was at his home in Lavallette at the time of the murders. The bluefish were running in Barnegat Bay that weekend and he wouldn't miss that for the world. He was there, fifty miles away, and he had witnesses to prove it, just as the State had witnesses to prove he was in New Brunswick.

There was some concern on Mrs.

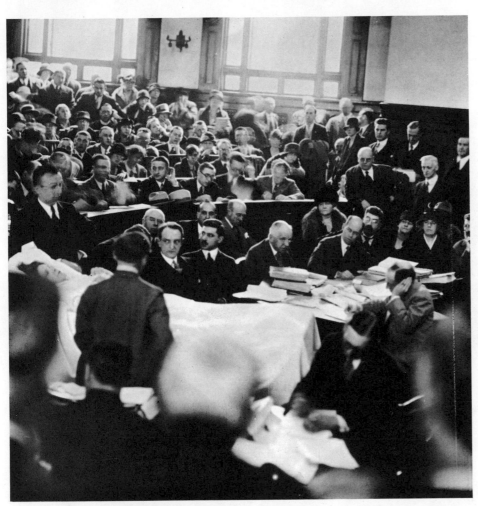

Seriously ill, the Pig Woman testified from a hospital bed.

Jane Gibson, the Pig Woman, was the key witness against Frances Hall and her brothers, Willie and Henry Stevens, but the defense tied her up in all sorts of contradictions and memory lapses.

Willie Stevens (center) awaits his turn to face Prosecutor Alexander Simpson. Supposedly a dim-witted fellow, Willie furnished one of the high moments of the Hall-Mills trial by parrying Simpson's razor-edged questions with the utmost skill, patience and indulgence. Far from wilting under examination and helping the State's case, as most people anticipated, Willie's straightforward testimony scored telling blows for the defense.

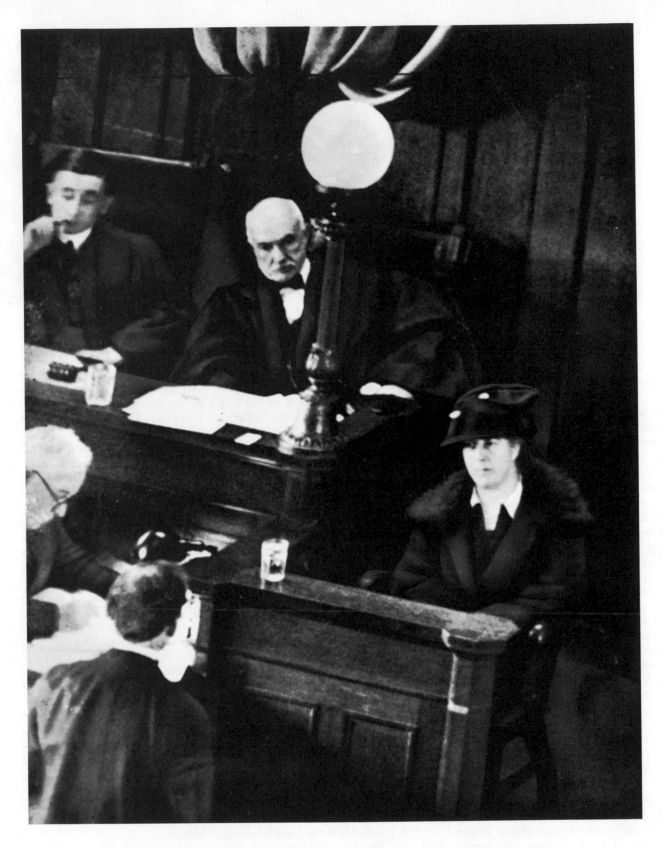

Frances Hall on the stand. She went through the ordeal with icy, stone-faced calm—until the Prosecutor asked whether the Rev. Mr. Hall, who betrayed her, always had been "a loving, affectionate husband." The widow wept as she murmured her one-word answer: "Always."

The Widow Hall is flanked by her brothers, Willie and Henry (right).

Hall's features as the eccentric Willie Stevens took the stand. People always made fun of Willie. He rode around town with Engine Co. No. 3, wearing his own oversized red helmet, and he ran errands for the firemen and bought them things out of his forty-dollar allowance. Sometimes he rode the laundry wagon to pass the time, looking so comical in his wing collar. People said he wasn't altogether right in the head and he was a burden to Mrs. Hall.

But Willie, a pudgy fellow with a walrus mustache and a chowder head, took good care of himself on the stand. If he was the village idiot, you'd never know it from his testimony. He was calm, courteous, direct, and the soul of patience. He had the air of a man who wanted to help the prosecutor if he possibly could. He had no hard feelings. Where was he on the night of the murders? He was in his room, sir. He just went out for a little while, sir, when his sister asked him to go to the church with her and look for the Reverend. In the morning, when he heard that Mr. Hall was dead, he dropped his *New York Times* and cried. Willie got good notices in the papers. Dudley Nichols, the *World* man, later a top Hollywood writer and producer, noted Willie's "childish delight" in courtroom theatricals and the "irresponsible rotundity" about him. He seemed like "a small boy" to Nichols. Willie, in a word, set the stage perfectly for his sister.

Poised, well-bred, a touch of white in the collar over her black widow's weeds, Mrs. Hall answered the ques-

tions evenly as they were put by Robert H. McCarter, former Attorney General of the State and one of its top trial lawyers and now part of the "million-dollar" defense. (It cost $400,000 actually.)

Q—Now, Mrs. Hall, did you kill your husband? A—I did not.

Q—Did you play any part in that dreadful tragedy? A—I did not.

Was Eleanor Mills once in her own Sunday school class? Yes. Did she pay the bills when Eleanor Mills had a kidney operation early in 1922? Yes. Did she send flowers for her room? Yes. Did she drive Mrs. Mills home from the hospital? Yes. Did she sometimes invite Mrs. Mills along on family picnics? Yes. Did she have any but the kindliest feelings towards Eleanor Mills in all that time? No, sir. Did she ever have the least occasion to suspect her husband and the choir singer? Certainly not.

Prosecutor Simpson, five feet tall but a giant in the courtroom, took over. He moved close to Mrs. Hall. He had lots of questions. He tore into every angle of her story. Could she swear she was not in De Russey's Lane with her brothers that night? Absolutely. Did she tell James Mills the next morning that she thought the Reverend and Mrs. Mills had met with foul play? No, she didn't think she had. Was there a scratch on her face that morning, as a witness testified? No, sir. Why had she sent her brown cloth coat to a dyer in Philadelphia after the murders? She needed a coat for the mourning period and always sent things to that firm.

Was the coat stained with anything? Certainly not. Why did she ask the police about "casualties" when her husband failed to return home that night? "It means accidents," she said. "It means death also, doesn't it?" Simpson stormed back. "I do not know that it does," the witness said. Was Reverend Hall always "a loving, affectionate husband"? The lady replied, almost inaudibly, with one word: "Always."

Now there were tears in her eyes. It was plain that the Iron Widow, through the long nightmare, had some good memories to go with the bad.

Despite the mass of testimony, the jury was out only five hours. The verdict was not guilty. There remained only some details: The standing indictment against Henry Carpender would be thrown out. Mrs. Hall and her brothers would sue the *Daily Mirror* for three million dollars and accept an out-of-court settlement. Phil Payne, the managing editor who broke the story, would die the next year in the disappearance of the monoplane Old Glory, flying to Rome. The Pig Woman would die four years later. The widow and her family would retreat into the close-knit privacy they had always known.

Somebody figured out that the words filed out of Somerville on the Hall-Mills story could have filled twenty-two novels. This was undoubtedly so, but there was no last chapter in the mountain of prose. The question would go down through the years: Who killed the little pastor and his favorite choir singer?

A TEMPLE OF GOLD

"I am being crucified by the very bats of hell..."
—SISTER AIMEE

Aimee Semple McPherson, colored spotlights 'n' all.

Aimee Semple McPherson pulled into Los Angeles in 1917 in an old jalopy carrying one hundred dollars in small bills, all her worldly goods, her mother, Minnie (Ma) Kennedy, and two small children. She came the long way. She had beat the bushes for sinners from Canada through the American backwoods to China to New Zealand and Australia before the Sodom and Gomorrah called Hollywood came into her consciousness. Here wickedness flourished; here, without a tent she could call her own, she would stand and do battle.

The Land of the Gold Bathtub proved a fertile battleground. Within five years Sister Aimee herself was surrounded by much splendor. Her "International Institute of Four-Square Evangelism" had prospered to the point where she could build the

$1,500,000 Angelus Temple, seating 5,000 and complete with a $75,000 radio studio, a club for lonely hearts, a Cradle Roll Chapel for babies, a Miracle Room for discarded crutches and braces, and a $7,000 weekly payroll. Pretty good going for a soulsaver off the sawdust trail who always insisted that she was "not a healer" but "only the little office girl who opens the door and says 'Come in.'" Aimee at times professed concern over the glamor and abundance about her. "Sometimes," she would say, "I wish I didn't have to carry on the Lord's work in such a conspicuous capacity."

Sister Aimee was hefty without being fat and made a vibrant, exciting appearance in the pulpit in her flowing white satin gowns. She had special colored lights play over her during her sermons and this Hollywood effect set

off her blond locks nicely. She billed herself as "The World's Most Pulchritudinous Evangelist," an item which must have made Harold McPherson wonder what he had given up. McPherson had parted from Sister Aimee because he wanted to settle down and take root in the grocery business, while she insisted on riding the tent circuit for Jehovah. She had married the dedicated grocer in New York after her first husband, Robert Semple, a boilermaker turned Holy Ghost revivalist, died in China on their missionary turn among the Orientals.

The Sister attained her greatest fame in the spring of 1926 with an incident that started as a drowning, became a "kidnaping" and finally took on the appearance of a romantic Odyssey. The story broke in late May when Emma Schaeffer, her secretary, reported the evangelist missing after a dip in the ocean from a lonely spot at Venice, outside of Los Angeles. Sister Aimee had gone to the beach for a day's peace and quiet, throwing up her own tent as a combination dressing room and a haven for meditation. Miss Schaeffer said the Sister commissioned her to go on an errand to a nearby hotel and then started for the water. She saw the ample figure in the green bathing suit dip beneath the waves and bubble on the surface but when she came back, no evangelist.

Ma Kennedy, a Salvation Army lass in her own younger days in Canada, summoned the faithful legions to Angelus Temple that very night. "We know she is with Jesus," said Sister Aimee's mother. "Pray for her." The congregation not only prayed but ante'd up a barrel of cash so that a $25,000 reward could be set aside for all or any persons contributing to the evangelist's return. Among the scores who thereupon flung themselves into the waters at the point of Sister Aimee's departure, one youth drowned and another died of exposure, while a girl in the congregation reportedly killed herself out of grief for her missing spiritual leader. After a while, Ma Kennedy prepared the people for the worst and had a small plane scatter lilies over the Sister's watery resting place. A single memorial service drew eleven thousand persons.

But Sister Aimee, while somewhat tuckered out, proved to be very much alive as the outbreak of public mourning limped into its thirty-second day. On June 23, the evangelist emerged from the desert outside of Douglas, Arizona, and furnished the world with this play-by-play account of her ordeal:

While Emma Schaeffer was on that errand at Venice, a man (Steve) and a woman (Rose) approached her on the beach and said their baby was dying in a car nearby; would she come and pray for the infant? When she reached the car there was no baby, only a man (Jake) at the wheel, with the motor running. She was tossed into the sedan and passed out. She was also drugged. Her captors drove down to Mexico and stashed her away in a shack in a little village across the Arizona border. Steve said that if she didn't produce half a million dollars in ransom he would sell her to a Mexican named Felipe, otherwise uniden-

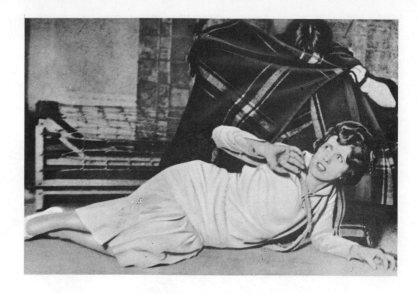

Always willing to help the newspaper photographers, Sister Aimee here re-enacts the "kidnaping" which dimmed her reputation in 1926. The authorities insisted that the evangelist went off on a romantic journey with her radio operator and then made up the abduction tale.

tified. Steve burned her with cigars when she wouldn't answer questions she deemed too personal. But her captors relaxed their vigilance at noon on June 22 and she slipped away and made the thirteen-hour march across the burning, sun-baked desert to sanctuary in Douglas.

In the hospital, made comfortable in a pink silk dressing gown, Sister Aimee exhibited burns on her fingers, bruises on her ankles where she said she had been shackled with cord, and blisters on her feet. The story didn't take. Desert-wise observers deemed the blisters much too mild for the kind of hike Sister Aimee had described. It was also noted that her walking shoes were hardly scuffed and her dress bore little dirt or damage. Someone else thought it odd that the evangelist had not asked for water upon reaching Douglas; she should have been at least a little thirsty. District Attorney Asa Keyes came up from Los Angeles and went over the desert trail with the evangelist and king-sized doubts filled his mind, too.

Then the dirty linen began to fly.

It turned out that Kenneth G. Ormiston, the radio operator at Angelus Temple, had vanished from all of his familiar haunts—including his wife's

home—some time before Sister Aimee dropped out of public view. Ormiston was still missing, but the District Attorney had quite a dossier on the man's recent travels. He said that during late May and most of June, Ormiston and a blond companion had checked in and out of a number of hotels in West Coast beach resorts under a variety of "Mr. and Mrs." aliases. The prosecutor said the woman answered the description of Aimee Semple McPherson.

Sister Aimee, newly welcomed home to her tabernacle by a tremendous throng of well-wishers, issued a public appeal to the amorous radio operator to come in and clear her tarnished name. "It would seem," said the Evangelist's manifesto, "that any true man who knew the diabolical attempts to assassinate my name and great work by linking it with such a story would come out with a clear statement, or communicate directly with our office. Will you do this?"

Ormiston stayed away but the "clear statement" came forth, addressed in particular to a portion of the District Attorney's story dealing with a ten-day idyll at Carmel during which grocery orders were said to have been signed in a hand resembling Sister Aimee's. Ormiston's mailed affidavit submitted

On a visit to New York, Sister Aimee stopped at Tom Noonan's Bowery Mission to save some souls.

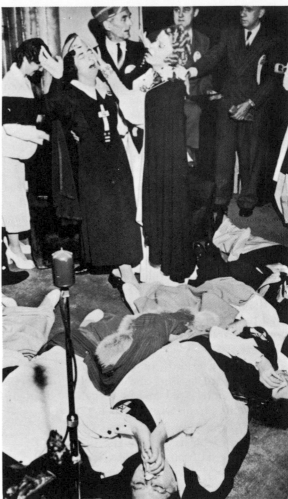

Bedecked with flowers and her hair freshly marcelled, Sister Aimee comforts a worshipper about to swoon at a rally of her International Institute of Four-Square Evangelism. Note the women on the floor, felled by religious frenzy and sobbing violently.

Once the sturdy McPherson frame was assailed by tropical fever in Mexico. When the word was conveyed back to Los Angeles, the faithful sent up prayers for their stricken shepherdess.

the intelligence that he was not in Carmel with Aimee Semple McPherson, no sir, but with a fair companion he would prefer to identify as "Miss X" lest any further embarrassment ensue.

Keyes got Sister Aimee and her mother indicted on a charge of obstructing justice during the long saga of the "disappearance" and "kidnaping." The evangelist responded with a newspaper serial charging that unnamed vice lords were conspiring against her because she had lured too many prospective prostitutes onto the straight and narrow. The series was titled, "Saint or Sinner—Did I Go from Pulpit to Paramour?" Sister Aimee explained everything as follows:

"I have waged unrelenting battle with the *Batlike Demons From Hell* and they fear me and revile me as the Devil hates holy water. What brought about District Attorney Keyes' change of belief?

"Did the overlords of the underworld who are fighting me and who are heavily interested in Los Angeles have anything to do with it?

"I am being crucified by the very bats of hell, who have gone the limit in perfidy; brutal, conscienceless, hardly human. They have gone to the extent of the mummer's art in 'making up' women to look like me and pose in questionable places as Sister Aimee."

The Angelus Temple radio station spread the same gospel over the West Coast. On the lighter side, Sister Aimee scoffed at the possibility that she could have disappeared because of an affair of the heart. "The man I marry has not appeared on the scene yet," she said. "He must be good looking. He must be six feet tall or more. He must be a preacher. He must have certain rigid standards. He must play the trombone and be a good singer and he must be a good and holy man." Ormiston could not have met many of those qualifications, obviously.

Come the trial itself, the embattled evangelist showed up in a demure outfit of powder-blue and white and announced, "I am like a lamb led to slaughter." Undaunted, Keyes produced an assortment of chambermaids, house detectives, and other trained observers to identify the Sister as the party of the second part on Ormiston's hotel stopovers during the anxious days when the hordes were beseeching the blue Pacific to yield up the McPherson remains. Ormiston himself was located in Harrisburg, Pennsylvania, while

these revelations were pouring forth, but then something strange happened. Keyes suddenly moved for an acquittal and Ormiston was not called. Keyes never explained why.

Her ordeal over, Sister Aimee took to the road again, ranging as far as Europe to repair her fences. She had the old Hell-robbing spirit and the very same ardor for tackling the forces of Satan, but the tour fell flat; something had gone out of her audiences. She tried the Orient again for a year and then came back to Los Angeles. A marriage to a radio man named Dave Hutton, not a trombone player and in no sense the beau ideal she had mentioned during the Ormiston mess, got her back into the papers briefly. But the union didn't last long. Sister Aimee, now past forty, shed Hutton when another woman accused him of toying with her affections and asked for $200,000 damages. After that the evangelist dropped out of the news again. In September, 1944, she was found dead in Oakland, California, possibly from an overdose of sleeping pills.

Years later, in Isabel Leighton's book, *The Aspirin Age*, Carey McWilliams blamed the times, not the evangelist, for all the newsprint used up on her in 1926. McWilliams noted the dandy ingredients in the mixture—"sex, mystery, underworld characters, spooks, kidnapers, the ocean, hot desert sands, an escape, and a thrilling finale"—and concluded:

"It was a story made for the period, a period that invested the trivial with a special halo, that magnified the insipid, that pursued cheap sensationalism with avidity and passion. While admittedly quite a story, the 'kidnaping' of Sister Aimee became invested with the proportions of a myth and the dimensions of a saga in the great vacuum of the age. It was a kind of compendium of all the pervading nonsense, cynicism, credulity, speakeasy wit, passion for debunkery, sex-craziness, and music-hall pornography of the times."

It was, indeed.

Sister Aimee, Lloyd Morris said, "fused economics and ecstasy, showmanship and salvation, carnival and contrition." Here she is in her silks and satins ready to go forth and do battle with the Devil.

The Big Bath

*"Let us have wine and woman,
Mirth and laughter,
Sermons and soda-water
The day after."*

—BYRON

Joyce Hawley: she got wet in a manner frowned upon by the Prohibition people.

Earl Carroll, the *Vanities* producer, had occasion to throw a party early in 1926. He wanted to honor the Countess Vera Cathcart, who had just battled her way past an Immigration Service attempt to bar her from these shores for "moral turpitude" because of her sensational London divorce from the Earl of Cathcart. Carroll summoned several hundred people to an after-hours gathering in his theater and there unveiled what seemed to him the very thing that Dry America needed to liven up its drinking soirees. He had a bathtub wheeled on stage and while he held an opera cloak in front of it, Joyce Hawley, seventeen and blue-eyed, shed her clothes and tiptoed in. As he dropped the cloak with a flourish, Carroll invited the revelers to step forth. The tub contained champagne as well as the tall and shapely bathing beauty. One could scoop up the bubbly water in tumblers or just feast one's eyes on Joyce Hawley radiantly awash in the vintage. While it was that simple, the idea failed on two accounts:

I—Miss Hawley burst out crying for the shame of the thing just as the perfect host's guests approached the interesting porcelain fixture. Carroll forthwith ordered the tub wheeled off stage—champagne, bathing girl and all.

II—The snoopy Prohibition people heard about it and had the producer summoned before a Federal Grand Jury, since it was patently illegal in 1926 to possess or take a bath in anything containing more than 1.5 per cent alcohol. Carroll said heck, it was just ginger ale, not champagne. The jury indicted him anyway.

While the trial was pending, Miss Hawley accepted an engagement to reenact her performance at the Greenwich Village Follies—minus the champagne, minus the tears and minus the total nudity. She was billed as "The Queen of the Bath" and the ads promised viewers a "Sensational Tub Tableau." For a girl who was only a hog-butcher's daughter from Chicago, still

only a year away from the smell of the stockyards, the statuesque young model showed a highly professional business sense. For example, she issued a scale of prices for her services, as follows:

INTERVIEW	$100
ONE PICTURE	$ 50
SET OF FIVE PICTURES FOR MOVIE STRIP	$200
TRUE LIFE STORY	$500
LIFE STORY AND INSIDE PEEPS BEHIND THE SCENES OF A LINGERIE SHOW AND NUDITY REVIEW	$1000

plus share of all syndicate rights

Come the trial, Miss Hawley, formerly Teresa Daughelos, testified that

Kathryn Ray and Earl Carroll demonstrating the Charleston.

Carroll promised to pay her one thousand dollars to soak in the champagne. She said she had posed nude for artists but never for large assemblages and wouldn't have accepted the bathtub engagement except that she needed the money. While on that point, she said that Carroll never did pay her.

The producer was found guilty of perjury for denying his unique violation of the Volstead Act. He was fined two thousand dollars and sentenced to a year and a day in the Federal Prison at Atlanta and served four months. And Joyce Hawley went home to mother. "I'm going to college," she said, "and I'm going to help my parents." She escaped notoriety after that.

Mr. Carroll and friends.

"Peaches."

Peaches and Daddy

The aging Edward West (Daddy) Browning, who had nothing but time and money, dropped in on a sorority dance in New York one day in 1926 because his romantic tastes ran to teen-age girls. On this particular expedition his sheep's eyes lit upon Frances (Peaches) Heenan, a plump Washington Heights schoolgirl who managed to look just a trifle beyond her 15 summers. In due course, Peaches was being driven to class in a peacock blue Rolls Royce furnished by the eccentric 51-year-old real estate millionaire.

"He showered me with flowers, deluged me with candy and gifts," the girl said later. "My boy friends were forgotten. I had glances for none save Mr. Browning, my silver-haired knight, his gentle caresses, his quiet dignity, his *savoir faire*."

The wedding took place on April 10.

The child bride fled her well-heeled knight on October 2 and touched off a legal battle that scorched the town's newsprint.

Daddy, suing for a separation, offered himself before the bar as an unkissed and deeply wounded groom. He said his wife's cries for "Mama" made the marital chamber a place of utter frustration.

The hefty Peaches didn't deny her strong attachment to Mama but told quite another story. She alleged that Daddy romped around their honeymoon premises in the nude and insisted on the same simple fashion for her, even at the breakfast table. She said Daddy flew into a rage and pinched her when she pressed her girlish right to enjoy her oatmeal more formally—say, in a nightgown. She said Daddy further distressed her by gamboling around the bedchamber on his hands and knees, again without the encumbrance of any wearing apparel.

Since photo journalism happened to be in its infancy at the time, the *New York Evening Graphic* undertook to illustrate Peaches' testimony with its own patented "composographs" (see sample on this page). Short of this fake picture device, the other local tabloids managed to give the story a display befitting its vivid content.

The principals appeared to enjoy the spectacle as much as the public itself.

Daddy won the suit and Peaches, cut off without a farthing, shed 40 pounds and hit the vaudeville trail.

This sort of thing earned Peaches as much as $8,000 a week and furnished a nice nest egg for her and Mama against the time Daddy passed away in 1934 and the ex-Mrs. Browning could claim a widow's share of the estate.

Confronted by a historian in the employ of the *New York Post* three marriages and three divorces later, Peaches was quite candid about her brief idyll with Mr. Browning:

Q—Were you in love with him?

A—Not at all.

Q—Why did you marry him?

A—I haven't the faintest idea. How can you account for the actions of a 15-year-old?

That was in the winter of 1955 and even then, like the song said, there was something lonesome and blue about Peaches Browning. She died the next year after a bad fall in her bathtub. She was 46, and there was no evidence that she had ever known any happiness in the headline-scarred journey from middle-class Washington Heights to Manhattan's plush East Side.

Edward "Daddy" Browning, with "Peaches" (right) and his adopted daughter Dorothy, at left.

Browning and a woman reporter exchange banter.

The famous Honk! Honk! composograph.

"Trudy"

An Amazon named Gertrude (Trudy) Ederle, daughter of a New York delicatessen owner, triumphed over the rip tides and choppy waters of the English Channel, swimming the treacherous twenty-two miles between Cape Gris-Nez and Dover in fourteen hours and thirty-one minutes. She was the first to do it. She came back to New York to the wildest ticker-tape welcome ever staged for a woman.

All in all, it was an event that epitomized the trail-blazer aspect of the Lawless Decade. It was a "first," it was a new kind of achievement for a woman, and it was done by employing new devices planned to overcome or reduce the known difficulties—note Trudy's goggles and the grease smeared over her body to insulate her from the killing chill of the Channel waters.

Gertrude Ederle swam the English Channel that year . . .

The welcome in New York, with Official Greeter Grover Whalen presiding . . .

The Big Parade up Broadway. Lindbergh's would top it.

IT HAPPENED IN 1926 . . .

The Sixth Year of the Drought accounted for an unusual story on Capitol Hill. Dr. Samuel Harden Church, president of the Carnegie Institute of Technology, went before a senatorial committee and described the Demon Rum as "one of the greatest blessings that God has given to men out of the teeming bosom of Mother Earth." He also observed, with much nonchalance, that hip flasks were quite common among the students on his campus. A Dry witness then charged that Dr. Church had said those things only because he was miffed at the Prohibition Service for intercepting some honest-to-goodness liquor coming down from Canada for his own larder . . . U. S. Attorney Emory R. Buckner of New York put a figure on the nationwide bootleg trade: $3,600,000,000 a year . . . The Supreme Court split five to four to uphold the law limiting doctors' prescriptions of whiskey to one pint every ten days per patient . . . President Coolidge told Congress we had to have teeth in the Volstead Act or else . . . The Drys said more people were buying their babies shoes now that they couldn't spend their money on alcohol . . . Wayne B. Wheeler, general counsel for the Anti-Saloon League of America, admitted that the League had paid some congressmen to lecture in the cause . . . Mrs. Mabel Walker Willebrandt said Prohibition was being enforced with increasing success. She was in charge of enforcement at the time . . .

* * *

The textile workers of Passaic, New Jersey, sixteen thousand strong, struck against a 10 per cent pay cut. The strike, marked by much violence, lasted a year and both sides claimed victory . . . There were twenty-three lynchings during 1926 . . . Ford dropped the Model T for the Model A . . . The stock market dipped but came back strong . . . Dr. Ales Hrdlicka, the anthropologist, said a new type of American man was developing: less spare, taller and also more sanguine . . . The first telephone calls between New York and London took place . . . The Navy added chewing gum to its ship's stores, ending a fifteen-year ban . . . The Massachusetts Supreme Court denied a new trial to Sacco and Vanzetti . . . Henry Ford put in the five-day week in his plants . . .

Sinclair Lewis refused to accept the 1925 Pulitzer Prize for his novel, *Arrowsmith*. He said literary prizes

A scene from the play *Broadway*, by Philip Dunning and George Abbott, produced by Jed Harris, starring Lee Tracy.

tended to make writers "safe, polite, obedient, and sterile" and charged that the judges weighed books less upon literary merit than upon the moment's code of good form . . . DuBose Heyward's *Porgy* came out. George Gershwin picked it up one night because he couldn't sleep. He read it through and wrote Heyward and said he would like to build an opera around the Catfish Row story sometime . . . John Erskine's *The Private Life of Helen of Troy* and Warwick Deeping's *Sorrel & Son* were No. 1 best-sellers but Hemingway's *The Sun Also Rises* and Faulkner's *Soldier's Pay* weren't . . . In non-fiction, Bruce Barton's *The Book Nobody Knows* joined *The Man Nobody Knows* on the lists. George A. Dorsey's *Why We Behave Like Human Beings* also made it, along with Milton C. Work's *Auction Bridge Complete* . . . The Book of the Month Club and the Literary Guild were started . . .

Anita Loos produced a best-seller in 1926 and added a phrase to the language: "Gentlemen Prefer Blondes." Alice White and Ruth Taylor drew the roles in the movie. In our time the girls were portrayed—with more bulges—by Marilyn Monroe and Jane Russell.

Ann Pennington. Her dimpled, beautifully rounded knees were famous.

In the musical, *Americana,* on Broadway, Helen Morgan did a torch song, "Nobody Wants Me," while sitting atop an upright piano. It would become her trademark . . . Fredric March appeared in *The Devil in the Cheese,* William Harrigan in *The Great God Brown,* Lee Tracy in *Broadway,* Lenore Ulric and Henry Hull in *Lulu Belle,* James Rennie in *The Great Gatsby,* Spencer Tracy in *Yellow,* Helen Hayes in *What Every Woman Knows,* Eugene and Willie Howard and Ann Pennington in *George White's Scandals* . . . Eva Le Gallienne opened her low-priced Civic Repertory Theatre on Fourteenth Street . . . In Hollywood, Marion Davies, riding high, felt the need of a hideaway on the beach. She bought two little homes on the Santa Monica shore and decided to build a hallway to connect them. It was going to cost $7,500 but Miss Davies got more ambitious ideas as the work progressed. Four years and $1,750,000 later the pretty blond star had herself a mansion that was one of the world's showplaces—and she was still building. She called the place Ocean House and imported furnishings — and guests — from all over the world. In time, prac-

tically completed, fully furnished and staffed by an army of 32 servants, Ocean House represented a tidy $7,000,000 investment. Hollywood society frolicked over the premises for fifteen years before Miss Davies, longtime friend of William Randolph Hearst and shareholder in some of his publishing enterprises, moved to a smaller mansion in Beverly Hills. Eventually Ocean House went to rot and ruin. Some of the buildings—there were five when Miss Davies called off the architect — faced demolition in 1956 to make way for a motel . . . The Charleston was the rage. Hope Hampton demonstrated the dance on the deck of the *Leviathan* for a group of Oxford students and Gimbels basement did a rush business in "Charleston flare dresses." Price: $1.58 . . .

* * *

George Gershwin.

Eugene O'Neill.

Marion Davies.

William E. (Pussyfoot) Johnson got his chums in the Dry lobby angry with an overcandid memoir in *Cosmopolitan.* "I had to lie, bribe, and drink to put over Prohibition," Pussyfoot wrote, adding that he would do it again if he had to.

A Charleston endurance contest at the Parody Club.

MURDER
FOR
MONEY

Albert Snyder: the victim.

"Ruth Snyder was so like the woman across the street that many an American husband was soon haunted by the realization that she also bore an embarrassing resemblance to the woman across the breakfast table."
—ALEXANDER WOOLLCOTT

It was the year of the Long Count, starring Dempsey and Tunney. It was the year of the Atlantic flights, starring Lucky Lindy. It was the year of the Home Run, starring Babe Ruth. It was the year of the Executions at Charlestown, starring Sacco and Vanzetti. It was the year of the Unwed Mother, starring Nan Britton and Warren Harding. But 1927 began with the sordid story of a straying suburban housewife and a fun-loving corset salesman. Ruth Snyder and Judd Gray became quite famous by taking a sash weight to Albert Snyder and then fighting bitterly over who had the idea in the first place. They made murder—and possibly even illicit love—unpopular that year.

The deed was unfurled on a Sunday morning in March in the Snyder row house in Queens Village, New York. Mrs. Snyder, bound and gagged, pounded on her daughter's door shortly after 2:00 A.M. and screamed, "Get help!" Lorraine, nine, called a neighbor. Snyder, $115-a-week art editor of *Motor Boating* magazine, lay smashed to death on his bed. His wife blamed a burglar; she said the man also hit her over the head and tied her up. But all the things she listed as stolen turned up in secret caches around the house and the unemotional Mrs. Snyder cracked that night. She named Judd Gray as her collaborator in the badly fumbled murder plot—"Poor Judd," she said. "I promised not to tell"—and the police found him upstate in a Syracuse hotel.

The traveling salesman professed total innocence. "My word, gentlemen," he said, "when you know me better you'll see how utterly ridiculous it is for a man like me to be in the clutches of the law. Why, I've never even been given a ticket for speeding."

But he wasn't nearly as hard to break as his paramour. He confessed on the train going back. He said that when the time came to smite Snyder, he weakened and had to have help from Mrs. Snyder. She had said that her courage departed at the appointed hour and Gray—she used to call him "Lover Boy"—had to wield the bludgeon all by himself.

Ruth Brown Snyder, thirty-two, was a slim and nicely curved peroxide blond with good features marred only by a hard jaw and an icy look. Henry Judd Gray, thirty-four, who had a wife and eleven-year-old daughter in Orange, New Jersey, wore shell-rimmed glasses and had a mild, gentle look. He could have passed for a Sunday School teacher.

The tragic journey began in the summer of 1925 when a mutual friend introduced the Queens matron to the corset impresario in a restaurant in midtown Manhattan. Mrs. Snyder, oddly, happened to be in the market for a corselette and Gray took her back to his office. "She removed her dress and I tried on a garment to see if it was the right size," he said, "and she was very

badly sunburned and I offered to get some lotion to fix her shoulders, and..."

Thereafter the pair met in hotels with much regularity and compared notes on married life and items like that. The plot on Albert Snyder's life —and some companion discussions about taking out a fat insurance policy on the easy-going artist—thickened amid a strong romantic aura and ample helpings of bootleg whiskey. But there would never be any agreement on the details: the lovebirds squabbled bitterly in court that April.

End of the Affair
"Does not he to whom you betray another know that you will at another time do as much for him?"

—MICHEL DE MONTAIGNE

The trial of Ruth Snyder and Judd Gray in the Queens County Courthouse at Long Island City started out like a replay of the Hall-Mills story. The chamber overflowed with outside observers, some of them holdovers from the elaborate newspaper coverage of the earlier epic. The list included Mary Roberts Rinehart, Billy Sunday, David Belasco, D. W. Griffith,

1927

Peggy Hopkins Joyce (presumably as an expert on marriage), Will Durant (then on the best-seller lists with *The Story of Philosophy*), Dr. John Roach Straton, and Aimee Semple McPherson.

The latter pair drew the strongest moral and religious lessons from the murder melodrama. Dr. Straton's examination of the record satisfied him that "literally every one of the Ten Commandments" had been trampled along the tawdry path of the crime. Sister Aimee used the columns of the *New York Evening Graphic* to enjoin God to teach young men to say, "I want a wife like mother—not a Red-Hot Cutie." It took brass for "The Beautiful Sister Aimee of the Silver Tongue" to utter such a lofty sentiment within a year after starring in a red-hot scandal of her own, but nobody was surprised.

The proceedings opened with violently conflicting presentations. Edgar F. Hazleton, Mrs. Snyder's counsel, told the jury he would show that not only Gray but also the late Albert Snyder had contributed to his fair client's descent into the morass. He said that Snyder "drove love from out that house" by pining over a departed sweetheart of his youth and that Gray worked out the murder and the $50,000 double-indemnity insurance policy that sweetened the package.

"We will prove to you," Hazleton said, "that Ruth Snyder is not the demimondaine that Gray would like to paint her, but that she is a real loving wife, a good wife; that it was not her fault that brought about the condition that existed in that home . . ."

Samuel L. Miller, one of Gray's attorneys, had it the other way. He offered the jury "the most tragic story that has ever gripped the human heart." He said Gray was such a peace-abiding citizen that Ruth Snyder had to give him fifteen or twenty shots of whiskey to steel him for the murder.

"He was dominated by a cold, heartless, calculating master mind and master will," Miller said. "He was a helpless mendicant of a designing, deadly, conscienceless, abnormal woman, a human serpent, a human fiend in the guise of a woman. He became inveigled and drawn into this hopeless chasm, when reason was gone, when mind was gone, when manhood was gone, and when his mind was weakened by lust and passion."

Ruth Snyder took the stand in a simple black frock characterized by the ladies among the 120 working reporters as "chic but decorous." She said Snyder spent most of his time on such manly sports as boating and fishing and barely took her out, except to an occasional movie, but she maintained the best possible home for him nonetheless. She said she was the one who read the Bible to their daughter Lorraine and took her to Sunday school.

Then Hazleton came to the chance meeting with Gray and the hurry-up romance that ensued. "He was in about the same boat I was," Mrs. Snyder testified, a microphone carrying her words to the overflow throng in the corridors. "He said he was not happy (at home)." She said Gray drank heavily when they went to hotels or such Prohibition-time resorts as the Frivolity Club or the Monte Carlo but she hardly ever finished a drink and didn't even smoke. She swore that Gray got her to take out the heavy insurance policies on Snyder. "Once," she said, "he sent me poison

The Snyder home in Queens Village, N. Y., where the murder occurred.

Ruth Snyder: the wife.

and told me to give it to my husband." When the witness came to the murder itself she lost her composure and wept, while the stone-faced Gray suddenly came to life and chattered eagerly to his legal battery.

On cross-examination, Assistant District Attorney Charles W. Froessel hit hard on the men in Ruth Snyder's life, including other roving salesmen of her acquaintance, but the witness swore Gray was her only lover. The women

in the courtroom, hostile to Mrs. Snyder from the beginning, snickered often during this line of questioning but the prosecutor didn't spare the woman in the chair.

Q—You thought that while you were

carrying on with the defendant Gray you were putting it all over on your husband, didn't you? A—No, I did not.

Q—You thought you were doing him a favor? A—No, I did not.

Q—You knew you were doing wrong, did you not? A—Yes.

Q—He had full confidence in you, did he not, Madam? A—Yes.

Q—And you betrayed that confidence, did you not? A—I did not.

Q—Well, you betrayed it with Gray, did you not? A—Yes.

Q—You hated your husband, did you not? A—No, I did not.

Q—You loved him. A—I didn't love him but I didn't hate him.

Q—Of course, you did nothing in your married life to make your husband unhappy, did you? A—No.

Q—In other words, you want the jury to believe that you were a perfect lady. Your answer is that you did nothing to make your husband unhappy. A—Not that he knew about it.

The big, hulking prosecutor took the witness over every step of the way, up to the murder, detail by detail, tearing her story to shreds. When he let her go she staggered from the stand badly shaken.

Judd Gray took the uneasy seat five minutes later, wearing a double-breasted business suit touched off by a white handkerchief in the lapel pocket. Occasionally he would glance from the stand to his aged mother, Mrs. Margaret Gray, sitting alongside no less a personage than Nora Bayes, the actress, there to see some real-life drama. Gray said he was perfectly happy at home until Ruth Snyder entered his life in search of a corselette. He said he hardly knew her well when she started talking about disposing of her husband. "We had a terrific argument over the thing."

Gray's recital transformed his ex-lover into a modern Borgia and made Albert Snyder, up to a point, the most durable of husbands. The salesman said Mrs. Snyder—he called her "Momsie" in better times—once tried to kill Snyder with gas because nothing happened when she put knockout pills in his prune whip. "I told her I thought she was crazy," he testified. He said she gave Snyder poison for a case of hiccups but it only made him violently ill. "I said to her," Gray swore, "that was a hell of a way to cure hiccups." He said that when she told him about another abortive gas attempt he "criticized her sorely." He said she tried to kill Snyder with overdoses of sleeping

powders at least twice. He said that once she showed him some arsenic with which she was going to spice "the Governor's" diet and another time she asked him if he would shoot Snyder for her. Gray said the woman simply wore him down to the point where he couldn't refuse when she asked him to bludgeon the artist to death. He said she worked out the insurance policies herself. He said she struck the first blow with the sash weight. Here Ruth Snyder sobbed so heavily that Gray glanced her way.

As the salesman finished, the dead man's brother, Warren Schneider, collapsed in the corridor outside and his wife's screams pierced the little courtroom, so Supreme Court Justice Townsend Scudder called an adjournment.

When the summations came, Gray wept over his attorney's eloquent appeal to the jury and Mrs. Snyder broke down when District Attorney Richard S. Newcombe likened her to a "wild beast of the jungle."

The jury deliberated ninety-eight minutes before condemning the once-loving pair. It was not a hard verdict to reach; no double prosecution had ever received quite as much help from the defendants themselves.

Gray went to the electric chair professing contentment. His wife, who had shunned him since the day of his arrest, sent him a letter of forgiveness—co-signed by her mother—as the end neared. When he got it, he said, "I am ready to go. I have nothing to fear."

Ruth Snyder died, on that bleak night of January 12, 1928, with a prayer on her lips. She had said in the Death House earlier that God had forgiven her and she hoped the world would.

Judd Gray (center) poses with defense attorneys Samuel L. Miller (left) and William J. Millard, who portrayed him as a love-sick weakling easily drawn by Ruth Snyder into the plot to kill her husband. Mrs. Snyder in turn accused Gray of masterminding the deed. In the Death House at Sing Sing the church-going corset salesman wrote a book called *Doomed Ship* in which he counseled men against infidelity and wicked ways.

THE LINDY HOP

"In the spring of 1927, something bright and alien flashed across the sky. A young Minnesotan who seemed to have nothing to do with his generation did a heroic thing, and for a moment people set down their glasses in country clubs and speakeasies and thought of their old best dreams . . ."

—F. Scott Fitzgerald

Charles A. Lindbergh, Jr., called Slim, flew the St. Louis-Chicago mail run. He got $350 a month and $100 in allowances and picked up a few more dollars stunt flying at county fairs and as a captain in the Missouri National Guard. In 1927 it occurred to him to try for the $25,000 prize put up by hotel man Raymond Orteig for the first nonstop flight from New York to Paris. He got the *St. Louis Globe-Democrat* and some local businessmen to stake him. When he reached New York, the papers were full of stories about two much more celebrated fliers preparing to make a bid for the eight-year-old Orteig prize—Navy Commander Richard E. Byrd and his three-man crew in their Fokker, and Clarence Chamberlain and his passenger, Charles A. Levine, in their Bellanca.

Byrd and Chamberlain were still poring over the Atlantic weather charts and fussing with their planes when the impatient kid went out to Roosevelt Field on Long Island before dawn on May 20. There was a sleet storm upstairs but the lanky upstart figured his little gray-and-white monoplane could fly through it. He took on 451 gallons of gas (and some coffee and sandwiches) and pointed for France at 7:52. The groundmen were surprised that he could get off with such a load, but he had no trouble. Nor did a thousand miles of snow and sleet bother him over the lonely ocean as he neared Paris. He put *The Spirit of St. Louis* down at Le Bourget, on the other side, thirty-three hours and twenty-nine minutes later—"I am Charles A. Lindbergh," he said—and found 100,000 Frenchmen waiting in a chill and nasty wind. He was carried around the arc-lit field on the mob's shoulders for half an hour, losing his cap and getting mussed up in the process. Paris staged the wildest demonstration since the Armistice, but it was nothing com-

pared to what lay ahead for the twenty-five-year-old flier.

Back in the States, the editorial writers were hailing him in extravagant terms. The *New York Evening World* wondered whether his 3610-mile flight shouldn't be classified as "the greatest feat of a solitary man in the records of the human race." The *Tucson Citizen* had no doubt about it: "One must go back to the fictive times of the gods who dwelt on Mount Olympus for a feat that will parallel that of Captain Lindbergh." And the song writers said it with music. George M. Cohan tapped out "When Lindy Comes Home" and Eddie Dowling and Jimmy Hanley called their hosanna "Hello, Yankee Doodle." There would be others, such as "Lucky Lindy," and even a new dance just for him, the Lindy Hop.

With seven years of scandal, crime and the Prohibition Follies under its belt, America was ready for a genuine All-American pin-up. It was ready for a collective love affair with someone nice, like a clean-living boy from the Midwest who wouldn't know a hip flask from a night club doll. Lindbergh fit the bill perfectly. Neither the editorial writers nor Tin Pan Alley had overstated the case.

When the flier got to New York 1,800 tons of ticker tape and shredded newspapers and phone books showered down in welcome as he was driven up lower Broadway to Fifth Avenue. The crowds were so dense that Trudy Ederle, who had her own parade the year before, couldn't get past the police lines for a glimpse of America's new hero. It cost the city $16,000 to clean up when the big street party was over. For Lindbergh, the party was just starting.

A movie company offered "The Lone Eagle" a million dollars if he would find himself a girl and get married on

"I am Charles A. Lindbergh."

a sound stage. Another studio offered him a half million to sign a year's contract—no marital strings attached. A vaudeville circuit offered him $100,000 to go on the two-a-day for twenty-eight days. The Roxy Theatre in New York offered him $25,000 for one week. (LINDY LOST TO SHOW BIZ, *Variety* mourned when the flier decided to stick to what he knew best.) He got 14,000 gifts, and marriage proposals by the hundreds. He got 3,500,000 letters (and there was $100,000 in return postage in them). He got 100,000 wires and 7,000 separate job offers. A group

Lindbergh and the little monoplane that carried him to fame, "The Spirit of St. Louis."

Clarence Chamberlain was preparing to take off across the Atlantic with Charles A. Levine when Lindbergh beat him to the take-off. Chamberlain and Levine (left) made the flight later but the real glory was gone.

Amelia Earhart was the first woman to fly the Atlantic—as a passenger in 1928. Here she is being met by Navy Commander Richard E. Byrd back in New York, where an elaborate official welcome awaited her. In 1932, Miss Earhart flew the Atlantic solo. In 1937, she vanished over the Pacific on an around-the-world flight.

of promoters offered him $2,500,000 for a round-the-world flight.

Lindbergh shook everyone off and went on the payroll of the Guggenheim Foundation for a series of good-will tours through the Americas for $2,500 a week, which had a modest sound compared to the amounts flying around in the headlines. On the side, the ex-air-mail pilot took pieces of TWA—"The Lindbergh Line"—and Pan-American World Airways and coined large sums writing for *The New York Times* and the *Saturday Evening Post*. He would never know need again but he might not know contentment either. The future held heartbreak and tragedy, bitterness, self-exile, disillusion, massive wrong guesses on World War II, and severe political troubles.

The tragedy came first. Charles A. Lindbergh, Jr., born to the flier and Anne Morrow in 1930, the year after their marriage, was kidnaped from their New Jersey estate on March 1, 1932. The Lindberghs paid $50,000 in ransom, but the baby was found dead in the woods near their home in Hopewell. It took two years to trace the ransom money to Bruno Richard Hauptmann, and another year to convict the Bronx carpenter and put him in the electric chair. When their long ordeal was over, the Lindberghs slipped aboard a boat for England with their second son, Jon, leaving a hint that they would never again live in the United States.

Abroad, Lindbergh formed a strong friendship with Dr. Alexis Carrel, the French scientist who was a believer in the Superman ideal and a devotee of totalitarianism. In 1936 the flier went to Germany to see the New Order for himself as the guest of Hermann Goering. He accepted military decorations from the Hitler Government and as World War II approached he warned Britain's Prime Minister, Stanley Baldwin, that the German Air Force was unconquerable. Back in the States in 1940 and 1941, he became the darling of the isolationists and the pro-German forces and sometimes found himself as a speaker on the same platform with such rabble rousers as Joe McWilliams and Gerald L. K. Smith. It was rather strange company for Lindbergh because his father, a one-time Congressman from Minnesota, had helped found the Farmer Labor Party before his death in 1924.

When America went in on the Allied side, President Roosevelt's Secretary of War, Henry L. Stimson, turned down Lindbergh's offer to serve. The flying hero had been made a Colonel in the Air Force years before, but official Washington, bitter over his political activities on the Far Right, made him wait quite a while to don uniform. When he did, he served with distinction in the Pacific in a non-combatant role. But he wasn't Lindy any more. He was Colonel Charles A. Lindbergh, Jr.

Bruno Richard Hauptmann paid with his life for the kidnap-murder of the Lindbergh baby but protested his innocence to the end.

The ladder used by the kidnaper of Charles A. Lindbergh, Jr., rests against the boy's bedroom window on the flyer's secluded estate in Hopewell, New Jersey.

Nan Britton
AND THE
PRESIDENT'S DAUGHTER

"The author tells of her great love for my brother. If she loved him as she says she did, would she have written such a book about him after his death?"
—ABIGAIL (DAISY) HARDING, *talking about Nan Britton*

Nan Britton said she told all only to help other unwed mothers get legal recognition for their children.

Nan Britton waited until four years after the death of President Harding to tell her story. When she did, in July of 1927, she dedicated it "with understanding and love to all unwed mothers, and to their innocent children whose fathers are usually not known to the world." The book, *The President's Daughter,* became a kind of bootleg best-seller overnight. Many stores kept it under the counter, as if it were a collection of French postcards between covers, but 50,000 Americans paid five dollars apiece for it that summer and fall. It was not hard to reason why. Nan Britton had a true-life story matching anything in the spicier novels of the twenties: her romantic backdrop embraced both the conventional hotel room and the White House itself.

Back in 1910, when she was 14 and he was 45, Warren Harding was Nan Britton's "Ideal American." She clipped his portrait from a campaign poster—he was making his losing bid for Governor of Ohio—and hung it in her bedroom. Before then, she had to peer through the plate-glass window of the *Marion Star* to feast her eyes upon the publisher-politician; now she only had to look up from her pillow. Nan's father, a physician, had no occasion to question his pretty teenager's worship of the graying Harding. The two families were acquainted and this was just a schoolgirl crush the girl would get over. But she didn't get over it, not even when Harding went away to Washington to serve in the Senate.

In 1917, a young lady now and finishing a secretarial course in New York, Nan Britton wrote to Senator Harding and asked if he could help her get a start in the business world. The Senator not only remembered the girl fondly but came to New York—this was in May, with the Capitol ablaze over our impending entry into the war—and took her to see his friend Elbert H. Gary at the United States Steel Corporation. In his capacity as Chairman of the Board, Judge Gary was able to find an office job for the Senator's shapely protégée.

Miss Britton said that a number of get-acquainted hotel sessions between her and the Senator, accompanied by un-fatherly kisses and vows of undying love, took place during the early discussions of her future. But the book related that she did not become "his bride"—Harding had a more formal one in Washington—until July 30, 1917. The book said that event took place in

a Seventh Avenue hotel in Manhattan and was capped by the arrival of a pair of decidedly unromantic house detectives. Miss Britton said the Senator paid them twenty dollars to forget the whole thing and confided to her that he would have been willing to pay a thousand. From that point on *The President's Daughter* went into infinite, kiss-by-kiss detail on their secret life over a seven-year period, complete with names, dates and places in New York, Washington and elsewhere and lacking only the love letters she said she and Harding agreed to burn. Mark Sullivan observed that the book, "coming after exposures of financial corruption on the part of his Administration, made Harding's memory almost a rag in the gutter."

Miss Britton said that she bore Harding's daughter in Asbury Park, New Jersey, on October 22, 1919, and named her Elizabeth Ann Christian (Harding had a male secretary named

Mr. Harding never saw the baby.

keep. At other times, according to her account, any funds she needed were delivered by a Secret Service man on the White House staff; she used a thinly-veiled pseudonym for the agent.

Miss Britton said she maintained the most pleasant relations with Mrs. Harding and the President's family in Marion all through the romantic alliance. For years everyone had looked upon her affectionately as an adopted "niece" of Ohio's favorite son. (On that score, Miss Britton said Harding had often checked her into hotels with him as his niece.)

The book had a rocky time coming out. None of the publishers wanted it and John S. Sumner's Society for the Suppression of Vice, waving a warrant, seized the plates from the Manhattan print shop that undertook the job. The author had to go to court to get them back.

What accounted for Nan Britton's eagerness to get the story of her own shame into the records? She said she wrote *The President's Daughter* to raise money for the Elizabeth Ann Guild, set up to crusade for "legal and social recognition" for all children born out of wedlock. But the anti-Britton press—and it was substantial—questioned the degree of her concern in this area. The book itself described her extensive efforts to get the President's family to support Elizabeth Ann, so some newspapers observed that if the necessary money had been forthcoming there would have been no book and no Elizabeth Ann Guild. That part of the debate, of course, did not go into the main burden of the woman's heavily documented story.

Miss Britton said that Harding's sister Abigail, better known as Daisy, believed her prepublication account enough to give her eight hundred dollars and promise to raise a fifty-thousand-dollar trust fund for Elizabeth Ann, but then changed her mind. When the family broke its long silence on the scandal, Dr. George T. Harding, the President's brother, denounced the Britton book as "infamous" and insisted that no Harding had ever heard of an illicit love affair in the departed President's life. Daisy Harding, for her part, simply observed that if Nan Britton had loved her brother she never would have written such a book. That hurt Nan Britton. She remarked that Daisy Harding had been her grammar school teacher in the old days and she certainly wanted

Christian). She said the beaming father ransacked his memory and agreed with her that the girl had been conceived on a couch in his Senate office. She said that Harding, fifty-four and childless in his union with Florence King, never saw Elizabeth Ann, but eagerly received regular reports on her progress. The book made a somewhat weightier point too. Miss Britton said she was with Harding in Chicago during the 1920 Republican National Convention—an interesting item because it recalled that the GOP elders had asked Harding whether any "impediment" in his personal life stood between him and the Presidency and he had deliberated ten minutes before saying no.

As Nan Britton told it, Harding had a way with "impediments" anyway.

She said that when she visited him in his White House office he even found a way to escape the prying eyes of the armed guard on patrol outside his window. "He introduced me to the one place where, he said, we *might* share kisses in safety," Miss Britton wrote. "This was a closet in the anteroom, evidently a place for hats and coats ... We repaired there many times in the course of my visits to the White House, and in the darkness of a space no more than five feet square the President and his adoring sweetheart made love."

Miss Britton said she brought the President snapshots of Elizabeth Ann on her journeys to Washington and that he would dwell on them affectionately. At times, she said, he reached into his drawer and gave her a couple of hundred dollars towards the baby's up-

Nan Britton (left) took much pride in her friendly relationship with Mrs. Harding and the President's family.

President Harding and his wife, Florence, in the White House rose garden.

to continue being friends with her. This produced no noticeable reaction from the battleground in Marion.

The family's chilly view of *The President's Daughter* did not diminish its sales immediately, nor limit its interest later as an item of curiosity. The book sold ninety thousand copies eventually and Miss Britton even talked of stage and movie rights. Nobody in the theater took the hint. And Will Hays, who had gone from the Harding Cabinet to Czar of Hollywood, said it would never, but never, be put on film.

Death spared Florence King Harding. She passed away in 1924, the year after her husband. But there was an ironic piece of timing in *The President's Daughter*. It was in 1927 that the eighty-thousand-dollar Harding Memorial in Marion was completed, and the twenty-ninth President and his wife were interred in it, side by side.

Sixty Homers

"It is part of our national history that all boys dream of being Babe Ruth before they are anyone else."
—Jimmy Cannon

The picture that needs no caption.

They called him the Babe, the Home Run King, the Sultan of Swat, the Bambino, the Behemoth of Swing and the Colossus of Clout. John Kieran, one of the more cultured sports journalists, compared him with Paul Bunyan on one occasion and the giant Gulliver on another. Paul Gallico, much as he loved him, was puzzled by his fame for an odd reason. "There has always been a magic about that gross, ugly, coarse, Gargantuan figure of a man and everything he did," Gallico wrote. "It is all the more remarkable because George Herman Ruth is not sculptured after the model of the hero . . . He was kneaded, rough-thumbed out of earth, a golem, a figurine that might have been made by a savage." Ban Johnson, president of the American League, had a vast respect for the man's talents but complained that "Ruth has the mind of a fifteen-year-old."

Johnson's statement reflected both the bitterness and concern the baseball magnates suffered over the Babe's conduct off the field. Ruth just couldn't be the Boy Scout type we look for in our sports heroes; he was cut from another mold. That kind of accident might not hurt too much in the case of run-of-the-mill athletes, but Ruth had millions of dollars in gate receipts riding on his broad back all through the twenties. Without his big bat to keep the fans coming, the Black Sox Scandal of 1921 might have reduced baseball to a penny-poor bystander in the Golden Age of Sports. Thus, when Ruth stayed out all night sampling bootleg liquor,

the club owners had the hangover. When Ruth ran around with flappers, the club owners fretted about the sagging morals of the time. When Ruth overate, the club owners had the belly aches. When Ruth gambled, the club owners wept for his strained purse. The New York Yankees, the organization that held his contract, took more tangible action, naturally, over Ruth's frequent breaches of baseball etiquette. He was benched, fined, suspended, or just chewed out, as the circumstances warranted. The Yankees never stopped trying to get the playful oaf in line—and never succeeded, either. His appetite for the high life, for everything the dollar could buy, was too deep-rooted even for the vaunted Yankee organization to chop off by front-office edict. Perhaps it was understandable.

Babe Ruth came up out of the streets and alleys of Baltimore. Folklore often

identifies him as an orphan but he was worse than that. He was a cast-off. His German-Irish parents either didn't want him or didn't know what to do with him. "I was listed as an incorrigible," he said once, "and I guess I was." In any case, the Ruths put him in a reform school when he was seven, in 1902, and he spent the rest of his boyhood shuttling between there and the miserable slum flat over his father's saloon. He was "out," as he put it, when his mother Kate died in 1908, so the elder Ruth sent him back to the institution—St. Mary's Industrial School. He was "out" again in 1911 and then back for good. His father wanted him to quit brawling and fighting and learn a trade, such as tailoring or shirt-making. The priests at St. Mary's despaired of making the overgrown rebel a tailor or a shirt-maker or a Little Lord Fauntleroy, but they saw a possibility for him in another direction—

Babe Ruth as a pitcher for the Boston Red Sox in 1919.

Used up by age (thirty-two, old for baseball) and fast living and supposedly six years past his prime, Babe Ruth pounded out sixty homers in 1927. No. 60, on the season's last day, moved sportswriter John Kieran to poetic ecstasy in *The New York Times*. "My voice may be loud above the crowd and my words just a bit uncouth," Kieran wrote, "but I'll stand and shout till the last man's out: 'There never was a guy like Ruth!'" Down through the years, it proved to be true. Hank Greenberg, Hack Wilson, Jimmy Foxx, Johnny Mize, and later such upstarts as Willie Mays and Mickey Mantle came close, but the mark still stood through 1956.

baseball. He was at peace with himself when he was pitching a ball or knocking the cover off it with a bat. Brother Benedict was so impressed that he got owner Jack Dunn of the Baltimore Orioles to come and look at him. Dunn signed the nineteen-year-old at once, but he never finished his apprenticeship in the minors. The Boston Red Sox paid $2,900 for his contract in mid-season.

The boy from St. Mary's proved to be a pretty fair left-handed pitcher who could also hit. Ed Barrow, the Boston manager, converted him to an outfielder in 1919 and it paid off. Playing every day, Ruth hit twenty-nine homers, a new record, and Col. Jacob Ruppert put out $125,000 to bring him to New York. There the spindly-legged six-footer proceeded to change the face of baseball and write its most tower-

ing and enduring legends. He hit fifty-four homers in 1920, and fifty-nine the next year. His big bat lured so many fans into the rented Polo Grounds that the team put up its own park—Yankee Stadium, "The House That Ruth Built." Ruth made the investment good. He was the heart of the New York club's celebrated "Murderer's Row" and he carried the game to new heights in 1927, when he smashed his own record and hit sixty homers.

In this process, the Baltimore urchin's salary—$600 a season with the Orioles, $1,300 up to $10,000 with the Red Sox, $20,000 to $52,000 with the Yankees—soared to $70,000, and then to $80,000. And Ruth lived on the money all the way. He made $1,425,000 in baseball, counting his World Series shares, and at least another half-million on the outside in such ventures as

Murderer's Row: Babe Ruth, Lou Gehrig, Bob Meusel, and Tony Lazzeri. The Yankee dynasty began when they were all together on the one batting order.

Yankee manager Miller Huggins shakes hands with Rogers Hornsby, the St. Louis Cardinals' awesome slugger. Hornsby held the National League batting championship seven times during the twenties and in 1924 set the major leagues' all-time BA—.424. In later years only a few hitters—such as Ted Williams, Joe DiMaggio, and Stan Musial—threw as much terror into pitchers as "The Rajah" did.

A familiar scene: Lou Gehrig (holding bats) offers the traditional handshake as Babe Ruth crosses the plate after hitting one into the right-field seats. This happened in the third game of the 1927 World Series. The Yankees swept the Pittsburgh Pirates in four games that year.

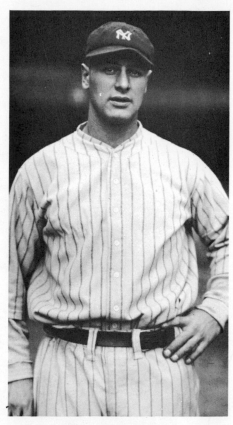

The pitcher who got by Ruth had another problem: Lou Gehrig (above). First baseman and clean-up batter in the Murderer's Row lineup, Gehrig hit the ball as hard and as often as Ruth but played out most of his career in the vast shadow cast by the Babe. He had forty-seven homers in 1927, only thirteen behind Ruth. His batting average dipped under .300 only in the first and last of his fifteen years in the game. His high marks were .379, .374, .373 and .363. A butcher's son, he came to the Yankees via the sand lots on New York's West Side, the High School of Commerce and Columbia University.

vaudeville, movies and indorsements. He used it all. One season he made $40,000 and had to borrow money to get back to training camp in the spring. Another time he got $25,000 for making a movie in Cuba and stuck the check into his vest and forgot it; when he remembered to cash it the company had dissolved. Once he confessed losing $35,000 on a single horse race.

Some of the Babe's extravagances required late hours, of course, and that kept him in constant trouble with Miller Huggins. When Huggins slapped him with a record $5,000 fine and suspended him in 1925 for breaking training on the road, Ruth publicly denounced the Yankee manager as incompetent and blamed him for the loss of the pennant the year before. Later the slugger was contrite. "I was a Babe

and a Boob," he said. Set down after his first season with New York, he went into the Palace with a vaudeville act and drew a blistering review from the *World*:

"All lip-rouged like a tight-wire lady, with a voice as sweet as a furnace shaker in action, hands that could not find a place on that whole stage to rest comfortably, a grace of carriage somewhere between John Barrymore and an elephant, Babe Ruth came out yesterday at the Palace. And the flappers flapped and the standees whooped her up until the poor chap stood on one foot, then the other, hoping they'd hurry and subside so he wouldn't forget his lines."

The Babe went back to baseball; battling Huggins and the umpires was easier than the two-a-day.

Through it all, and amid never-ending wails that his way of life might do irreparable damage to the nation's youth, the boy from the reform school went right on rewriting the records and jamming the turnstiles. He went through the Golden Age into the thirties before his legs gave out. The Yankees cast him off in 1934, after fifteen years, and he wound up his career with the Boston Braves and the Brooklyn Dodgers in the National League. The fans stayed with him to the end; he never hurt them, apparently, as much as he pained the baseball magnates. When cancer strangled him to death in 1948, eighty thousand grieving men and boys—and women, too—filed past his bier in Yankee Stadium. The Yankees retired his famous No. 3. The memory would never be retired.

Lou Gehrig hangs up his cap. The Yankee Iron Man took himself out of the lineup in Detroit on May 2, 1939. In fifteen seasons he set a never-equalled record for consecutive games played—2,130. Then a rare form of paralysis hardened his spinal cord and touched off a progressive shriveling of his muscles. He stayed in the lineup after the doctors had signed his death warrant, and Manager Joe McCarthy wouldn't bench him even when he began to miss easy grounders and his batting average dipped to .143. So Gehrig had to bench himself—in the saddest and most memorable day in baseball's history. The great first baseman died two years later.

T-H-E L-O-N-G C-O-U-N-T

"While I am not an authority on Shakespeare, I do not think there is anyone who had more appreciation of him than I. I worship at his shrine."

—GENE TUNNEY, *lecturing before*
Dr. William Lyon Phelps' class at Yale

Gene Tunney on the canvas in Chicago in 1927—for thirteen seconds—before he got up to keep Jack Dempsey from winning back his heavyweight title.

Gentleman Gene Tunney, country squire and dabbler in Shakespeare, looked back on it all with a show of disdain. "The laugh of the twenties," he wrote, "was my insistence that I would defeat Jack Dempsey for the heavyweight championship of the world. To the boxing public, this optimistic belief was the funniest of jokes. To me, it was a reasonable statement of calculated probability, an opinion based on prize-ring logic." And so it was. Tunney held to the theory, controversial but enduring, that the boxer could beat the . slugger. Brain vs. Brawn, Cunning vs. Brute Strength, Craftsman vs. Killer. In historical terms, Corbett vs. Sullivan (New Orleans, 1892, twenty-one rounds). Simple.

The ex-Marine with the lust for culture demonstrated his theory on two memorable occasions—one to win the title from Jack Dempsey and another to keep it. The first fight, in the pouring rain at Philadelphia on September 23, 1926, drew 120,557 fans and a record gate of $1,895,733. The brash, determined Tunney came out at the start and hit Dempsey a right to the jaw. "No one ever did that to me before," the champion told the challenger, forgetting Luis Firpo. Dempsey evidently felt that Tunney, the light-heavyweight titleholder, hit harder than his advance notices indicated. As it happened, the stories out of the challenger's training camp had dwelt less on his punching power, if any, than on the fact that he was finishing Samuel

Butler's *The Way of All Flesh* and dipping into the scribblings of Mr. Shakespeare as often as his strenuous physical exercises allowed. But Tunney didn't mean to win with sledge-hammer blows. He didn't have any in his arsenal. He meant to win with jabs and hooks, and he jabbed the champ silly. He danced around on the wet canvas as though it were a newly-waxed ballroom floor. He made Dempsey look old (he was thirty-one), slow and clumsy. He cut him up and won easily.

Back in his hotel, face smashed, left eye closed, Dempsey wept. He was richer by $990,000 but there was no more miserable man in the United States. "What happened, Ginsburg?" Estelle Taylor asked, using her pet name for him. "Honey, I forgot to

As champion, Tunney took the usual fling in the movies and on the stage. Here he is preparing to go on at Loew's State in New York.

Tunney and Tom Heeney shake hands before their championship fight.

duck," the fallen champion told his wife. Despite his three soft years since the Firpo fight, he had gone into the ring a four-to-one favorite over the underrated twenty-seven-year old Leatherneck from New York's Greenwich Village. He came out badly tarnished but immensely popular for a change. The fans weren't buying Tunney's Brains vs. Brawn propaganda.

Dempsey came back. In Chicago a year later, on September 22, he almost did what no heavyweight has ever done. He almost won back his crown, but that was the Battle of the Long Count. Remember that seventh round? Losing all the way, Dempsey floored Tunney with a long left hook. Tunney landed on his backside in a daze. The timekeeper started the count but Referee Dave Barry held back until Dempsey, standing menacingly over his fallen opponent, went to a neutral corner. There were four seconds lost that way —enough for Tunney to keep the title. He got off the canvas at "nine" and held Dempsey off. When his punches missed the weaving champion, Dempsey taunted him with words. "Come on out and fight," he said. But Tunney had other ideas. He had piled up enough points in the early rounds to win if he could stand up through the tenth. He did better. He was jabbing and hooking Dempsey at will toward the end. He was still the champion, but the title had no real luster: boxing fans would never forget that he was on the floor for thirteen seconds in that memorable seventh round.

Tunney didn't brood too much about the evident unwillingness of the masses to sweep him shoulder-borne into the glorious future. He had proved his point and and acquired a fortune in the process.

The Chicago fight drew 104,942 fans and a gate of $2,658,600, still the highest in boxing's history. Tunney's share of this haul, coupled with the usual indorsements and stage and movie money, earned him $1,101,939.92 in 1927. He wouldn't hang around the Street of Broken Noses very long. He had a taste for the quieter, more rewarding pleasures of the mind. He defended his title with an eleven-round KO of Tom Heeney, the Australian Hard Rock, in Madison Square Garden in 1928, and then hung up his sweaty gloves. He married a Connecticut society girl, Polly Lauder, and drank in Europe's cultural high spots, not forgetting to stop and say hello to George Bernard Shaw, another Shakespeare devotee. But don't take Gene Tunney lightly for running with the longhairs or for taking Will Shakespeare to the training camps when he was working at his trade. Gene Tunney was a very good prize fighter, brains or no.

Commander Gene Tunney. During World War II, he spent much time in the South Pacific teaching boxing and conducting boxing tournaments for the U.S. Navy.

"Those Anarchist Bastards"

"...Never in our full life could we hope to do such a work for tolerance, for justice, for man's understanding of men as we do by accident...That last moment belongs to us—that agony is our triumph."
—VANZETTI, *from the Death Cell*

Nicola Sacco

There was a crowd of reporters waiting on the State House steps in Boston when Governor Alvan Tufts Fuller arrived to conduct the day's business on August 23, 1926.

"It's a beautiful morning, boys, isn't it?" he said, smiling broadly.

"The Governor seems in excellent health and spirits," *The New York Times* man wired his paper.

But there was a strong question that day about the health and spirits of two other men in Massachusetts—Nicola Sacco and Bartolomeo Vanzetti, anarchists. They were in the Death House at Charlestown Prison waiting to keep an on-and-off date with the electric chair. They might have been pardoned a little uneasiness on that beautiful morning. It was meant to be their last.

The long, tortured night of Sacco and Vanzetti began with their arrest on May 5, 1920. The Red Raids were then in progress and the police questioned them about a memorial meeting for Andrea Salsedo, an anarchist who had plunged fourteen stories to his death from the Department of Justice offices in New York after an eight-week grilling. Sacco and Vanzetti both had loaded pistols on them and on May 7 the police began to ask if they knew anything about a hold-up murder in South Braintree on April 15. A five-man bandit band had seized a $15,-776.51 payroll belonging to the Slater & Morrill shoe factory after shooting down paymaster Frederick A. Parmenter and guard Alessandro Berardelli. Sacco and Vanzetti denied knowledge of the crime.

Questioned about an earlier payroll holdup, in Bridgewater, Sacco pro-

Bartolomeo Vanzetti

176

1921: Sacco and Vanzetti (second and third from left) leave court after their murder conviction in 1921.

duced a time-clock alibi: he was at his bench in the Stoughton shoe factory where he was an edge trimmer. But Vanzetti, a fish peddler, was tried in the Bridgewater holdup. The judge in the case was the Hon. Webster Thayer, an aging pillar of the Back Bay aristocracy and a violent foe of all things radical. His charge to the jury included an injunction which, while horrid in a judicial sense, was quite popular at the time. "This man, although he may not actually have committed the crime attributed to him," Judge Thayer said, "is nevertheless morally culpable, because he is the enemy of our existing institutions . . . the defendant's ideals are cognate with crime." Even though thirty witnesses testified that he was in Plymouth when the crime took place, Vanzetti was convicted and sentenced to twelve to fifteen years in prison.

Judge Thayer, now sixty-four, also presided in Dedham the following spring when Vanzetti and his friend Sacco were tried in the South Braintree case. The Commonwealth produced an array of eyewitnesses who placed the two aliens at the scene. For

the defense, nine witnesses from Boston put Sacco there on the day of the crime; the clerk of the Italian Consulate testified that he came in that day to inquire about getting a passport to Italy. In Vanzetti's case, six witnesses placed him in Plymouth that afternoon on his door-to-door rounds. The prosecution had 61 witnesses and the defense 107. The jury had to determine where the weight of truth lay.

The two men in the steel cage—both radicals, both slackers who had fled to Mexico during the war; Vanzetti with a brand-new criminal record in the Bridgewater holdup—were found guilty. The jury deliberated six and a half hours but the case reverberated around the world for the next six years. During that time, evidence piled upon evidence to throw massive doubts on the conviction, but Judge Thayer denied successive motions for a new trial, including one based on a convicted murderer's story that he could name the gang that committed the crime.

There were strong suggestions that the little Yankee Judge had something more than a mild distaste for the convicted men. While turning down the

appeals, he had freely referred to Sacco and Vanzetti as "Dagos" and "sons of bitches" in the confines of his golf club. During a Dartmouth football game he was overheard saying to a friend, "Did you see what I did to those anarchistic bastards?" Robert Benchley, the writer, quoted a mutual New England friend —"Webster has been saying those anarchist bastards down in Boston were trying to intimidate him." Frank P. Sibley of the *Boston Globe*, dean of the Massachusetts reporters, said that in thirty-five years around the courts he had never seen anything like Judge Thayer's handling of the Sacco-Vanzetti trial. "His whole manner, his whole attitude, seemed to be that the jurors were there to convict the men," Sibley wrote. Louis Stark of *The New York Times* said that in February, 1922, Thayer had said to him, "I hope *The New York Times* is not going on the side of these anarchists." Stark said the judge revealed to him an overwhelming abhorrence of radicals and foreigners. Other reporters also documented that point but it couldn't help win a new trial. The judge passing on that detail was Webster Thayer.

1927: Manacled together, the fish peddler and the factory worker hear the death sentence.

The Last Days of Sacco and Vanzetti

"I have known Judge Thayer all my life. . . . He is a narrow-minded man; he is a half-educated man; he is an unintelligent man; he is carried away with his fear of Reds . . ."
—WILLIAM G. THOMPSON, *for the Defense*

On April 9, 1927, the eyes of the world were focused on a little courtroom in New England. The day of sentence finally had arrived. When Nicola Sacco was asked what he had to say, he replied in halting English that his friend Vanzetti would speak for both of them. But then the immigrant factory hand looked up at the shriveled old man on the bench and words poured forth:

"I never knew, never heard, even read in history anything so cruel as this Court. After seven years' prosecuting they still consider us guilty. And these gentle people here are arrayed with us in this court today.

"I know the sentence will be between two classes, the oppressed class and the rich class, and there will be always collision between one and the other. We fraternize the people with the books, with the literature. You persecute the people, tyrannize them and kill them. We try the education of people always. You try to put a path between us and some other nationality that hates each other. That is why I am here today on this bench, for having been of the oppressed class. Well, you are the oppressor . . .

"You know it, Judge Thayer—you

Sacco's wife Rosina (right), mother of his two children, and Vanzetti's sister Luigia leave Charlestown Prison in Boston after visiting the condemned men. Vanzetti had no kin in the United States; his sister came over from Italy to plead his case with Governor Alvan T. Fuller.

Heywood Broun argued the Sacco-Vanzetti cause passionately in the *New York World* and broke with publisher Joseph Pulitzer, Jr., for suppressing further columns about the two doomed Anarchists.

Leading literary figures of the period joined the worldwide fight for Sacco and Vanzetti. Among them were poet Edna St. Vincent Millay (top) and humorists Robert Benchley (left) and Dorothy Parker (above). Through a New England friend, Benchley was able to furnish testimony bearing on Judge Webster Thayer's violent prejudice toward the two Italians.

know all my life, you know why I have been here, and after seven years that you have been persecuting me and my poor wife, and you still today sentence us to death. I would like to tell all my life, but what is the use?"

Vanzetti, forty-one, a prize student in Italy before he came to the United States—laborer, peddler, bricklayer, quarry worker, rope mill hand, and strike leader in this country, was even more eloquent than Sacco.

". . . I am not only innocent of these two crimes," he said, "but I never commit a crime in my life. I have never steal and I have never kill and I have never spilt blood and I have fought against the crime and I have fought and I have sacrificed myself even to eliminate the crimes that the law and the church legitimate and sanctify.

"This is what I say: I would not wish to a dog or to a snake, to the most low and misfortunate creature of the earth —I would not wish to any of them what I have had to suffer for things that I am not guilty of. But my conviction is that I have suffered for things that I am guilty of. I am suffering because I am a radical and indeed I am a radical; I have suffered because I was an Italian and indeed I am an Italian; I have suffered more for my family and for my beloved than for myself; but I am so convinced to be right that if you could execute me two times and if I could be reborn two other times I would live again to do what I have done already. I have finished—thank you."

Judge Thayer noted in a wispy voice that Massachusetts' Supreme Judicial

Court had upheld the verdicts and that death was mandatory. He set the week of July 10 for the executions but protests mounted with such force that Governor Fuller granted a reprieve until August 10 so that a special advisory commission could look into the case for him. He named Abbott Lawrence Lowell, president of Harvard University, Dr. Samuel W. Stratton, president of the Massachusetts Institute of Technology and ex-Probate Judge Robert Grant.

The Lowell Commission went over the record and heard a mass of testimony—some from prosecution witnesses recanting their 1921 stories, some throwing doubts on the veracity and character of other state witnesses, some backing the trial witnesses who had placed Sacco in Boston on the day of the South Braintree holdup, eighteen saying Vanzetti sold them fish in Plymouth that day, some to the effect that the court interpreter erred in translating key testimony. One witness swore that before the trial the man later made foreman of the jury had said, "Damn them, they ought to hang anyway."

Except for noting "a grave breach of official decorum" in Judge Thayer's oft-quoted off-the-bench remarks, the Lowell Commission found nothing to suggest a miscarriage of justice. The Governor accepted the findings but on August 10 he granted a twelve-day reprieve for final legal moves. The stay reached the Death House in Charlestown Prison just fifty-one minutes ahead of the executioner and served to touch off violent Sacco-Vanzetti demonstrations all over the world. There were forty persons hurt in a London riot. There were street fights in Paris and disorders outside the American Consulate in Geneva. The American flag was burned before our Consulate in Casablanca. There were riots in Berlin, Warsaw, Buenos Aires, Mexico, Cuba, Japan, Brest, Marseilles and elsewhere. Throngs wearing black mourning bands marched in Boston and New York. The voices of George Bernard Shaw, Albert Einstein, H. G. Wells, Romain Rolland, Anatole France and John Galsworthy joined with those of the American writers and intellectuals pleading for clemency. Heywood Broun, till then a leisurely observer of the American scene, tore into the Lowell Commission in his *New York World* column:

"What more can the immigrants from Italy expect? It is not every person who has a president of Harvard University throw the switch for him. If this is lynching, at least the fish-peddler and his friend, the factory hand, may take unction to their souls that they will die at the hands of men in dinner jackets or academic gowns, according to the conventionalities required by the hour of execution." The *World*, supposedly an oasis of liberalism in those days, held out succeeding Broun columns when he refused to write about more tranquil subjects than the two Italians in Death Row. Eventually it led to his leaving the paper.

Sacco and Vanzetti died on August 23, 1927. Governor Fuller spent the "beautiful morning" and the rest of the day entertaining eleventh-hour appeals for the doomed men, but did not act. The Commonwealth put an armed garrison around Charlestown Prison—thousands demonstrated to the last second—and the switch fell on schedule. Later Louis Stark summed it up this way: "The tragedy of the Sacco-Vanzetti case is the tragedy of three men—Judge Thayer, Governor Fuller, and President Lowell—and their inability to rise above the obscene battle that raged for seven long years around the heads of the shoemaker and the fish peddler."

It was greater than that. It was the tragedy of the whole United States in the Lawless Decade, because it happened in the very Cradle of Liberty and it suggested that in those days, in some places, the government itself held the law lightly.

End of the story: With the mourners limited lest further protest demonstrations occur, the Sacco-Vanzetti funeral cortege proceeds slowly through the streets of Boston on a dismal, rainy Sunday in August, 1927.

IT HAPPENED IN 1927...

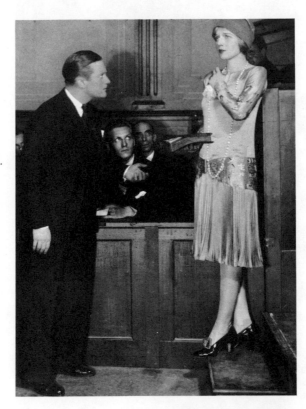

The woman taking the oath and about to ascend the witness stand is Ann Harding. The scene is from *The Trial of Mary Dugan.*

The Senior Council at Princeton quit because the trustees banned automobiles on the campus . . . Richard Barthelmess and Mary Hay were divorced . . . Alexander Kerensky, head of the provisional government that ruled Russia for a little while before the October Revolution of 1917, settled in New York . . . President Coolidge warned that the foundations of government and society would collapse if the people didn't pay more attention to the scriptures . . . The first demonstration of television took place. Walter S. Gifford, president of A.T.&T., in New York, and Secretary of Commerce Herbert Hoover, in Washington, talked on the telephone and watched themselves on a two-and-a-half-inch screen . . . Lisbeth A. (Lizzie) Borden, acquitted in 1892 in the celebrated ax murder of her father and step-mother, died in Fall River, Massachusetts . . . Ruth Elder crashed into the sea on a flight to Paris with George Haldeman, but was rescued . . . Fannie Brice divorced Nicky Arnstein . . . Isadora Duncan, the dancer, died in Nice when her scarf tangled in the wheel of a fast-moving sports car and dragged her out, breaking her neck.

❖   ❖   ❖

Aaron Sapiro, Chicago attorney, filed a $1,000,000 libel suit against Henry Ford because Ford's *Dearborn Independent* linked him to an alleged Jewish conspiracy to seize control of the nation's agricultural interests. The case ended in a mistrial. While a second trial was pending, in July, Ford issued an apology to the Jewish people for everything the *Independent* had said about them since 1920 and for republishing the fake Protocols of Zion. Ford also agreed to withdraw from circulation the book *The International Jew.* Sapiro dropped his suit . . . President Coolidge, speaking at Carnegie Institute at Pittsburgh in October, noted with satisfaction that America's wealthy men were devoting their riches to the spread of democracy and the development of the liberal arts.

❖   ❖   ❖

On the Prohibition front: The United States Supreme Court held that

The police shut down an item called *The Virgin Man* and in this photo three of the principals— Virginia Smith, Dorothy Hall, and Don Dilloway— are sitting in Magistrate's Court awaiting a lecture from a judge on stage morals.

bootleggers had to file income tax returns and could not plead self-incrimination to escape this responsibility. A similar ruling would be applied to bookmakers three decades later . . . Canada knocked out its Dry law after ten years . . . Medical Examiner Norris said that New York speakeasies outnumbered the old saloons. Police Commissioner Grover Whalen observed that

"all you need is two bottles and a room and you have a speakeasy" . . . New York's Committee of Fourteen said the speakeasies were worse than the saloons because the saloons at least barred women . . . The brave author and producers of a rather intimate epic called *The Virgin Man* all drew ten-day workhouse sentences. The members of the cast were simply told to go

The little lady in the center of the action is Helen Hayes in the 1927 hit, *Coquette*. The others (left to right) are Phyllis Tyler, Gaylord Pendleton, G. Albert Smith, and Eliot Cabot. Miss Hayes, a lustrous star, spanned the decades up to the present day and eventually saw a Broadway theater named in her honor.

and sin no more . . . On the nicer levels, Alfred Lunt and Edward G. Robinson in *The Brothers Karamazov*, Rose McLendon and Frank Wilson in *Porgy*, Katharine Cornell in *The Letter*, Jeanne Eagels and Leslie Howard in *Her Cardboard Lover*, Bela Lugosi in *Dracula*, Otto Kruger in *The Royal Family*, Ruth Gordon in *Saturday's Children*, Minnie Maddern in *Ghosts*, Walter Hampden in *An Enemy of the People*, Ed Wynn in *Manhattan Mary* and Eddie Cantor in the *Follies*.

* * * *

On the screen, Gary Cooper, college-bred son of a Montana judge, got his first lead in *Arizona Bound* (made in Nevada). The break came none too soon. Cooper had been falling off horses for ten dollars a day for three years. "Whether I was an Indian with Richard Dix, a Cossack with Rudolph Valentino, or an outlaw conspiring against Tom Mix," he recalled years later in his *Saturday Evening Post* biography, "my part had a certain sameness. When the time came for someone to be shot from a galloping horse, I was usually the one who took the tumble, often into a gulch filled with rock and prickly-pear cactus." The lanky Cooper went from *Arizona Bound* to a multimillion-dollar career . . . Norma Talmadge and Gilbert Roland appeared in *Camille*, Greta Garbo and John Gilbert were in *Flesh and the Devil*, Clara Bow, Richard Arlen and Buddy Rogers in the war film, *Wings*, Joan Crawford in *The Taxi-Dancer*, Emil Jannings in *The Way of All Flesh*, Joseph Schildkraut, H. B. Warner and William Boyd (Hopalong Cassidy) in DeMille's *The King of Kings*, and Ronald Colman and Vilma Banky in *The Night of Love*.

The girl is Barbara Stanwyck, who went on to fame in Hollywood. She is shown here with Paul Porter in the original New York production of *Burlesque*, in which Hal Skelly had the memorable lead role.

This was a highlight of the movie year—Charles Farrell and Janet Gaynor in the four-handkerchief love story, *Seventh Heaven*.

"Hello, Sucker"

Mary Louise Cecilia Guinan

"Texas Guinan combined the curious and admirable traits of Queen Elizabeth, Machiavelli, Tex Rickard and Ma Pettingill . . ."
—STANLEY WALKER

Texas Guinan never lost patience with the "revenooer" posses that rode her down for selling "likker" on the Glittering Gulch called Broadway. Quite the contrary, she tried to make them feel at home; sometimes she had the band strike up "The Prisoner's Song" when the Federal men arrived to haul her before the bar of justice. She kept the customers in high spirits too. Once she came back to her night club from court and sang this ditty:

> *Judge Thomas said, "Tex, do you sell booze?"*
> *I said, "Please, don't be silly.*
> *I swear to you my cellar's filled*
> *With chocolate and vanilly."*

Texas always insisted that she didn't have to sell the hard stuff because she got as much for sparkling water as people paid for Scotch before Prohibition. She said the customers brought their own whiskey, on their hips, and what could she do except provide set-ups? Of course, you could buy a booster in her joints if you knew the headwaiter, or if you looked as if you knew him, or if you knew somebody who was pretty sure he knew him, or maybe just if you were thirsty and didn't have the seedy look of the Dry agent.

Miss Guinan, a garish blonde with a brassy voice that could penetrate even the din of her own clubs, had a name for the customer—"Hello, Sucker"—and a slogan to go with it. "Never give a sucker an even break," she used to say. Hayseed or Wall Street broker, she flattered them all with the same high prices: $25 for a fifth of Scotch or $2 for a pitcher of water if you brought your own; $25 for champagne, $20 for rye. The "couvert" charge—an invention of the Lawless Decade—might run anywhere from $5 to $25 per head, depending on what the traffic would bear at a given time. Everybody paid with a smile. Well, nearly everybody; there were bouncers on hand to deal with the penny-pinchers.

Mary Louise Cecilia Guinan came off a ranch in Waco, Texas. Her parents hoped for a musical career for her but she went off and rode bronco in a circus instead. Then she drifted into vaudeville and found her way to Hollywood, where there was a demand for girls who could handle a hoss and lariat. For a while she did well enough in westerns to be called "the female Bill Hart," and she certainly was one of the more authentic lady gunslingers on the celluloid prairie. In those days she had a mop of black hair menacing enough to scare off the villain even without a six-shooter. But the movies were mute and Miss Guinan wanted to be heard. She came East for a Broadway musical early in the twenties, discovered the night clubs and got herself hired as mistress of ceremonies at the Beaux Arts. There her wisecracks and lung power caught the attention of Larry Fay, sometime entrepreneur, sometime racketeer, and he set her up at the El Fey Club. That was the beginning of a profitable partnership.

Miss Guinan went from El Fey to the Rendezvous, the 300 Club, the Argonaut, the Century, the Salon Royal, the Club Intime and any number of Texas Guinan Clubs, depending on how often the Prohibition people shut her down. Opening new joints after raids, Tex wore a necklace strung with gold padlocks just to show the Federals there were no hard feelings. One of her diamond bracelets featured a little gold police whistle.

The Guinan traps—and seventy or eighty other Manhattan spots of the time—were the forerunners of the sardine-packed night clubs that came in with Repeal. Her floors were so jammed that the dancing girls had to exhibit their wiggles, high-kicks and other charms right in the customers' faces. The "big butter-and-egg men,"

1928

Tex Guinan shares a cup of coffee in 1933 with an old business rival, Belle Livingstone, known in her early days as "the chorus girl with the poetic legs." One fashionable drinking oasis operated by Miss Livingstone boasted one floor decorated in a Japanese motif. The customers sat Oriental-style on expensive cushions as they indulged their thirsts with bootleg liquor. Belle had a reason for it, of course. "A man could get hurt falling off a bar stool," she said.

Tex Guinan boasted that she didn't shed her jewelry — always an abundant crop — even when she elected to give a hand to the kitchen help in her night clubs.

La Guinan as a movie gungirl before she turned her talents to the self-assigned task of keeping throats wet in Prohibition-time New York. Much as the Federal men hounded her, she was notably successful in this line and showed much charity towards her business competitors. She had an armored car escort Belle Livingstone back to the Great White Way after Belle did a brief bit in jail for purveying liquor to the better-fixed masses.

The Tex Guinan-Larry Fay emporium, The El Fey Club, is padlocked. The swastika on the entrance wall happened to be Fay's good luck emblem. He had copied it off a horse blanket some years before Adolf Hitler made it such a horrible symbol.

as Texas always called them, didn't seem to mind.

Miss Guinan's celebrated closing line for the chorus, "Give the little girls a great big hand," was only topped once. A gentleman in the audience arose and said, "Give the little girl a great big handcuff." It was another pinch, but the hostess laughed with the crowd: she owed her fame to her brushes with the Eighteenth Amendment. She would have been known to nothing more than a select group of free-spenders in the Big Town except for the fact that someone was always trying to put her in the pokey.

The frolicsome hostess didn't complain. She made a pretty good living out of her troubles—up to $4000 a week. Where it went, no one ever knew. When the thrice-married prohibition queen died in 1933, at forty-nine, there was $28,173 in her estate.

Larry Fay, a horse-faced dandy, originally set up Texas Guinan as a night club mistress of ceremonies. But in a career spanned by forty-six arrests Fay had many other interests —ranging from a legitimate taxicab fleet to rum-running to clip joints to a muscle-man setup that preyed on wholesale dairymen and rigged milk prices. For all of those activities, Fay's arrests seldom involved anything more serious than bawling out traffic cops or otherwise offending the peace and dignity of the city. His last night club was the Casa Blanca: an easily-aroused doorman shot him to death for cutting his pay as the bad times began to pinch in 1932.

THREE BAD BOYS

Vincent Coll, alternately called the Mad Dog and the Mad Mick and shown below with his lawyer, Samuel Leibowitz (right), owed his fall from grace to a $10,000 oversight. (Though some say the real cause was a woman.) Dutch Schultz put up the ten "big ones" to get him out into the fresh air when he was being held on a Sullivan Law charge. Coll jumped bail, so Schultz had his brother Peter killed, evidently as a moral lesson. Vincent in turn declared war on the Beer Baron. In a side engagement, gunning for another enemy, the Coll mob raked a Harlem street with bullets one summer day in 1931, killing a five-year-old boy and wounding three other children. A vast cry of indignation arose but a masterful defense by Leibowitz won Coll an acquittal. Later the underworld itself put a $50,000 price tag on the trigger-happy youth. Somebody with a machine gun collected it—or at least qualified for it—in due time. Coll met his doom in a downtown drug store while answering a decoy phone call.

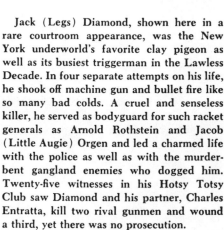

Dutch Schultz leaving court while on trial for income tax evasion. The man behind him on his left is J. Richard (Dixie) Davis, his mouthpiece, who later revealed to the Seabury investigation the links between Schultz and Jimmy Hines and blew the lid off the secret marriage between crime and politics in New York.

Schultz, born Arthur Flegenheimer, tended bar in a speakeasy in his native Bronx until 1928. Then he got himself a mob and took over the wholesale trade in needle beer. Tough, aggressive, hardly wary of gunfire, he moved into the multimillion-dollar Harlem policy game under Jimmy Hines' beneficent wing (the Tammany leader went to jail later for protecting the Schultz troop) and developed amicable trade relations with the Maddens and the Costellos and the other downtown racket dignitaries.

The Dutchman's wars with Legs Diamond and Vincent (Mad Dog) Coll spilled much blood as the Lawless Decade turned. Coll, an ex-employee with flaming ambitions and a terrible temper, took to dangerous diversions when he fell out with Schultz. He conducted wholesale raids on Schultz beer drops and kidnapped Madden's partner, Big Frenchy DeMange, for $35,000 ransom. Dutch's torpedos lured Coll into a Manhattan phone booth in 1931 and machine-gunned him to death. Schultz, plagued by then by Uncle Sam's tax collectors and on the lam, went on the spot with three bodyguards in a Newark bar in 1935.

Jack (Legs) Diamond, shown here in a rare courtroom appearance, was the New York underworld's favorite clay pigeon as well as its busiest triggerman in the Lawless Decade. In four separate attempts on his life, he shook off machine gun and bullet fire like so many bad colds. A cruel and senseless killer, he served as bodyguard for such racket generals as Arnold Rothstein and Jacob (Little Augie) Orgen and led a charmed life with the police as well as with the murderbent gangland enemies who dogged him. Twenty-five witnesses in his Hotsy Totsy Club saw Diamond and his partner, Charles Entratta, kill two rival gunmen and wound a third, yet there was no prosecution.

One of the assaults on the handsome gunman cut short a romantic interlude in the Hotel Monticello with his sweetheart, Follies girl Kiki Roberts, formerly Marion Strasmick. Diamond absorbed five bullets but was soon well enough to muscle in on the rackets in the Catskills while serving out an exile imposed on him by the Manhattan mobs. In 1931 he beat a trial upstate for kidnapping an uncooperative cider hauler but that night his luck ran out. Assassins caught up with Legs in Albany and blew his brains out while he was sleeping off the heavy effects of the celebration that followed his acquittal. The deed was generally attributed to the Dutch Schultz Gang. Diamond's wife, Alice, was the lone mourner at his funeral. She was mysteriously shot to death in a Brooklyn rooming house two years later.

Cut down by two sure-handed assassins firing .38's, Dutch Schultz presented this untidy picture in the Palace bar in Newark on Oct. 23, 1935. He was alive but elsewhere on the blood-spattered premises Lulu Rosenkrantz and Abbadabba Berman were very dead and a third Schultz handyman, Abe Landau, lay dying. The trapped quartet turned .45's on the enemy but was overwhelmed by the surprise attack.

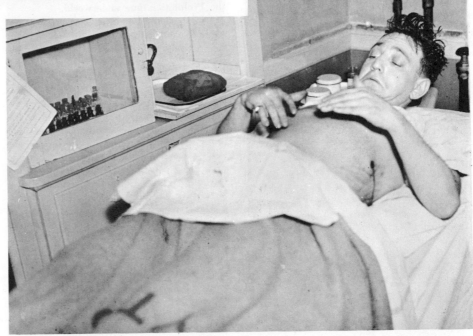

The Dutchman, mortally wounded, looks over the damage in the hospital. Schultz's deathbed ravings covered a wide range— all the way from mysterious million-dollar deals to assorted pals and double-XX guys to Communists, of all things. One sentence confounded everybody, even the poets: "A boy has never wept, nor dashed a thousand kim." What did the dying badman mean?

All shot up, the dying Beer Baron bequeathed the nation at least one high moral injunction in his bedside ravings. "Mother is the best bet," he said, "and don't let Satan draw you too fast." His mother had scrubbed floors so he could go to school.

OWNEY MADDEN

AND SOME SUPPORTING PLAYERS

Jimmy Hines.

Big Frenchy DeMange.

Waxey Gordon (Irving Wexler).

Owney Madden came to New York from Liverpool, England, and enrolled himself in the Gophers, the gang that ruled the theft-ridden West Side docks. He ran up 44 arrests during his young manhood but didn't have to do time until Little Patsy Doyle got killed shortly after he and his playmates in the Hudson Dusters had put five bullets in Madden during a dancehall quarrel. (He is shown appearing in court on a vagrancy charge.) Owney languished in Sing Sing from 1915 to 1923 and came out a mature, peace-abiding citizen of 31 ready for the refinements of the Prohibition-time underworld.

Once called "that little banty rooster out of hell" and later known as "Owney the Killer," now he attained a measure of respectability. Staked by Larry Fay, he went into rum-running, moved into the laundry and coal rackets with such true-blue pals as Tammany Leader Jimmy Hines standing behind him, and rose to a directorship in the Big Seven. In this combination, the hierarchy atop all organized Eastern crime, the now peace-abiding Madden stood alongside such rising powers as Lucky Luciano, Frank Costello, Waxey Gordon, Longy Zwillman of Newark, and the Lepke & Gurrah and Bug & Meyer mobs.

In the fashion of the day's mobsters, Madden also moved into the night clubs and the ever-tarnished fight game, joining Big Bill Duffy in piloting Primo Carnera to the heavyweight title. Jailed briefly for parole violation in 1932, Owney soured on the bad life (57 arrests by then) and retired to the quieter environs of Hot Springs, Ark. He's still there, a country squire with all kinds of memories.

Primo Carnera with Bill Duffy (left) and Louis Sarcese (right).

Lou (Lepke) Buchalter (left) and Jacob (Gurrah) Shapiro came out of the twenties intact, moved on into New York's labor and industrial rackets on a grand scale and emerged as two of the more terrible movers and shakers on the ruling board of Murder, Inc. The law didn't catch up with them until 1944. Lepke, the one on the right above, went to the electric chair. Gurrah got life in prison, but died in 1947.

Benjamin ("Bugsy") Siegel. He was just an apprentice mobster in the twenties. But in later years he worked his way nearly to the top. He had Las Vegas staked out as his private preserve until an unfriendly but quite accurate bullet marked Bugsy's spot.

Lucky Luciano. His star was rising in the twenties. He was one of the "syndicate," the "Big Seven," the "combination" controlling all vice, gambling and crime in the East.

Frank Costello came onward and ever-upward from Prohibition times to the present, attaining such affluence that in 1951 the U. S. Senate Crime Investigating Committee called him the "Prime Minister of the Underworld." Before then Costello was known as the Slot Machine King but that label hardly defined his true eminence. He stood at the very heights in the nationwide crime cartel when the government started to bring him down on assorted perjury and income tax charges, not to mention pending deportation proceedings. In the Lawless Decade, nobody thought to use the deportation device against the alien mobster in our midst although the alien radical—real or fancied— was kicked out quite casually.

THE HOUSE OF MORGAN (HELEN)

Helen Morgan sits on her own bar to toast the arrival of Repeal. The great sob singer wore an appropriate gown for the occasion— black velvet.

Once there were two Houses of Morgan in New York—J. P.'s and Helen's. Helen's was more popular. She sold booze and sad songs. J.P. dealt only in money. James Montgomery Flagg, the artist, probably explained Helen Morgan best. He said she was a composite of all the ruined women of the world. She had the music to go with it—such enduring torch numbers as Jerome Kern's "Can't Help Lovin' Dat Man," "Bill" and "Why Was I Born?" They all came out of *Show Boat* with La Morgan, permanently identified with her husky contralto tones. In her clubs, towards the end of the Lawless Decade, men paid the highest prices in town to sip bad liquor in a cloud of smoke and foul air and sob softly as the proprietress perched on a piano and let the music come.

That was the difference between Texas Guinan and Helen Morgan. You went to Guinan's for horseplay—Tex herself might play leapfrog with the out-of-town buyers if the spirit moved her. You went to Morgan's for the blues-in-the-night, washed down with illicit happy juice. Sometimes, as in the Guinan places, there was an extra added attraction: raiders. The more spectacular forays occurred at Chez Morgan. Major Maurice E. Campbell took a platoon of agents in one night, wrecked the club with axes and carried off everything that wasn't nailed down. The courts made the Prohibition watchdog return what he hadn't smashed to bits. On another occasion, Miss Morgan had her eight-piece band play a dirge while Federal men in boiled shirts, paying guests up to that moment, stripped the joint clean. The more sincere customers booed the agents lustily, all the way to the moving vans outside. But the lady herself grew weary of the battle after awhile. She quit the night club business towards the close of the twenties, saying the wear and tear on the nerves, let alone the high cost of her gowns, was too much for her.

Miss Morgan, Tex Guinan, Belle Livingston were among the more notable women who dominated the night clubs and other rendezvous of revelry in the twenties. But the pattern persisted all over the country—speakeasies and "intimate" spots featured women torch singers and piano players. That is what the night-life public wanted. And in the Lawless Decade the night-life public was no longer predominately male. The women wanted their fun, too, their share of whoopee—a word that's almost obsolete probably because the wild, hectic, abandoned and aggressive kind of gaiety it described is also almost obsolete now. Let's face it: By contrast with the drinking traps of the Prohibition Era, today's after-dark resorts often border on the genteel.

"Joe Sent Me"

"We couldn't take the word of two Prohibition agents against Miss Morgan."
   —An anonymous juror, after Helen Morgan beat a liquor charge.

The classic peephole. You rang the bell. A slit opened and you were sized up. If the man inside knew you, or if you could persuade him you were "regular," you'd get in.

"I commend the use of non-alcoholic fruit juices," Ella Boole said, "because they appeal to the taste, are attractive to the eyes, refreshing to the spirits and have only good effects the morning after."

For the millions of Americans who elected not to take the WCTU leader's counsels, the Prohibition decade offered a variety of alternatives. There was Bathtub Gin, made according to your own formula in your own happy home. There was the friendly neighborhood bootlegger, always around when you needed him. And, finally, there was the speakeasy—denounced, condemned, defamed, raided, padlocked, boarded up but always there, or maybe around the next corner.

In New York in 1929 Police Commissioner Grover Whalen's men counted the speakeasies and came up with a nice round number: 32,000. But that was admittedly a low figure for the number of illicit oases serving the teeming metropolis of 6,000,000. You couldn't count the speaks because there were too many of them—in the basements of fashionable Manhattan mansions, in penthouses off Park Avenue, in Greenwich Village cellars, in Wall Street office buildings, in brownstone rooming houses, in tenements, in two-family dwellings in the Bronx, in Bay Ridge hardware stores, in . . . well, the speak was everywhere. There was one on New York's East Side with an exterior that made it look like a synagogue. There were any number set up as soft drink parlors, and any number operating as restaurants or tearooms; all you needed to know to get the hard stuff in those places was the right word, or maybe the right wink.

The out-and-out-speakeasy, free of concealing adornments, was by far the most interesting of the illegal resorts. The showmanship in these operations intrigued a *New York Times* operative in the spring of 1929—

"The intricate and mysterious rites observed before patrons are allowed to enter seem to be chiefly intended to add romantic excitement to the adventure, since the authorities are not likely to remain long unaware of their existence. Introduction by someone who has been there before is usually required. Then there is the business of registering the new patron's name and perhaps the issuing of a card of admittance to be presented on the next visit.

It is sometimes made even more important looking by a signature or a cabalistic sign on the back of the card. Many persons about town carry a dozen or more such cards.

"The devious means employed to protect the entrances to speakeasies probably adds to the general mystification. Bells are to be rung in a special way. A sliding panel behind an iron grill opens to reveal a cautious face examining the arrivals. . . ."

The face behind the sliding panel wasn't always the warmest one in town, especially when total strangers rapped on the door. The proper card or the proper word ("Joe sent me") would open the portals, of course. Once inside, a man was among kindred souls. The speakeasy was nothing like the bar we know today. It was more like a club. You could talk to the elbow bender alongside you quite easily because he had the same entree, the same special status that you had. He was "one of the boys" in a closely knit group of insiders foregathered in the interest of some temporarily illicit good fellowship. He was your ally in a mild piece of lawbreaking. He was your friend and the next round was on him.

A graphic demonstration. In midtown New York the iron grillwork door was almost the sign of the speakeasy. Because there were so many like that, particularly on West Fifty-second Street, revelers did not hesitate to ring the bell at any hour of the night and insist on gaining admittance. This householder did the best he could to protect his peace and quiet.

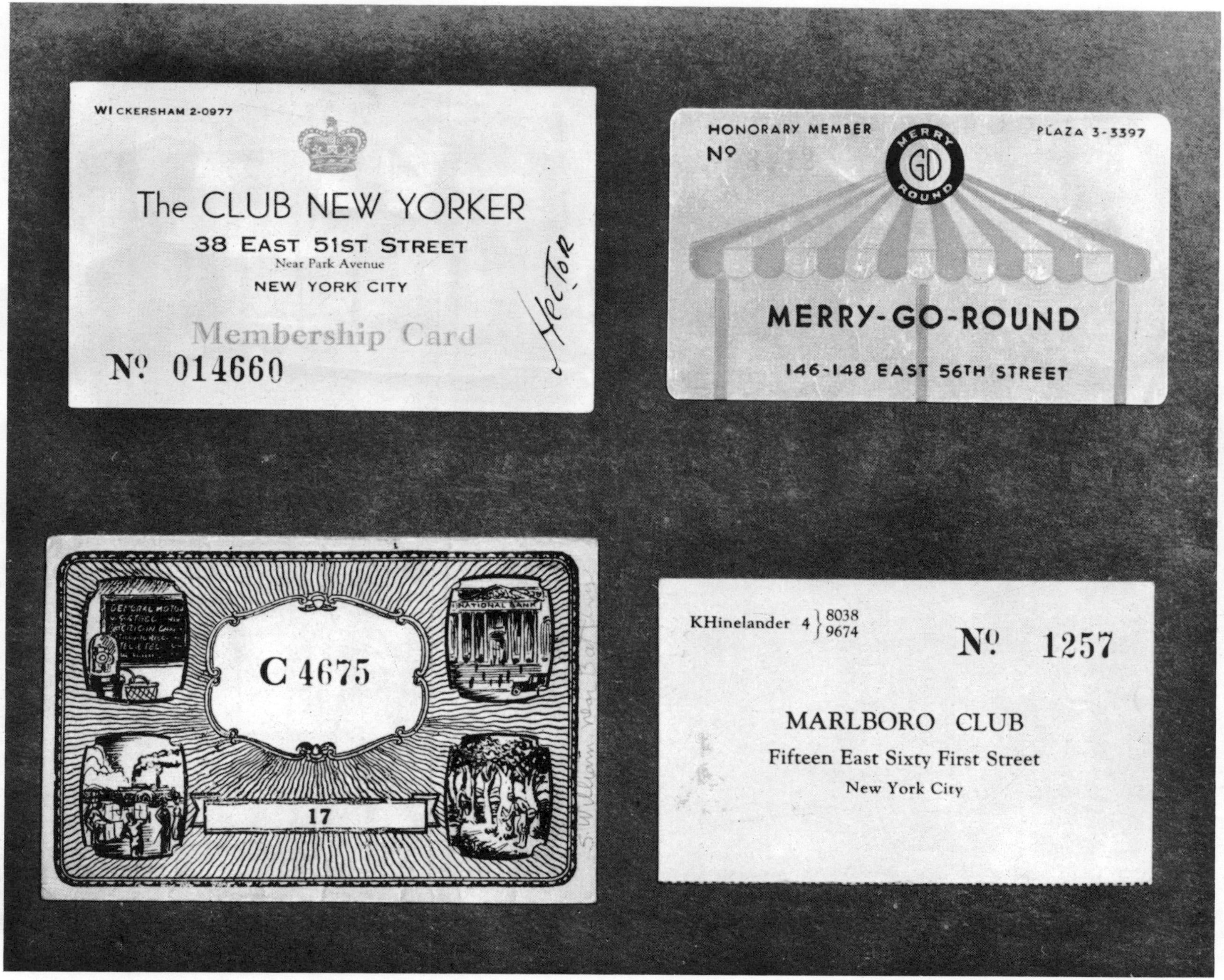
WICKERSHAM 2-0977
The CLUB NEW YORKER
38 EAST 51ST STREET
Near Park Avenue
NEW YORK CITY
Membership Card
Hector
Nº 014660
HONORARY MEMBER
Nº
PLAZA 3-3397
MERRY GO ROUND
GD
MERRY-GO-ROUND
146-148 EAST 56TH STREET
C 4675
17
KHinelander 4 8038 9674
Nº 1257
MARLBORO CLUB
Fifteen East Sixty First Street
New York City

Speakeasy cards. A card from a well-known speakeasy in good standing would get you into almost any other joint in town.

In New York there were all sorts of speak-easies: Above, a run-of-the-mill joint on East Forty-first Street. Below, a most elegant place on West Fifty-third Street.

The Stork Club on West Fifty-eighth Street.

The speakeasies added something else that was new: women, traditionally barred by customs from the saloons but a decidedly welcome fixture in the new-style oasis. There was more than one kind of woman in the joints, as it happened. There was the woman in the carriage-trade speak, on the arm of her escort and quite possibly in evening clothes if she was coming from a theater date or a party. And there was the woman in the flesh-for-sale trade, using the less discreet watering places as a base of operation for pickups.

That sort of thing often brought down more condemnation on the speakeasies than the traffic in bad booze. New York's Committee of Fourteen, led by highly distinguished citizens, sent a flock of sleuths into Harlem in 1928 and reported that prostitution was rife in the night clubs and the underground drinking traps. The Committee said that while street soliciting was on the wane and the hotels were being reasonably cautious about the ladies of the evening, the speakeasies almost invariably stocked female companions for their lonelier clients, sometimes as "hostesses," sometimes as

The Mansion on West Fifty-first Street

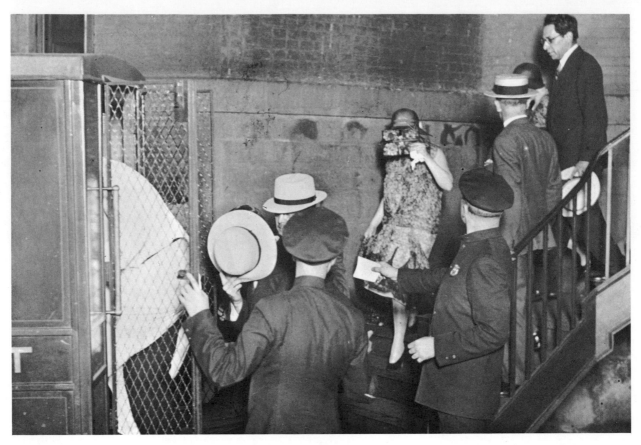

A raid on the Central Park Casino. Waiters, guests, proprietor — all prisoners — enter the police patrol wagon.

Long Beach raiders examine a fine haul.

A policeman guards the liquor seized by dry agents on raids in the Broadway sector.

A detective inspects the liquor in a Harlem bar raided by Federal agents.

Officers have fun pouring into the gutter 228 gallons of "moonshine" seized in a raid on an Atlanta, Georgia, home.

cigaret girls, sometimes as checkroom girls, sometimes as pure and simple hustlers—if you'll pardon the expression. This state of affairs left the Committee aghast, of course, but produced no other noticeable effect. The local police took the view that the speakeasies were a Federal problem but the Prohibition Bureau assigned only 200 sleuths—not all of them incorruptible —to ferret out the 32,000 traps in the sprawling city.

In that situation, a speakeasy might get shut down now and then, as its luck or connections ran out, but an enterprising owner could always re-open very quickly and let word-of-mouth advertising bring back the faithful. The chances were they would not have far to go; the speak that ran afoul of the authorities generally set up again in the same vicinity, sometimes only a few doors away from its old location.

For one thing, most of them had what amounted to a neighborhood trade; for another, any venture into new areas had to run the risk of severe competition (or maybe strong-arm stuff) from the oldest established places. In midtown Manhattan, for a while, this competition was excessively tough because an adventuresome group of Prohibition agents set up a speakeasy of their own. This resort, called the Bridge Whist Club, flourished on West Forty-Fourth Street for seven months before it was exposed. The dry sleuths, somewhat embarrassed, lamely said that they had opened the place simply to garner evidence against the bootleggers. It was a hard story to take—then and now—but it was scarcely surprising in view of the widespread official corruption bared during the Prohibition Era. From the drinker's point of view, of course, you couldn't knock it.

Al Smith

BROWN DERBY TO SILK HAT

Alfred E. Smith came Catholic-born from the sidewalks of New York. He went all the way from a Lower East Side tenement to the Governor's Mansion. He left enduring marks along the high road: his daring, far-reaching social legislation lighted the path for the liberal Democratic tradition in the Empire State. In the nation, another kind of history envelops his name; his star-tipped chariot smashed against the twin roadblocks of prosperity and intolerance in the national elections of 1928. He could understand the first roadblock — Herbert Hoover's campaign packet contained a guarantee of four more years of gilt-edged, ready-to-serve Republican prosperity. The second roadblock stunned Smith. He could not believe that the American people would slam the White House door in his face because of his religious faith.

The anti-Catholic whispers made a mess of the Presidential contest and left a deep scar on Al Smith and a still deeper scar on the American conscience. The mark is still there: In its 1956 convention the Democratic Party came within 38½ votes of nominating Senator John F. Kennedy as vice-presidential candidate and then switched to Estes Kefauver. Kennedy had everything to recommend him as Adlai Stevenson's running mate—youth and looks, a splendid war record in the Pacific and a good voting history in the Senate—but he was a Catholic. In the last moment of balloting, the terrible memories of 1928 intervened to deny him the nomination; the specter of Al Smith haunted the party after nearly three decades. However lacking in courage or in awareness of the new

Smith: "Let's look at the record."

levels of tolerance in America, the party's fears were understandable. Consider this excerpt from Irving Stone's study of the nation's Presidential campaigns, *They Also Ran*:

"For pure virulence there was nothing in all American history to equal the whispering campaign inaugurated against Al Smith: he was building a tunnel which would connect with the Vatican; the Pope would set up his office in the White House; the Catholics would rule the country, and no one could hold office who was not a Catholic; Protestant children would be forced into Catholic schools; priests would flood the states and be in supreme command; Smith would set himself up at the head of a Catholic party which would supersede the old Democratic party!

"A flood of letters, pamphlets and

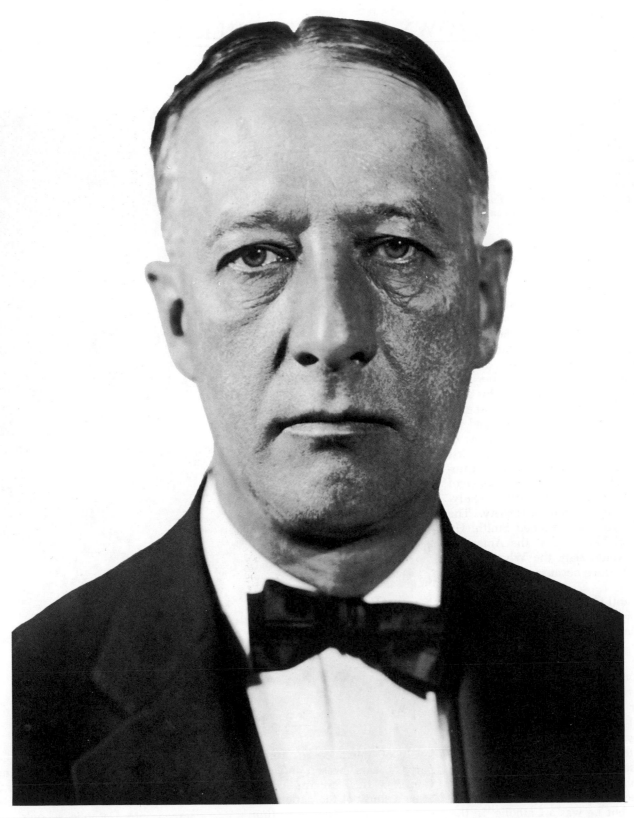

"Victory is his habit," Franklin D. Roosevelt told the convention, "the happy warrior, Alfred E. Smith."

The man and the derby.

anonymous newspapers swept across the South, rehashing the worst libels against the Catholic church that had been circulated in the United States during the period of 1840-60. One Democratic chairman of North Carolina reported that the anti-Catholic literature that poured into the state must have cost at least half a million dollars . . . In addition Smith was accused of being a habitual drunkard,

an illiterate, a rough, crude, uncouth tobacco-spitting bully of the East Side, a flunky of the corrupt Tammany of the Tweed days, an ignoramus who would disgrace the White House and make the United States the laughing-stock of foreign ambassadors."

What was fought in 1928, actually, was the classic battle between Rural America and the Big City, between Dry and Wet, between the true-blue

Protestant and the shanty Irishman. Al Smith was the essence of the political-moral-religious bigot's enemy. His political home—Tammany Hall—drew its great strength from the very melting pot so feared and hated by the legions in the hinterland. His spiritual home was the Roman Catholic Church. His morals were candidly outrageous: he was against national Prohibition and he said so, let the votes fall where they may. He was against the Women's Christian Temperance Union and the Anti-Saloon League and he was against the Ku Klux Klan, and he told it to them to their faces during the campaign. There were no whispers on his side; he shouted. His gravel-voiced tones, touched with the coarse accents of the city streets, resounded over the land, into the very Bible Belt itself. He spoke from sheer fighting courage and passionate conviction. He spoke from the depths of a heart that was breaking.

The religious issue actually predated the campaign by twenty months, going back to the time the boom began for the man in the Brown Derby. Charles C. Marshall, a New York attorney versed in canon law, wrote an open letter to the *Atlantic Monthly* in the Spring of 1927 in which he questioned whether a Catholic could function as President of the United States and stay within the teachings of his faith. The letter, scholarly rather than intolerant, contended that under Papal Law a Catholic President would have to place his loyalty to the Pope above his patriotic duty to the state. Smith sat down with the Rev. Francis P. Duffy, the "Fighting Chaplain" of World War fame, and drafted a forthright reply challenging the Marshall thesis from start to finish.

"I recognize no power in the institutions of my church to interfere with the operations of the Constitution of the United States or the enforcement of the law of the land," Smith wrote. He said his own creed granted freedom of conscience and worship to all men. He said he believed in the absolute separation of Church and State. He said he regarded the public school "as one of the cornerstones of American liberty." He said he did not view the encyclicals of the Pope as articles of Catholic faith binding upon the individual Catholic. "I believe," he concluded, "in the common brotherhood of man under the common fatherhood of God."

In 1924 the Democrats had denied

the nomination to Smith because they feared the combination of a Catholic and a Wet meant certain disaster at the polls. That convention went to 103 ballots before John W. Davis emerged as the candidate. Four years later the situation was vastly different. Franklin D. Roosevelt put the smiling man in the Brown Derby before the Houston convention this way: "We offer one who has the will to win—who not only deserves success but commands it. Victory is his habit—the happy warrior, Alfred Smith." The delegates picked Smith on the first ballot; he was the first Catholic to carry either major party's banner but the Democrats deemed him the only man with any chance, however faint, to oust the Republicans from the White House.

In the campaign, the religious issue emerged above the surface in reverse, for the most part. The bigots usually mentioned Catholicism openly only by way of protesting that Al Smith's faith was the furthest thing from their minds; they always said they were against him for a variety of other reasons. Herbert Hoover disavowed any discussion of religion. So did the Republican National Committee, but here and there an individual committeeman publicly charged that Smith would be nothing more than a Vatican stooge if he got to the White House. Bishop James Cannon, Jr. of the Methodist Episcopal Church added fuel to the issue by accusing the Catholics themselves of intolerance. The Dry bishop charged that the campaign was being waged "on the mystical body of Christ rather than of the man Alfred Emanuel Smith" and insisted that all "Catholic lovers of Christ" were "feverishly praying" for Smith to win. In the anti-Smith underground, the cry of "Rum and Romanism" resounded across the nation right up to election day.

There will always be a question as to how much difference it made that year. The Republicans were at the crest of their popularity and had a substantial candidate in the Quaker-born Hoover. As Secretary of Commerce in the Harding and Coolidge regimes the man in the high collar had a strong identification with the fat years. Beyond that, his own campaign pledges made the boundless prosperity of the retiring Coolidge look like nickel-and-dime stuff. "We in America today," Hoover said, "are nearer to the final triumph over poverty than ever before

in the history of any land. The poorhouse is vanishing from among us. We have not yet reached the goal, but, given a chance to go forward with the policies of the last eight years, we shall soon, with the help of God, be in sight of the day when poverty will be banished from this nation . . ." The Republican National Committee topped that with paid ads promising the voters "A chicken in every pot, a car in every garage." Some party spokesmen doubled this IOU: *two* chickens in every pot and *two* cars in every garage.

So Al Smith really had to go against a formidable variation on the three Rs —Rum, Romanism and Riches. It was too much even for the Happy Warrior, despite his remarkable record as the three-term Governor of New York. All he had to talk about were the liberal reforms that had done so much for the little people. These items had no impact around the nation in 1928; they represented small gains at a time when everybody was talking about big money, not just some tiny forward steps on the social front. Besides, what did it mean? It meant that Al Smith was a Good Governor, whereas in Herbert Hoover the Republicans had a Great Engineer, pledged to engineer some more good times.

The result was a landslide.

Hoover drew 21 million votes to 15 million for Smith. He carried all but eight states and got 444 electoral votes to Smith's 87. He cracked the Solid South, taking Texas, Virginia, North Carolina and Florida. He captured such doubtful Border States as

Oklahoma, Tennessee and Kentucky. He even took Smith's own New York—the worst blow of all.

No one quite like Al Smith had ever run for President before. Son of a horse-and-wagon teamster, he had no book-learning beyond the parochial school levels because he went to work at fourteen to help his widowed mother. He toiled in New York's Fulton Fish Market before he went into Tammany Hall and moved up through menial political chores to the State Legislature and the Governor's chair. He was crude and rough. In his derby, with a cigar sticking out of his face, he looked more like a machine boss than the potential master of the old mansion on Pennsylvania Avenue in Washington, but he wanted to get to that house very badly. He took his defeat hard and when the Democrats refused him renomination in 1932 and picked Roosevelt to make the easy race against the depression-tarnished Hoover, he went into a towering rage. Four years later he was still angry enough to campaign for the Republican Alf Landon against the man who had first called him the Happy Warrior.

He fought Roosevelt again in 1936 under the banner of the ultra-conservative Liberty League, and still again in 1940. In time, grown rich as the $50,000-a-year president of the Empire State Building and a director in several corporations, his political philosophy grew more akin to the Republican Old Guard's than to FDR's. In defeat, Al Smith had moved all the way uptown.

Roosevelt and Smith parted company in 1932.

IT HAPPENED IN 1928...

Ben Hecht, famous novelist, dramatist, movie writer. He and his friend Charles MacArthur had a great hit in *The Front Page*.

The Methodist Board of Temperance, Prohibition and Public Morals reported that high school and college students were drinking at parties, dances, hotels and in parked cars . . . In Lansing, Michigan, Etta Mae Miller drew a life term as a "habitual criminal" upon her fourth conviction for selling whiskey . . . The Bar Association of the City of New York resolved that "The Eighteenth Amendment is inconsistent with the spirit and purpose of the Constitution and in derogation of the liberties of the citizens . . . as guaranteed by the first ten amendments thereto" . . . A Treasury Department report showed that between 1920 and 1928 the Government had fired 706 Prohibition agents and prosecuted 257 others for taking bribes. Elmer L. Irey, Chief T-Man, termed the snooper band a "most extraordinary collection of political hacks, hangers-on and passing highwaymen". . . In New York, Captain Daniel Chapin lined up the agents on his staff and ordered them to extend their hands. "Now," he said, "every one of you sons of bitches with a diamond ring is fired." That took in about half of them . . . The Drys said the people were buying more and more washing machines now that they weren't spending all their money on booze . . . The bootleg cup-that-cheers killed 1,565 Americans during the year.

* * *

Just for larks, four Philadelphia society women played eight hands of bridge in a plane flying over the Quaker City . . . Five working women poisoned by radium in a New Jersey factory won awards of $10,000 each, plus medical costs, counsel fees and $600-a-year pensions . . . Calvin Coolidge fished all summer in Wisconsin. In an article for the St. Louis *Post-Dispatch* he said the nation needed a summer White House, preferably in the nearby hills, so that the President could escape Washington's heat . . . The Methodist Episcopal Church's Board of Bishops listed drunkenness, abuse and lack of morals as equivalent to adultery . . . Mayor Jimmy Walker of New York, disturbed by disclosures of graft in the Street Cleaning Department, called in all bureau heads and told them to root out the dishonest or quit . . .

The textile strike in Gastonia, N. C., produced much violence . . . The Briand-Kellogg pact, outlawing war, was signed at Paris . . . Gov. O. Max Gardner of North Carolina blamed dieting women for the drop in farm prices . . . New York police closed another Mae West show, *Pleasure Man* . . . Bernarr Macfadden warned the male population: "If you are looking for future happiness, avoid the girls who wear high heels." Devitalizing, Macfadden said. Not the girls, the heels.

* * *

Thornton Wilder's *The Bridge of San Luis Rey* led the fiction best-sellers. Hugh Walpole (*Wintersmoon*), S. S. Van Dine (*The Green Murder Case*) and Vina Delmar (*Bad Girl*) made the list. Andre Maurois' *Disraeli* topped the non-fiction books, along with Katherine Mayo's *Mother India*, Aloysius Horn and Ethlreda Lewis' *Trader Horn*, Emil Ludwig's *Napoleon* and Charles A. Lindbergh's *We*. Shaw put out *The Intelligent Woman's Guide to Socialism and Capitalism*. Stephen Vincent Benet's *John Brown's Body* and Upton Sinclair's *Boston* were moving nicely in the stores.

On the stage, Lee Tracy and Osgood Perkins starred in MacArthur and Hecht's *The Front Page*, Lynne Fontanne in O'Neill's *Strange Interlude*, Katharine Cornell in *The Age of Innocence* with Franchot Tone, Eva Le Galienne and Nazimova in *The Cherry Orchard*, Fay Bainter in *She Stoops to Conquer*, Laurette Taylor in *The Furies* and Jack Dempsey and Estelle Taylor in *The Big Fight*. The big musical was *Making Whoopee*, with Eddie Cantor, and the title song swept the nation. On the screen, Walt Disney's Mickey Mouse made his debut. Also Mickey Rooney.

Bernarr Macfadden: Beware of girls in high heels.

Trader Horn

Slaughter on Clark Street

"I want peace and I will live and let live."
—AL CAPONE

St. Valentine's Day in Chicago, Feb. 14, 1929.

There were seven men in the garage at 2122 N. Clark Street, Chicago, on February 14, 1929—St. Valentine's Day. Five of them were in the Bugs Moran gang and they were waiting for the boss, who wanted a consignment of liquor convoyed from the Canadian border through the Prohibition force's paper curtain. Moran had survived the five bloodiest years of the underworld wars to emerge as the successor to his executed chums—Dion O'Banion and Hymie Weiss—in command of the anti-Capone cabal on the North Side.

But the black touring car that pulled up outside the garage at 10:30 that morning wasn't carrying the affluent Mr. Moran. It looked more like a police car. There was an alarm bell on the running board and a gun-rack behind the front seat. And out of it, moving briskly in the light snow and 18-degree cold, stepped two men dressed as policemen and two in civilian clothes. A fifth man in uniform stayed at the wheel. Inside the garage, the quartet whipped open their overcoats and produced two sawed-off shotguns and two machine guns. Somebody barked out an order—"Line-up! Put your noses to the wall!"—and then the artillery began to go off. The seven men standing against the red bricks were cut down in a withering cross fire.

1929

The four messengers of death left in a deceptive formation. The two in civvies came out first, hands high, herded by the two in uniform as though they were under arrest. Sam Schneider, the tailor next door, heard the great clatter and saw the quartet depart; he thought the cops were simply taking in an errant pair trapped in gunplay in the cavernous booze drop. Witnesses in the rooming house across the street had the same idea.

The real police arrived in force in due time and tiptoed into the giant pool of blood in the garage. There lay the ripped-up bodies of Pete Gusenberg, James Clark, Adam Heyer, John May and two casual visitors, Al Weinshank and Dr. Reinhart H Schwimmer, a young optometrist who knew some

The Brothers Gusenberg, Frank and Pete, were the most prominent victims of the St. Valentine's Day massacre. Frank (above) survived for a few hours but didn't tell the police anything. Pete's photo is below.

had hijacked some Moran booze and then decided to knock him off lest he tattle. The Federal people promptly transferred the talkative Silloway to a less sensitive post far from the stormy shores of Lake Michigan.

Someone else said the Purple Gang of Detroit had staged the mass executions—the worst in the whole gory history of the underworld—over some business spat with the Moran organization, but Bugs himself would have none of it. "Only the Capone gang kills like that," said the hardy North Side beer baron.

Moran had a point. His troubles with the racket overlord had been multiplying for months because he had allied himself with the Aiello Brothers' gang in a struggle to take over the Unione Siciliana. Moran was suspect in the slaying of two Unione Siciliana presidents, Anthony Lombardo and

his predecessor, Pasqualino Lolardo, knocked off in his own living room after four of his supposed pals had sipped his rare wines one afternoon. Beyond that, Bugs had been having troubles with Vincenzo Demora, better known as Machine Gun Jack McGurn, who had been raiding North Side liquor drops on harrying missions ordered by Scarface Al.

On February 27, thirteen days after the killings on North Clark Street, the police brought in McGurn and John Scalise, ace artilleryman of the Terrible Gennas when they presided over the Unione Siciliana. McGurn furnished an effective if unchivalrous alibi. He said he had spent St. Valentine's Day in a cozy room in the Hotel Stevens with his best girl, so the indictment was thrown out. Scalise hadn't thought to furnish such an iron-clad story and was held for trial, but un-

of the Moran boys. Frank Gusenberg, with fourteen slugs in him, had crawled twenty feet toward the garage door and was still alive. In the hospital Lieutenant Tom Loftus, a long-time authority on the bad Gusenberg boys, stood over his cot:

"You're dying, Frank, and Pete is dead. Tell us who did it."

"Coppers," the gunman answered. "It was coppers."

"What coppers?"

"I didn't know them."

"Tell me the truth, Frank. The men who did this ought to go to the gallows. We wanna hang 'em."

"That's all I know. Coppers done it."

Loftus kept up the soft, gentle interrogation for three hours. Finally, Gusenberg gasped out his last: "It's getting dark, Tom. I'm cold—awful cold. Pull the covers up over me."

Frederick D. Silloway, the Prohibition administrator in Chicago, submitted that the murderers were indeed policemen—five sinful gendarmes who

This was not an uncommon sight in Chicago in the twenties. In this case the arrow points to Anthony Lombardo, Capone-installed president of the Unione Siciliana, cut down with bodyguard Joseph Ferraro at busy State and Madison Streets on Sept. 27, 1928. The Bugs Moran gang was among the suspects, so the St. Valentine's Day carnage may have been a special kind of memorial to Mr. Lombardo.

The man the executioners were looking for in the garage—Bugs Moran. He didn't happen to be there and his gangland enemies never did get around to killing him. He managed to last all through the gangland wars and did not die until 1957.

John Scalise (left) and Albert Anselmi, Capone artillerymen, were questioned about the bloody goings-on in the garage but nothing came of it. As it happened, it didn't matter; Capone himself disposed of them in due time.

Ed Fletcher (left) of Detroit's Purple Gang, and George F. Lewis, another suspect, held in Detroit for questioning in the St. Valentine's Day Massacre. They beat the rap.

friendly hands saved the state the expense.

Scalise and his torpedo mate, Albert Anselmi, were done in with ball bats and pistols along with Joseph Guinta, newly installed by Capone as head of Unione Siciliana. Capone supposedly threw a small private banquet for this trio and then, when they were groggy on vino and high-calory viands, bashed in their heads and sent some boys out to finish the job with revolvers. The story was that Capone was unhappy about the St. Valentine's Day bloodletting and doomed Scalise, Anselmi and Guinta for being so frisky.

What Capone feared was that the spectacular massacre would turn on too much heat; he was right. Chicago's tattered forces of decency got madder than ever. The newspapers compared the Midwestern metropolis to the wildest frontier towns of the old West and talked of a complete breakdown of law 'n' order. There were suggestions in Congress that the Marines be sent out to take the situation in hand.

And now the outcry took hold.

The end was at hand for Al Capone.

Machine Gun Jack McGurn, shown with his wife, Louise Rolfe, was another prime suspect in the St. Valentine's Day bloodletting. He was a trusted Capone sharpshooter but he had a satisfactory ailbi.

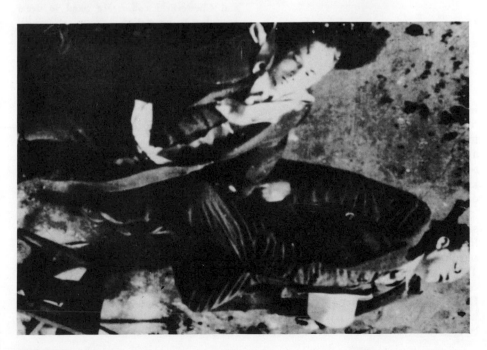

A widely circulated close-up view of the massacre. Printed upside down this way, it saved the reader the trouble of turning the page to identify the victims.

PUBLIC ENEMY
No. 1

"They talk about me not being on the legitimate. Why, lady, nobody's on the legit when it comes down to cases, you know that."

—AL CAPONE

Al Capone never could have made it as a model for collar ads. He had a flat nose, thick lips, a bull neck and a scar from his left ear to his lip. He liked to call it a war wound but it really was a memento of a knife fight in a Brooklyn dance hall. Al only made the fourth grade in school but he proved that a diligent, dedicated man could go far without formal education. He came up the hard way: street fights, petty thefts, warehouse heists, rough stuff in New York's Five Points Gang, two murder raps to shake off. In this process, the boy from Naples developed a suitable boldness for the years ahead.

Johnny Torrio brought Al Capone to Chicago in 1920. The stocky hoodlum started out as a mere bodyguard but soon was put in charge of the Four Deuces Café, the South Wabash Avenue pleasure dome where Torrio maintained his headquarters. The café had a saloon on the first floor, gambling traps on the second and third and girls-for-hire on the top story—for those who got past the lower plateaus both solvent and willing. Capone, then known as Scarface Al Brown, handled the café and other chores so well that Torrio put him in charge in 1923 when the Syndicate branched out into Cicero and the other neighboring towns tapped for exploitation. Pretty soon Scarface was wearing Chesterfield overcoats and monogrammed shirts and looking very much the gentleman.

Cicero, mother lode of the suburban gold mines, was an empire unto itself. It stood so high above the law that the Syndicate designated its own dummy candidates for public office and then put gunmen in the polling places to see that they got voted in. The Chicago police interfered in one election there and Frank Capone, Al's brother, died

Man to man: Ever gracious and friendly, even when the authorities had occasion to take up his valuable time with questions, Mr. Capone turns on the charm for Assistant State's Attorney Frank Mast. Note Al's spats and Chesterfield collar. He liked to dress according to his station.

in the ensuing gunplay. The Syndicate retained control. Indeed, Capone's iron rule was such that the police stood amiably by one day when he lost his temper over some trifling matter and knocked down Mayor Joseph Z. Klenha on the City Hall steps.

Even with that kind of Hollywood-style melodramatics the nation paid little attention to Cicero and the lesser baronies outside the Windy City. There was too much going on in Chicago itself: the assassination of Dion O'Banion ("His head got away from his hat," Capone said), the war between the O'Banion heirs and the

House of Genna, the attempt on Torrio's life, the battle over the Unione Siciliana and the political warfare between Big Bill Thompson's corrupt Republican machine and the reform administrations of Mayor Dever. So Capone stayed out of the papers, for the most part, until the chilly, bullet-riddled afternoon of September 20, 1926, when an armed convoy rode down on him in Cicero.

There were eight touring cars in the deadly battalion that raked the Hawthorne Hotel, the Capone GHQ. The wonder was that nobody got killed in the great clatter of machine-gun fire

In his public utterances, Scarface Al always professed a taste more suited to culture than gangland warfare. "With me," he said, "grand opera is the berries."

A visiting British newspaperman described Al Capone as America's "Nineteenth Amendment." The gangster didn't like that kind of press. "There's lots of grief attached to the limelight," he complained.

The people of Chicago put Big Bill Thompson back in City Hall in 1927 on his pledge of a "wide-open town." But maybe it wasn't wholly the voters' fault: hoodlums patrolled the polling places in great force to make sure Big Bill won.

as the sedans rolled slowly by. Capone hugged the floor of the hotel's restaurant and emerged with nothing more than flecks of dust on his tailor-made suit. "What shooting?" he asked when the ever-friendly local police came by. Then Cicero's Duce took steps to see that a neutral casualty—a woman hurt by stray bullets and flying windshield glass—received proper medical care. He boasted later that he spent $10,000 saving the lady's eyesight.

The daylight raid on Fortress Capone generally was attributed to Deanie O'Banion's avenging angels, Hymie Weiss, Schemer Drucci and Bugs Moran. Weiss paid with his life three weeks later. He was cut down by six assassins opposite the Holy Name Cathedral in Chicago, and Capone himself wrote the epitaph. "Hymie is dead because he was a bullhead," he said. "Forty times I've tried to arrange things so we'd have peace and life would be worth living but he couldn't be told anything." Drucci followed

Weiss to the grave by a curious route— a young cop blew his brains out in a quarrel of sorts while taking him to a station house for questioning over some election-day polling-place bombings.

A period of comparative peace and quiet set in after that. Government agents estimated that the new tranquility boosted the Capone empire's cash take to unexplored heights in 1927. This was the breakdown:

Beer, liquor, home-cooked alcohol, $60,000,000
Gambling places and dog tracks, $25,000,000
Brothels, dance halls and inns, $10,000,000
Miscellaneous rackets $10,000,000

The cold statistics, however mountainous, hardly told the Capone story in terms of its real impact on the American scene in the Lawless Decade. A garden-variety hood spawned in the poolrooms and gutters of New York, Scarface Al rose to heights never before scaled. He was the New Power,

bigger than the city and bigger than the state. He was the Mayor, Governor and Machine Boss all rolled into one. He gave the orders; the people's elected servants carried them out and kept their mouths shut. Capone's iron rule embraced not only Chicago but whatever other parts of Illinois he had the time and inclination to exploit. His authority was so great it could not be measured.

Thus two men were convicted in gang murders in a four-year period during which Capone and his mob rivals knocked off 227 men. Thus Big Bill Thompson ran for Mayor of Chicago against the reformer Dever in 1927 with a crystal-clear pledge of a wide-open town. "We'll not only re-open places these people have closed," Thompson said, "but we'll open 10,000 new ones." It sounded more like a promise to Capone than to the electorate, and it figured. The Syndicate stood behind the Thompson campaign with a fortune in cash and a formidable armed force besides. James M. Ragen, the racing-wire magnate, later murdered, termed the Capone mob "as strong as the United States Army." It wasn't, of course, but it surely was as strong as the City of Chicago itself after Thompson ousted the old-fashioned Dever. How strong? Fred Pasley, Capone's biographer, referred to the swarthy racket overlord as "the municipal cabinet member without portfolio—Commissioner of Lawlessness. To the upright Drys he was anathema, to the downright Wets a public benefactor, to the politicians Santa Claus." No power either as brazen or as great as Al Capone's ever existed before in an American metropolis. Perhaps none would again; the underworld syndicates that came in his wake, while formidable indeed, never ran quite as wild and free as Capone's.

The payroll of the Midwest underworld czar's private army—including the lavish "ice" handouts to the police and political fixers that stood behind the Syndicate, left Capone an estimat-

Enroute to the world championship, heavyweight Jack Sharkey saw nothing wrong in posing with Al Capone while in Florida for his fight with Young Stribling in 1929.

Capone managed to smile for the cameras when Deputy Police Commissioner John Stege (right) called him downtown. Stege, always a nuisance to the Syndicate, was called "Honest John." It was the kind of nickname few Chicago cops earned during the Lawless Decade.

Federal men stand by as an expert applies the acetylene torch to a safe seized from the Cotton Club, a Capone resort in Cicero, Ill. Records turned up in raids such as these put the Big Guy behind bars on tax charges.

ed $30,000,000 or so for his own purse. That's a staggering figure, but the man himself kicked around some towering numbers. He said in 1929 that in the brief years of his greatest prosperity his personal gambling adventures—he liked horses and dice—cost him $10,000,000 in pocket money. With or without his private vices, he had tastes that might be considered extravagant even for the Get-Rich-Quick Era. He had an 11½-carat diamond ring that cost $50,000 and his custom-built 7-ton limousine, steel-plated to discourage assassins, cost $30,000. He maintained a suitable town house in Chicago's Grand Crossing District; his Irish wife and son and the whole Clan Capone never wanted for the comforts befitting great wealth.

Capone enjoyed so much affluence in 1927 that he turned up in the official greeting party when Commander Francesco da Pinedo, Mussolini's round-the-world goodwill flyer, arrived in Chicago. The municipal authorities said the mobster was on hand only to

Alfred J. (Jake) Lingle, veteran police reporter of the Chicago *Tribune*, was shot to death in 1930 (photo at right) on his way to catch a racetrack train. The reward offers, starting with $25,000 from his paper, mounted quickly to $55,000. The first theory was that the underworld had rubbed out Lingle for exposing too many of its secrets. But when he died Lingle was wearing the kind of diamond-studded belt Al Capone gave to his closest friends and benefactors. A further airing of the awful facts showed that while the *Tribune* was paying him $65-a-week Lingle enjoyed a net income of $60,000 a year, had a chauffeur-driven Lincoln, plunged in Wall Street and on the turf, put $18,000 into a summer home on the Michigan lake shore and occupied space in the fashionable Stevens Hotel. The evidence indicated that the popular reporter had strong ties with the Capone empire, apparently stemming from the excellent municipal connections he had built up over the years, and may have been the underworld's liaison man with the police and politicians. The murder shook up the town. Capone professed to be broken up by it. "Jake was a dear friend of mine," he said.

After Lingle died, it turned out that he had a financial interest in gambling operations which went on behind such innocent facades as this cigar store.

Harry Koman (left), an eyewitness, tells Detective Sergeant Dan Kenny how Jake Lingle's assassin picked the reporter out of a subway-bound crowd.

Dominick Aiello (panama hat), one of the nine much-feared Aiello Brothers of Chicago's North Side, was questioned in the Lingle murder but let out.

discourage anti-Fascist demonstrators from showing up. The more cynical observers said the gang overlord was there as a distinguished compatriot of the Italian air ace, period. Capone also cut quite a figure in Florida, where he had a 25-room bayside villa at Palm Island. When he attended the Stribling-Sharkey fight in Miami Beach, his ringside pew was dusted off by no one less than Jack Dempsey, official greeter for the affair. Westbrook Pegler interpreted this tableau as "a gesture of good fellowship and an exchange of amenities between two professions having much in common."

The St. Valentine's Day massacre came as a jarring note during one Capone sojourn in the Florida sun. Since it suggested a new round of inter-gang violence, the Big Guy summoned a Council of Peace in the Hotel President in Atlantic City. But the friendly delegates from Chicago couldn't offer any guarantees that the anti-Capone factions would behave themselves with so much blood already spilled on their side. Indeed, they told the boss that he might be on the spot marked X.

Prisoner's Song

"I haven't had any peace of mind ... it's a tough life ..."

—AL CAPONE

  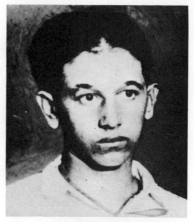

  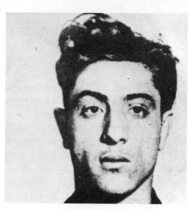

This gallery of rogues came through the swinging station house doors (in and out, of course) in Chicago's futile investigation into the gang slaying of the high-stepping Jake Lingle: (left to right, top) Mike de Pike Heitler, James Belcastro and James J. Adduci, (bottom) John Genaro, Pasquale Tardi and Louis Clementi. Heitler was an old time gambler who turned up in the Capone vice cartel. He once admitted paying off the police at the rate of $50 to $150 for each brothel doing business on the West Side. For thus corrupting the forces of law and order, the tender Chicago courts levied a $50 fine on Heitler. Belcastro earned an imposing nickname—King of the Bombers—in the days when the mobs were tossing "pineapples" at merchants who resisted Mr. Capone's "protection." Adduci survived a string of arrests to get elected to the Illinois House of Representatives, where he fought anti-crime legislation with much zeal down through the years. Belcastro and Adduci were among those questioned when Heitler himself went on the spot in 1931. Genaro, Tardi and Clementi never achieved the eminence of the other three.

Enroute from Atlantic City, supposedly on the way back to Chicago to take things in hand, the paunchy Al Capone got arrested in Philadelphia. It looked prearranged. Two detectives encountered Alphonse and a bodyguard, Frank (Big) Cline, outside a movie and after the proper introductions and flashing of badges Capone said, "Oh, bulls. All right, here's my gun." Indicted the very next day, Capone pleaded guilty on the gun charge and drew a year in jail. "He was running away from a gang which was out to kill him," Mayor Harry A. Mackey said. "If he hadn't been glad to go to jail, I think he would have fought the case to the last." Major Lemuel B. Schofield, Philadelphia's Director of Public Safety, talked at length to Capone and got a first-hand picture of a gangland Goliath suddenly smitten with disquieting reflections.

"I'm like any other man," said the Quaker City's distinguished guest. "I've been in this racket long enough to realize that a man in my game must take the breaks, the fortunes of war. Three of my friends were killed in the last three weeks in Chicago. That certainly isn't conducive to peace of mind. I haven't had any peace of mind in years. Every minute I was in danger of death. Even when we're on a peace errand we must hide from the rest of the racketeers . . . Why, when I went to Atlantic City I registered under a fictitious name."

Capone said he had been trying to quit the mobs for two years.

"Once in the racket you are always in it, it seems," Schofield quoted him. "The parasites will trail you begging for money and favors and you can never get away from them no matter where you go. I have a wife and a boy who is eleven—a lad I idolize—and a beautiful home in Florida. If I could go there and forget it all I would be the happiest man in the world. I want peace and I will live and let live. I'm tired of gang murders and gang shootings . . . it's a tough life to lead. You fear death every moment and, worse than death, you fear the rats of the game who would run around and tell the police if you don't constantly satisfy them with money and favors."

The lament ended on a plaintive note that was fraught with historical oversights in its more significant passages:

"I was never able to leave home without my bodyguard. He has been with me constantly for two years. I have never been convicted of a crime, never, nor have I ever directed anyone else to commit a crime. I don't pose as a plaster saint, but I never killed anyone. And I am known all over the world as a millionaire gorilla."

Capone had a reasonably comfort-

Frank Biege, a Capone lieutenant, had some embarrassing moments in 1929 when his wife turned talkative and caused a reopening of the investigation into the slaying of Assistant State's Attorney William McSwiggin. Mrs. Biege told the authorities that Biege had told her that Mr. Capone himself wielded the machine gun when McSwiggin, a man of mysterious affairs, was cut down with two gangster companions in Cicero in 1926. Biege, alias Frank Perry, denied that he had ever said such a naughty thing, even in the confidence of the marital chamber. "My wife is a woman of great imagination," he added, "I haven't seen her for a year." As it turned out, nothing came of the woman's sensational charges.

Captain John (Honest John) Stege hounded the Chicago mobs during the brief flurries of reform in the twenties. He is shown here unpacking machine guns to be issued to detectives on special duty at election booths. When Louis Alterie openly threatened to shoot it out with the men who murdered his pal Dion O'Banion, Stege walked up to the gangster, slapped his face and took his gun away. But Stege had his ups-and-downs on the detective force; when the Thompson machine was in power he was banished to outlying districts where he couldn't annoy the racket guys.

able time in the pen. He managed to keep in touch with his many enterprises over the warden's phone and in his moments of solitude he read *Country Life* magazine, dipping into the nicer cultural levels of the twenties. When he got out, Genevieve Forbes Herrick of the *Chicago Tribune* obtained an audience with him.

"You know, lady, I'd rather the newspapers wouldn't print a line about me," Capone said. "That's the way I feel. No brass band for me. There's a lot of grief attached to the limelight. Say, if I was just plain Izzy Polatski, living in Chicago, I'd not stand out in the gutter trying to get a peek at Capone. I'd attend to my business and let him attend to his; no use making a laughing-stock of the city . . . All I ever did was supply a demand that was pretty popular. Why, the very guys that make my trade good are the ones that yell the loudest about me . . . They talk about me not being on the legitimate. Why, lady, nobody's on the legit, when it comes down to cases; you know that."

Fred Pasley heard variations on the same theme when he talked to the mobster in his office in Chicago's Lexington Hotel—under photos of the man's two heroes, George Washington and William Hale Thompson, the soul of tolerance and understanding whenever he was Mayor of Chicago.

"All I ever did," said Scarface Al, "was to sell beer and whiskey to our best people . . . Why, some of the leading judges use the stuff . . . If people did not want beer and wouldn't drink it, a fellow would be crazy for going around trying to sell it. I've seen gambling houses, too, in my travels, you understand, and I never saw anyone point a gun at a man and make him go in. I never heard of anyone being forced to go to a place to have some fun . . ."

There was at least one item the suddenly loquacious badman overlooked when he drew his self-portrait as an earnest tradesman catering to Dry America's thirst. No less than 500 murders occurred in Chicago and the Syndicate's captive suburbs during the Lawless Decade. Alphonse Capone didn't start signing the death warrants until he inherited the golden quill from Johnny Torrio in 1925, so he couldn't be taxed with all the carnage. He did have a clammy paw in some of it—the lion's share, let's say. In short, he really was not a nice boy, no matter how much he yearned to serve his fellow citizen's craving in the booze, gambling and flesh marts.

Uncle Sam Steps In

News item, vintage '29: *Al Capone, citizen of Chicago, offered the government $4,000,000 to settle his income tax delinquencies. The government turned it down.*

Herbert Hoover was barely settled in the White House in the spring of 1929 when he was visited by Colonel Frank Knox, publisher of the Chicago *Daily News,* and some troubled citizens. The delegation acquainted the new President with the more terrible facts of life in their town and asked for federal help. Hoover, distressed, thereupon told Andrew Mellon, Secretary of the Treasury, to see if the T-Men could break Al Capone's iron grip on Chicago. Mellon called in Elmer L. Irey, chief of his enforcement branch, and gave him the assignment.

The T-Men had a nice running start on the case. For years they had been trailing around after Al's big brother Ralph, called Bottles, in an effort to shake him loose from some paltry income tax payments. Their inquiries showed that Bottles, a gambler and horse fancier, had deposited $1,751,-840.60 in a single bank account from 1924 to 1929 while alternately ignoring the tax laws or pleading poverty. Bottles drew a three-year prison sentence and a $10,000 fine in the winter of 1929 and then Mellon called in Irey again. Irey set down the conversation in his book, *The Tax Dodgers:*

"Mr. Irey," Mellon said, "do you know about President Hoover's medicine-ball cabinet?"

"I've read about it." It was the kind of group of men who later would be called a "Brain Trust," who gathered each morning at the White House to toss medicine balls with the President, and incidentally plot the course of the nation.

Mellon went on. "Do you know how those sessions start and finish?"

That was easy. I didn't.

"Well," the Secretary said, "when the exercising starts Mr. Hoover says, 'Have you got that fellow Capone, yet?' And when exercise is done and everybody is leaving, the last thing Mr. Hoover always says is, 'Remember, now; I want that man Capone in jail.'"

"Yes, Mr. Secretary," I said as I left.

Irey sat down with Arthur P. Madden, the Intelligence Unit Agent-in-Charge in Chicago, and two of Madden's men, Frank Wilson and Pat O'Rourke. Wilson was assigned to check on all the books and records seized in Chicago gambling raids over a period of years. The tougher job went to O'Rourke. His orders were to acquire the trappings of an eastern hoodlum and worm his way into the Al Capone gang, which he did. The early Wilson-O'Rourke researches put two of the mob's top lieutenants in jail on tax charges—Jake Guzik and Frank (The Enforcer) Nitti. This so unnerved the Boss that he dropped in on Wilson and announced that he certainly wanted to pay his own just debts —up to $4,000,000 or so—if Uncle Sam thought him delinquent in his tax payments.

But it was too late for deals. Capone was accused of tax evasion for the years 1924 through to 1929. The indictments, touching only on the barest portions of the gangster's enterprises, charged that Johnny Torrio's one-time $75-a-week strong-arm man owed $215,030.-48 on an income of $1,038,654.84 during the dandy years. The Department of Justice, suddenly aroused, chimed in with 5,000 separate indictments for bootlegging. Capone was tried in the tax cases in October, 1931, and found guilty. Judge James H. Wilkerson sentenced him to eleven years in prison, $50,000 in fines and $30,000 in costs. In the courthouse elevator a few minutes later, Capone ran into Pat O'Rourke. "The only thing that fooled me was your looks," he told the agent. "You look like a Wop."

The Big Guy hardly seemed angry.

Capone was sent to the Federal Prison at Atlanta, where he worked in the overall shop. Later he was transferred to Alcatraz. With time deducted for good behavior, he got off the Rock in mid-January, 1939, but by then he was a human wreck. He had spent eight years behind bars in deadly, quaking fear of his life and towards the end an old case of syphilis affected his brain. He came out a paretic and retired to his Miami Beach estate, his empire taken over by the formidable post-Prohibition syndicates led by such peace-abiding outlaws as Frank Costello. Capone lingered until 1947 and when he died, at 48, he was only a dim memory to most Americans. He may have had the last laugh at that: He trampled on the law for ten years but it took nothing less than the national government itself to smash his monumental authority; he could buy local and state governments as he pleased. Quite a note for a simple immigrant from Naples.

Al Capone takes some needed relaxation fishing in the waters off his Florida estate.

The Night Mayor of New York

"There are three things a man must do alone—be born, die and testify . . ."
—JIMMY WALKER

Jimmy Walker in 1925. He took a Florida vacation just after he was elected Mayor.

The playboy Mayor takes part in a Press Club show.

Midway through the Lawless Decade and having a wonderful time, Baghdad-on-the-Subway ousted the stuffy John F. Hylan and got itself the right Mayor for the right moment. James J. Walker, called Jimmy, eased his trim frame behind the big colonial desk in City Hall on the first day of 1926 and looked impishly around the musty, high-ceilinged room; he would not spend too many of the precious hours in those dim-lit, austere precincts.

So Jimmy Walker turned on his puckish Irish grin, called for his walking stick and his gray spats and silk topper and went uptown where the lights were brighter. He went up to Broadway, where he was at home. The town came to know him as the high priest of live-and-let-live—in all the departments, including the increasingly less sacred institution of marriage. The Man-About-Town stopping at the Central Park Casino for a nightcap with his best girl, not to be confused with his lawful wedded wife, could take comfort that the Night Mayor was also on the premises—with *his* best girl.

The vast Walker fame did not derive solely from his lively taste in the fair sex, of course. He came into City Hall with a solid 14-year record in the State Legislature behind him. He wrote the bills that legalized boxing in New York and let the theaters stay open on Sundays. Cast in the liberal image of his political sponsors, Gov. Al Smith and Senator Robert F. Wagner, he fought for the 5-cent fare, for the eight-hour day for working women, for workmen's

compensation laws, for tenement safeguards. Quick on the tongue, he killed a move to censor novels with one swift wisecrack: "I have never yet heard of a girl being ruined by a book." Between times Tammany's dandy little lawmaker managed to string together the lyrics of a ditty that, like some of his municipal deeds, would live after him —"Will You Love Me in December as You Did in May?"

Always a familiar figure around Tin Pan Alley and the adjoining hot spots, Walker unfailingly selected his female partners from behind the footlights. He picked pretty little Janet Allen out of a chorus line in 1912 and made her his wife, only to stray after a while when songstress Yvonne Shelton came into view. Miss Shelton—"Vonnie" or "Little Fellow" to her favorite swain—had to be sacrificed in 1925. Al Smith was afraid that the open dalliance might cost Walker the election, so the candidate dutifully went back to his wife. The political patch only held the union together for a year, or until the Mayor's bedroom eyes alit on beautiful Betty Compton, playing a small role on Broadway in Gertrude Lawrence's starring vehicle, *Oh, Kay!* This May-December romance—the actress was just half the eternally boyish Mayor's 46 years—was the big one for Walker.

The 1929 campaign, coming after four more years of bad booze, hot jazz and wonderful nonsense in the Big Town, effectively laid to rest Mr. Smith's early fears about the effects of open amours on the voting populace. The Night Mayor, also known as the

In dead earnest here, he broadcasts a plea to the public.

At the 1927 Kentucky Derby. That's Mayor Thompson of Chicago at Walker's right.

The New York Boxing Writers' Association in 1946 voted Jimmy Walker a plaque marking his service to boxing. Commander Benny Leonard, U.S.M.S., is at the right. Al Buck of the *New York Post* made the award as Dr. Richard Neil looked on.

Late Mayor because he seldom got to City Hall before high noon and almost never kept an appointment on time, ran for re-election against the popular Fiorello H. LaGuardia and won by half a million votes. Everybody loved the smiling Irishman from Greenwich Village. Nobody expected him to work his fingers to the bone in that municipal factory downtown; he belonged to the Great White Way, or maybe on Fifth, marching up the golden avenue in the van of some parade or other.

And then along came Samuel Seabury, the good, gray, solid rock of respectability, poking around in the dungeons of the gay and prospering metropolis . . . rattling the skeletons . . . tracking down the vice cop's ill-gotten gains to find out why the town was wide-open for the streetwalker legions . . . turning the bus franchises and the sewer contracts and the stock deals over to a platoon of investigators and accountants . . . making magistrates squirm as they tried to explain why they were always so kind to policy runners and other politically-favored defendants . . . asking razor-edged questions . . . digging deeper and deeper and ever deeper.

Not all the murky trails led to the man in City Hall—not by any means—but the tireless Judge Seabury and his bright young helpers did turn up some embarrassing items directly involving Jimmy Walker. "Little Boy Blue is going to blow his horn—or his top," said the brash and dapper $40,000-a-year Mayor on the way into the hearing room. But he came out tarnished. He couldn't explain—at least not with any conviction—how he happened to make $26,535.51 in oil stock deals with taxicab impressario J. A. Sisto without having to invest a dime of his own. Nor why J. Allan Smith, contact man for a bus company, staked him to a European jaunt in 1927 with a $10,000 letter of credit and an extra $3,000 to cover an overdraft. Nor how he happened to pick up a $246,000 bonanza in a joint stock account with Paul Block, Brooklyn financier and publisher. Block's own story didn't help; he said that his 10-year-old son once observed that the world's richest city didn't pay its Mayor enough, so he decided "to make some money for Jimmy."

On the way to Palm Springs, in 1931, he wasn't worried about efforts to oust him.

In South Bend, at Knute Rockne's funeral.

The ex-Mayor shuffles a different kind of board.

The mounting Seabury revelations prompted Governor Franklin D. Roosevelt to set up hearings to determine whether Walker should be removed from office, but the Mayor didn't wait for the ax to fall. On Sept. 1, 1932, he resigned and fled to the Continent. He had Betty Compton by his side, as ever, and soon he was able to make it legal when Janet Walker obliged him, after all those years, and got a Florida divorce. Walker and Miss Compton were married at Cannes, France, even while the ink was settling on the decree. The union only lasted until 1941, when Miss Compton got a divorce of her own.

Jimmy Walker never talked for publication about the events that led to his downfall. Asked about the high old days in sinful Manhattan, he said somewhat wistfully that he wished he knew where all the money was that he supposedly had stolen while he was at the helm, but that only made the untold story a little more intriguing; it didn't tell anything. The plain citizen of New

Betty Compton.

Jimmy Walker on the stand. Samuel Seabury waits for his answer to an embarrassing question.

York, for his part, looked with much tolerance on the tainted record. When Walker came back from exile in 1935, satisfied that he would not be brought to trial, his great popularity hardly seemed dimmed; the welcome mat was out. In no time at all he was the town's favorite after-dinner speaker and again a familiar figure in public places.

If he had any massive guilts, either about his private or official life, he kept them to himself. In the days when the storm clouds were thickest, he went before a huge banquet audience and put his case this way:

"I have lived and I have loved. The only difference is that I was a little more public about it than most people. After all, maybe it isn't a mistake to be one's self and take chances. With all my misgivings, my countless mistakes, with all my multiplicity of shortcomings, I have a single regret. I have reached the peak of the hill and must start the journey downward. I have carried youth right up to the 50-yard mark. I had mine and made the most of it."

Maybe Gene Fowler, his biographer, said it even better than the eloquent Walker. He said Jimmy "wore New York in his lapel like a boutonniere." In those days, mixing a Prohibition that didn't work with a who-gives-a-damn prosperity that didn't last, a man could do that.

"EVERYBODY OUGHT TO BE RICH"

(newspaper clipping)

TRANSACTIONS ON THE NEW YOR[K ...]

TUESDAY, SEPTEMBER 3, 1929.

	Day's Sales.	Friday.	Thursday.	A Year Ago
	4,438,910	4,571,960	3,476,140	3,724,856

	Year to Date.	1928.	1927.	1926.
	731,288,280	528,139,384	367,709,467	306,215,22[?]

"The fundamental business of the country is on a sound and prosperous basis."
—HERBERT HOOVER, Oct. 25, 1929

"In January of 1929," Stewart Holbrook said in *The Age of the Moguls*, "there was no one to look over the edge of the cliff and note how far it was down to the bottom of the canyon."

Nobody wanted to look. America was in the Big Bull Market, getting richer minute by minute since 1924, save for only an occasional setback. Now stocks only went one way—UP—and there was no reason why they shouldn't keep going that way. There was no reason why Coolidge Prosperity shouldn't go on forever. Mr. Coolidge himself said so in his State of the Union message as he prepared to turn over the White House to its new tenant, Herbert Hoover. "No Congress . . . ever assembled," said the President, "has met with a more pleasing prospect than that which appears at the present time. In the domestic field there is tranquility and contentment . . . and the highest record of years of prosperity."

Oh, there were some areas lacking in tranquillity, contentment or even easy money. There were people who hadn't yet quite recovered from the depression of 1920-1921—the farmers, notably. There were sharecroppers in the South taking the barest existence out of the soil. There were men in the mines and mills in the great industrial centers earning hardly enough to feed their broods.

Nobody looked that way. The Wall Street tickers tapped out a symphony of golden wealth. It was the mood music of the times, the climactic tones of the Get-Rich-Quick Era; millions danced to the dizzy strains or fed on the lush printed prose that accompanied them. John J. Raskob sat for a *Ladies Home Journal* interview entitled, in his own words, "Everybody Ought to Be Rich." Raskob was vice-president of General Motors, an ally of the DuPonts and a director of the

Bankers Trust Company and American Surety and the County Trust and—well, he came solidly qualified. This is what he said:

"Being rich is, of course, a comparative status. A man with a million dollars used to be considered rich, but so many people have at least that much in these days, or are earning incomes in excess of a normal return from a mil-

lion dollars, that a millionaire does not cause any comment . . . In my opinion the wealth of the country is bound to increase at a very rapid rate . . . Anyone who believes that opportunities are now closed and that from now on the country will get worse instead of better is welcome to the opinion—and whatever increment it will bring. I think that we have scarcely started . . . I am firm in my belief that anyone not only can be rich but ought to be rich . . . Prosperity is in the nature of an endless chain and we can break it only by refusing to see what it is . . ."

There was plenty of chapter and verse in the Raskob thesis that sunny August of 1929. The financier pointed out that anyone who had the foresight to put $10,000 into the common stocks of General Motors in 1919 "now would be worth more than a million and a half dollars." He said that anyone who started then and there to put $15 a month into common stocks and let the dividends accumulate would in 20 years "have at least eighty thousand dollars and an income from investments of around four hundred dollars a month."

Compared to some of the other super-salesmen of the time, Raskob seemed conservative. Edwin LeFevre, a familiar Wall Street figure, told of one nameless plunger who ran $100,000 into $20,000,000 and another who went in with a mere million and made it multiply thirty times in eight months. "Never before have such fortunes been made overnight by so many people," said LeFevre. But he was talking about investors with substantial stakes. The stories about the little man were much more enticing: the peddler who ran $4,000 up to $250,000; the butler who listened in on a financiers' cigars-and-brandy session and picked up a fast $150,000; the chauffeurs-with-big-ears

Ticker tape tells the Wall Street story.

This is Samuel Insull, shown aboard the steamer Exilona as he came back from Turkey in 1934 to face trial in the collapse of his multibillion-dollar Midwest utility empire—one of the towering financial marvels of the twenties.

Insull's story made the Horatio Alger novels look like the tamest kind of rags-to-riches fiction. Humbly born in London, he quit school at 14 to go to work as an office boy for $1.25 a week. Later he became a clerk for Thomas A. Edison's London agent, who was so impressed that he urged the inventor to hire him. The boy—21 then—arrived at Castle Garden in 1881 and went to work as Edison's secretary; he was soon handling the organization of the various Edison companies. By 1902 he was president of Chicago Edison and by 1907 he had merged all the light and power companies there into Commonwealth Edison.

Then, striking out on his own, he moved into other Midwest utilities. By the late twenties he was president of 11 companies, board chairman of 65 others and director in 85 more and had 72,000 employees in utility operations extending through the Midwest down the Mississippi Valley into New England.

Insull weathered the stock market crash by shoring up his intricate combine with his own $100,000,000 fortune and every dime he could wangle from relatives and friends. But then Cyrus Eaton, Cleveland magnate, tried to buy up control of the Insull properties and Insull went into the market to buck him. Insull won, but he lost $60,000,000 in the process and then he couldn't survive the deepening post-crash economic depression. His empire fell apart in June, 1932, with estimates of the investors' losses running as high as $750,000,000.

Broke at 72, Insull went to Paris to live out his days on $21,000-a-year in pensions due from three of his companies that survived the debacle. Indicted here later on mail fraud and embezzlement charges and facing multi-million-dollar suits from creditors, he fled France to escape extradition. The Greeks gave him sanctuary for a year before ordering him out in response to demands from the United States. The old man chartered a tramp steamer and drifted on the Mediterranean for 11 days but had to put in at Istanbul for food and water. There the Turks held him and he was brought back for trial with his brother Martin.

When the government couldn't prove its case, Insull returned to Paris. He dropped dead there on the streets at the age of 78. He left $1,000 in cash and $14,000,000 in debts—another charge against the dizzy whirl America took during the Lawless Decade.

who got healthy buying what the boss talked about on the way to his brokerage house in the morning; the Stock Exchange clerks and pages who brought home feedbox stuff for everybody on the block and ran small pools into silver streams.

Once the hallowed money mart at Broad and Wall was more or less off-bounds to the little man. It was the resort of the professional speculator, the "insider." Now everybody was solicited to come in and put his money on the line—and it wasn't gambling so much as an investment in the glorious American future, an expression of faith in the endless, wondrous prosperity that blessed the land. Only the hardiest spoilsports rose to protest that the wild and unchecked speculative fever might be bad for the country, and the merry hum of the tickers drowned out their voices. Why not? The money lay in stacks in Wall Street, waiting to be picked up. You had to be an awful deadhead not to go get some.

It was such a glorious time that the National Association of Merchant Tailors ordained a well-dressed American should have twenty suits, a dozen hats, eight overcoats and twenty-four pairs of shoes. That was for Just Plain Bill, 1929 model. The association said the man "of social position" should run through six sack suits a season and stock his wardrobe with two full-dress suits, a single and double-breasted tuxedo and some tropical evening wear for the good old summertime.

The tailors weren't alone. There were ads tempting the masses—let's say the *upper masses*—with $50,000 Russian sable coats, $45,000 duplex apartments, slender, low-slung Pierce Arrows at $8,200 and women's suits starting at $450. As 1928 roared to a happy close, the *New Yorker* carried a double-page spread from Black Starr and Frost (Fifth Avenue, Paris, Palm Beach) offering a rose-pink pearl necklace that had a rather expensive sound. "For more than one hundred years this house has collected pearls," said the breathless text, ". . . for more than one hundred years it was believed impossible to assemble a large single necklace in which each pearl would have the highest lustre and be perfectly, exquisitely matched . . . and now, as the culminating achievement of our history, we have reached this goal. This necklace is conceded by experts and connoisseurs to be the finest in existence . . . Price $685,000."

It didn't seem unreasonable at that moment. If you read John J. Raskob, everybody ought to have had $685,000, or a running start on it, anyway.

John J. Raskob saw prosperity as "an endless chain" but that winter the chain snapped.

THE CRASH

"October. This is one of the peculiarly dangerous months to speculate in stocks. The others are July, January, September, April, November, May, March, December, August and February."

—*Pudd'nhead Wilson* (Mark Twain)

Margin is a pretty wonderful thing. Simple, too: you borrow money to buy securities and you put up the securities as collateral for your loan. If the securities go up, you collect the dividends, which is also known as clipping coupons. If the securities go down, you raise some more cash—margin—to cover your investment. So many people were buying on margin in 1929 that there was six billion dollars outstanding in brokers' loans as compared with one billion in 1920 and 3½ billion in 1927. The Federal Reserve Board in Washington took to brooding about this item and got into a lovers' quarrel with the banks about it. The gentlemen in the capital wanted to raise interest rates to make borrowing a little tougher. But the banks had no qualms at all about the mountainous speculative tides; they were doing nicely, thanks.

Thus Charles E. Mitchell, president of the National City Bank and a director of the New York Federal Reserve Bank, took a very dramatic step in March when the growing talk of a curb on loans led to a break in the market. As more than eight million shares changed hands in a wave of scare selling, Mitchell announced that his institution stood ready to put out 25 million dollars in call loans. "We feel," Mitchell said, "that we have an obligation which is paramount to any Federal Reserve warning, or anything else, to avert any dangerous crisis in the money market." The Federal Reserve people laid back until August before raising their interest rates to 6 per cent. It was too late then; prices were on the rise again and the prophets of doom, their honor besmirched by the rampaging tickers, were on the run. Mr. Hoover himself said things were sound.

The theatrical weekly told the story in its own language.

On September 3, 1929, the all-time high was reached. Steel soared to 261, compared to 138 the year before. General Electric went to 396, against 128 the year before; A. T. & T. to 304, against 179; Westinghouse to 289, against 91. Nobody knew how many people were in Wall Street by then; the estimates ran from 1,000,000 to 25,000,000. As the new peaks were scaled, Roger Babson put out a sober warning. "Sooner or later," the economist said, "a crash is coming and it may be terrific." Professor Irving Fisher of Yale entered a quick dissent. The professor had just announced that stocks had reached "a permanently high plateau," so he evidently regarded Babson's dire prediction as a personal affront. Other Wall Street authorities wrote off Babson as an impractical longhair who didn't know what he was talking about.

Babson was right. The nightmare began September 5, although none of the market specialists in attendance read the symptoms correctly. Steel and other key issues fell off in a brief but heavy wave of selling. On October 4, securities dipped from 2 to 30 points and margin calls began to be heard on every hand. October 21 an avalanche of selling set in but was checked be-

fore the tickers closed. "I know of nothing fundamentally wrong with the stock market," Charles Mitchell said, and some of the financial editors talked of the trading mart's "merry comeback."

There was no real comeback. On October 23, fresh selling smashed values down by five billion dollars. All the leaders dipped but it was only a prelude to the calamity that lay ahead. The next day—Black Thursday—selling orders jammed the trunk lines into the Exchange. The ticker ran close to an hour late that morning and the quick fortunes of the New Era began to dissolve. The soothsayers poured not only words but money on the troubled waters. "There has been a little distress selling," said Morgan partner Thomas W. Lamont, Sr., "but reports from brokers indicate that margins are being maintained satisfactorily." The nation's banking giants assembled in the House of Morgan and pooled 240 million dollars to stick a cushion of buying power under the sagging market. The pool's emissary, the imposing Richard F. Whitney, strode onto the Exchange floor at 1:30 P.M. and bought 10,000 shares of Steel with theatrical flourishes. Then he began to snap up other issues. He said he might buy 20 to 30

Curious throngs rushed down to Wall Street as the disaster unfolded in the money marts.

Richard F. Whitney, the essence of conservative respectability, was the man selected by the Banker's Pool to buy up millions of dollars worth of stocks on Black Thursday in an effort to instill confidence and stop panic selling. This move slowed down the crash but couldn't stop it. In the early thirties, in trouble on investments, Whitney juggled the accounts of his own bond house, using investors' money to meet his losses. He went to Sing Sing for it and never came back to Wall Street.

million dollars' worth if time allowed. Psychologically, it was a master stroke. With the smart money buying instead of selling, the market steadied to hold off total disaster. On October 25 less than six million shares were traded—half the Black Thursday record—and fresh optimism flowed from high places.

"The fundamental business of the country, that is the production and distribution of commodities, is on a sound and prosperous basis," Herbert Hoover said. Andrew Mellon, Secretary of the Treasury and also the Aluminum King, predicted a speedy recovery for the badly shaken market. The Federal Reserve Board held two hurried meetings and reported there was no need for the government to act. "There is nothing

in the business situation to justify any nervousness," said Eugene M. Stevens, president of the Continental Illinois Bank. "The worst is over," said J. L. Julian of Fenner & Beane. "The selling was panicky, brought on by hysteria. General conditions are good." There was a point to the remark about hysteria. Police had to send reserves as curious throngs surged into Wall Street when the wild selling wave set in; there were thousands of little people, evidently, who wanted grandstand seats as their dreams of riches washed away in streams of ticker tape.

The soothsayers brought forth two days' respite in the marketplace, and the calendar furnished another—Sunday, no place to trade. On Monday, the panic was on again: 9 million shares sold on the Stock Exchange and 4 million on the Curb and losses exceeded ten billion dollars. The bottom fell out next day—Black Tuesday, October 29. Not even the Bankers' Pool, shoring up one fast-dropping issue or another, could hold back the whirlwind.

The bedlam that day on the floor was perhaps best described by a gray-haired Stock Exchange guard: "They roared like a lot of lions and tigers. They hollered and screamed, they clawed at one another's collars. It was like a bunch of crazy men. Every once in a while, when Radio or Steel or Auburn would take another tumble, you'd see some poor devil collapse and fall to the floor."

The toll was stupendous. The greatest of all selling waves—16 million shares on the Exchange and 7 million on the Curb—set off a panic that would destroy 30 billion dollars in open market values. Auburn fell off 60 points, DuPont 70. Steel, 205 when Whitney was snapping it up, dropped as low as 167. Westinghouse at one point fell to 100, almost one-third of what it was worth in September. The great investment trusts, led by Goldman Sachs, withered along with the old-line corporations. Now the market's big men, affluent enough to withstand the early shocks, went down with the tradesmen and clerks and shopkeepers who had taken their last pennies into Wall Street.

"Brother, Can You Spare a Dime?"
—Song by YIP HARBURG, 1932

The Wall Street Crash did not end on Black Tuesday. There were other bad days ahead in the great canyon in

Charles E. Mitchell, president of the National City Bank and thus one of the more highly-placed seers of the Get-Rich-Quick Era, also suffered personal disaster in the wake of the crash. He had to resign the lucrative bank job after a Senate hearing disclosed curious stock dealings with his wife in which he took huge "paper" losses to beat the government out of heavy income tax liabilities. The odd inter-family transactions led to Mitchell's arrest but he won an acquittal in a sensational trial early in 1933.

downtown Manhattan but they hardly mattered: the major shock was over. There was only a handful of people left to get hurt, and by then it was time to make jokes. The debacle only slightly diminished the peculiar American capacity for extracting laughs from the most ghastly shocks.

In the case of the overnight money shortage, as it happened, the first of the funnies was uttered in total seriousness, on October 30—the morning after—from no less a party than Bethlehem Steel's Eugene G. Grace.

"I," said Mr. Grace, "cannot see any reason for all this pessimism."

John D. Rockefeller, Sr. had a good one too: "There is nothing in the business situation to warrant the destruction of values that has taken place in

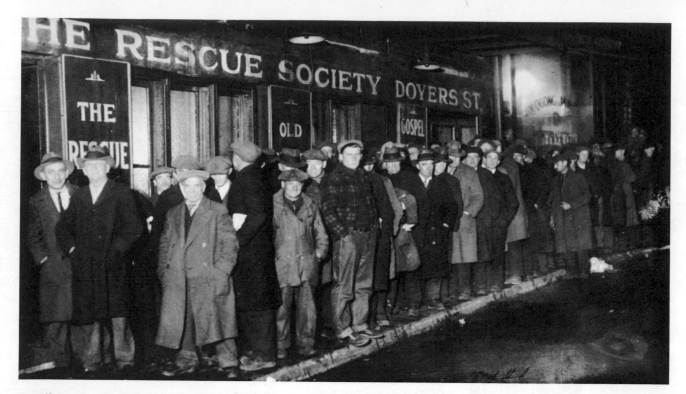

Breadline, New York City. Breadlines came
back to the American scene in 1929.

the past week, and my son and I have
for some days past been purchasing
sound common stocks." Eddie Cantor,
minus a couple of million himself, had
a fast answer for old John D. "Sure
he's buying," Cantor said. "Who else
has any money left?" Rockefeller was
not entirely alone, actually. John J.
Raskob, evidently having reread the
pearls of wisdom in his "Everybody
Ought to be Rich" sermon, said stocks
were at bargain prices and he was going to buy himself some choice issues.
Julius Klein, Assistant Secretary of
Commerce in the Hoover Administration, said everything seemed all right
to him and prosperity should go rolling
along. The Mayor of New York, Jimmy
Walker, appealed to movie exhibitors
to show pictures that would "reinstate
courage and hope in the hearts of the
people." (On Fifth Avenue, police
found a stray parrot screaming a message with a somewhat different moral
than Mr. Walker's. "More margin!" the
parrot cried. "More margin!")

The straight comics were more on
the grisly side. There was a rash of suicide jokes. "You stand in line to get a
window to jump out of," Will Rogers
complained. Then there was the standard gag about the cynical hotel clerk's

On the move. The crash and the depression that followed it spawned
a great migration. When job opportunities dried up, whole families
and groups of families pulled up stakes and traveled the great high-
ways in a search for a place to earn their daily bread. Above, sharecroppers (later known as "Okies") on the way west.

remark to incoming guests: "You want
a room for sleeping or jumping?" And
the one, widely told, about the two
brokers who took the hotel-window
plunge together because they had a
joint account. This kind of fun-making
did not produce universal laughter by
any means, because it had traces of
horrible fact. Not only broke but mort-

gaged or over-extended beyond repair,
some men did go out of windows, or
suck on gas pipes, or blow their brains
out. Nobody ever tried to add up the
toll. It remains just about the only
missing statistic in the smashing Third
Act closing Wall Street furnished for
the Get-Rich-Quick Era. Perhaps it's
just as well.

IT HAPPENED IN 1929...

The Drys held their torn and tattered banners high. Mrs. Mabel Walker Willebrandt said that Prohibition certainly could be enforced "but New York will be the last citadel to fall." She said the nation's capital already was on the water wagon, down almost to the last hostess: "The ribaldry of the cocktail shaker, the exchange of home-brew recipes and the florid eagerness for false stimulation from what is almost always questionable liquor are rapidly fading from the social hours in Washington . . . It has come to be more of a social achievement to establish the reputation for successful entertainment without cocktail, highball or liquors" . . . The government dropped its liquor cases against thirty New York night clubs, conceding that it couldn't get juries to convict . . . President Hoover clenched his fists and told a New York meeting that the Eighteenth Amendment simply had to be enforced. He said that too many people seemed to think that "laws are made for those who choose to obey them."

* * *

Henry Ford attended a dinner in honor of a Jewish philanthropist, David A. Brown, and paid tribute to "the great benevolence of the Jewish people, their philanthropy, their eagerness to make this world better, to educate the untutored, to heal the sick, to care for the orphans; their intent and intelligent participation in all that makes for civic righteousness and social justice stamps them a great people." The address was broadcast . . . Tex Rickard died . . . A Rutgers University freshman drowned in the Raritan Canal fleeing from a class rush; the Student Council then abolished class rushes and pajama parades . . . On May 6, Harry Sinclair went to jail for contempt of the Senate in the Teapot Dome scandal; on May 15, he was re-elected chairman of the Sinclair Consolidated Oil Corporation . . . Gray-haired Mrs. Mary Ware Dennett, 53, was fined $300 in Brooklyn for sending "obscene matter"—a pamphlet on sex, prepared for her children—through the mails. On appeal, she was cleared . . . Calvin Coolidge was elected a director of the New York Life Insurance Com-

pany . . . In an economy move, Herbert Hoover banished to Fort Meyer the seven horses quartered in the White House stables.

* * *

Babe Ruth's estranged wife, burned to death in Watertown, Massachusetts, left $5 to the Home Run King and $50,000 to their adopted daughter, Dorothy, 9 . . . Captain Frank Hawks set a record for the 2700-mile flight from Los Angeles to New York: 18 hours, 21 minutes and 59 seconds . . . The Graf Zeppelin flew around the world . . . Marshal Foch died with the

Huey (Kingfish) Long, Governor of Louisiana and rabble rouser with much potential, was just beginning to attract national attention in 1929. He went on to the United States Senate and attained a national following with a vague "Share-the-Wealth" program but in 1935 a young doctor, gone berserk, assassinated him in the State Capitol at Baton Rouge.

words *allons y* (let's go) on his lips . . . In Boston, Harry J. Canter drew a year in jail for criminally defaming ex-Governor Alvan T. Fuller by carrying a placard bearing the words, "Fuller, murderer of Sacco and Vanzetti" . . . Commander Richard E. Byrd planted the Stars and Stripes on the South Pole . . . The Ford Motor Company boosted daily wage rates from $6 to $7 . . . Americans bought $850,-000,000 worth of radios . . . There were 23,-000,000 cars on the roads . . . Two Southern governors, Theodore Bilbo in Mississippi and Huey Long in Louisi-

Bing Crosby, an unknown singer, was touring with Paul Whiteman's band the year the bottom fell out of the New Era.

Ring Lardner's "Round-Up" came out in 1929. Lardner went from baseball reporter to columnist to the short story and produced some of the humor classics of the twenties. He is shown with his wife.

Fred Allen, shown here with his wife Portland Hoffa, was a hit in *The Little Show.*

One of Broadway's big hits was *Journey's End*, a grim story of the war.

ana, began to attract national attention . . . Bing Crosby, a singer, was touring with Paul Whiteman's band . . . Major H. O. D. Seagrave set a new speed record for autos: 211 mph . . . Movie attendance soared to 100,000,000 per week . . .

On the literary front, Erich Maria Remarque's *All Quiet on the Western Front* led the fiction best-sellers, trailed by Sinclair Lewis's *Dodsworth* and such items as *Scarlet Sister Mary*, by Julia Peterkin, and *Joseph and his Brethren*, by H. W. Freeman . . . Also in the stores: Ernest Hemingway's *Farewell to Arms*, Thomas Wolfe's *Look Homeward, Angel*, William Faulkner's *The Sound and the Fury*, Ellen Glasgow's *They Stooped to Folly*, Ring Lardner's *Round-Up*

and W. R. Burnett's *Little Caesar*. In non-fiction, Abbé Ernest Dimnet's *The Art of Thinking* was the best-seller. The list also included Frances Hackett's *Henry the Eighth*, Lytton Strachey's *Elizabeth and Essex*, Walter Lippmann's *A Preface to Morals* and Robert L. Ripley's *Believe It or Not.* Bertrand Russell's *Marriage and Morals* also was in the stalls, along with the James Thurber-E. B. White essay, *Is Sex Necessary?*

* * *

In the theater, Elmer Rice's *Street Scene*, with Erin O'Brien Moore and Beulah Bondi, won the Pulitzer Prize. Laurence Olivier made his Broadway debut in *Murder on the Second Floor*. Bette Davis appeared with Donald Meek in *Broken Dishes*.

Libby Holman scored with the song, "Moanin' Low," in *The Little Show*, with Clifton Webb (and Fred Allen and Portland Hoffa). Eugene O'Neill's *Strange Interlude* was banned in Boston. *Journey's End*, the war play. was a big hit . . . Also on the boards: Gertrude Lawrence and Leslie Howard in *Candlelight*, Jacob Ben-Ami and Josephine Hutchinson in *The Sea Gull*, Edward G. Robinson in *Kibitzer*, Grace George in *The First Mrs. Fraser*, Walter Hampden in *Richelieu*, Jack Donahue and Lily Damita in *Sons O' Guns*, Cary Grant in *A Wonderful Night*, Jimmy Durante, Eddie Foy, Jr. and Ruby Keeler in *Show Girl*, and Ruth Gordon in *Serena Blandish* . . . On the screen, nearly everybody talked.

THE MORNING AFTER

New York, 1930: The people line up for bread. The same picture was duplicated all over the nation.

The calamity in Wall Street buried something more than the paper dreams and paper profits of the wildest binge in our history. It buried an era and a way of life. It buried the Get-Rich-Quick idea. It buried the What-The-Hell philosophy behind the dizzy ride so many Americans went on when the postwar kinks were ironed out and the good times came. It brought the nation to its senses: the gray tomorrow had to be faced.

It was very gray indeed.

The Great Crash ushered in the Great Depression.

Apple Annie showed up on one street corner and her husband on another.

The soup kitchen, pretty much in the discard since the mild rush of 1920 and 1921, expanded its facilities for an SRO clientele.

The breadline appeared in the American city.

The home relief office opened.

And an odd thing happened: the people turned to Washington. Virtually ungoverned since the war, free to write their own tickets not just in manners and morals but on all levels, free to borrow and burn as they chose, free to speculate on fly-by-night investments while the policing agencies in the capital looked the other way, the people turned to Washington to write some rules and regulations for the next

229

In the big cities, with no organized relief to meet the mounting unemployment that followed the crash, missions, gyms and church basements were converted to soup kitchens.

round. The people wanted the government to do something. The eight free-and-easy years of Harding and Coolidge, looking back, suddenly lost their luster.

Where was the government while we were running wild? Where was the government while the seeds of depression were planted? Where was the government while the Great Crash was in the making? That's the kind of question the man in the street began to ask in the wake of the debacle in Wall Street.

Herbert Hoover did not hurl the forces of government into the breach. He wheeled up the weapon he had used before the crash and during the crash: optimism. The country was "fundamentally sound"—that was the word from the capital. Recovery was just around the corner. Influential sections of the business world and all kinds of independent authorities supported this happy view. In the spring of 1930, the Harvard Economic Society took a long look at its graphs and charts and assured the republic that the worst was over: the recession had been checked. The general idea in all the high places was that if we just kept calm and didn't interfere with the wonderful self-healing processes of America's private economy, everything would straighten itself out.

It didn't, of course.

Millions of men lost their jobs—the total reached 4,500,000 during 1931 and tripled during 1932. Commodity prices dipped to new lows. The business index showed 50 per cent below normal. National income fell to half what it was before the dark October days of 1929. Forty per cent of the nation's farms were mortgaged and some long-suffering tillers of the Midwestern soil were threatening violence to ward off any more foreclosures.

Thus the whole edifice of the New Era crumpled into ruin. All the prophets of everlasting prosperity went with it. First, the gods of business, the legend of their infallibility smothered in the ticker tape avalanche. Then, the Great White Fathers in Washington. The nation passed harsh judgments: Warren Harding hadn't governed at all; he just played poker with the boys and hoped they wouldn't steal too much. Calvin Coolidge shut out the world and slept, confident that the businessmen would keep the good times rolling. Herbert Hoover looked the other way as economic disaster struck.

In this setting, the 1932 national election was no contest. Herbert Hoover went into the campaign like a loser. Franklin D. Roosevelt talked about vast social and economic reforms and Hoover protested that "the very foundations of our American system" would be imperiled if the man got in. Roosevelt talked about a New Deal for the "forgotten man" and Hoover inveighed against dangerous new philosophies of government. Roosevelt talked hope and bold action and Hoover was shrouded in despair. Roosevelt talked a new prosperity and Hoover looked longingly back on the old, the one that didn't stick. Roosevelt won in a landslide. It was a time for a change, and change came with staggering speed.

On Sunday, March 5, the day after his inauguration, the new President—smiling, self-assured, surrounded by a daring Brain Trust—ordered a bank holiday to furnish a breather for the nation's slowly collapsing banking structure. He got Congress to pass emergency legislation to put the resources of the Federal Reserve System behind the banks to prevent any more shut-downs caused by runs on deposits.

Then the New Dealers launched their massive assault on the depression. The Agricultural Adjustment Administration cut farm surpluses through production controls and subsidies. The National Industrial Recovery Act (NRA) set up codes of fair practice in industry, boosted wages by raising minimum pay and spread out jobs by shortening working hours. The Federal Emergency Relief Administration (FERA) allocated hundreds of millions of dollars to the states to help sustain the jobless. The Public Works Administration (PWA, later the Works Projects Administration, or WPA) put out billions to create employment on useful construction jobs. The Civilian Conservation Corps (CCC) put unemployed youths into reforestation jobs at $1 a day plus bed and board. The National Labor Board set up the first real playing rules between the unions and management. The Farm Credit Administration and the Home Owners Loan Corporation (HOLC) choked off the rising tide of foreclosures and evictions.

On the other levels, the Roosevelt Administration moved with the same breathtaking speed: the Reconstruction Finance Corporation, set up under

The apple vendors, men and women alike, appeared on the street corners in 1930. The sign in the bottom picture reads, "Mr. Glad will be at this corner this afternoon at 4 o'clock to distribute one thousand nickels to one thousand needy Men." You can see "Mr. Glad" there.

An Ohio farm goes on the auction block and angry neighbors gather to protest the fore-closing of the mortgage.

Battling back from the depression on the land with the help of Farm Security Administration loans, a New England farmer tells his story to a reporter for the *New York Post*.

Hoover but not much more than a fig-urehead agency, got vast amounts to lend to private investors. TVA, a trail-blazing experiment in low-cost public power, undertook the social and eco-nomic development of the Tennessee Valley. The Federal Deposit Insurance Corporation (FDIC) insured individual accounts up to $5,000 to restore confidence in the private savings institutions. The Securities and Exchange Commission (SEC) set up safeguards to protect investors in the stock market. The Federal Public Housing Administration (FPHA) started the first meaningful assault on the slums by subsidizing new, modern, low-rent apartments.

People made jokes about the way the alphabet was taking such a beating in Washington; there were suggestions that Roosevelt (FDR) would have to stop setting up new government agencies because he was running out of letters. And there were fierce protests too. "New Deal" took on an ugly sound in

F. D. R.

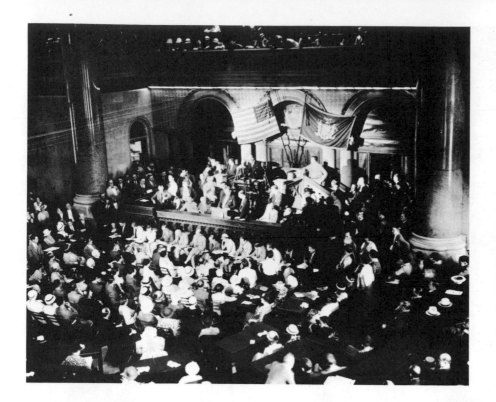

Repeal! The noble experiment was ended. Prohibition, the greatest single factor in the lawlessness of the Lawless Decade, ceased to exist in most states of the Union in 1933, when the repeal of the Eighteenth Amendment freed the States to decide for themselves whether they wanted to be Wet or Dry.

Upper left, New York State's special convention ratifies the repeal amendment.

Lower left, first deliveries of legal liquor attract a joyous crowd to a New York night club.

Below, the first drinks of the new legal liquor, to celebrate repeal. It was only Prohibition that was repealed. The New Freedom, the new attitude toward the Past and the Future could not be repealed. That was the Lawless Decade's bequest to the American people.

the board rooms where men looked back with longing on twelve years of delightful non-interference from government. The cry of "Socialism!" issued from high places.

It wasn't Socialism as we knew it then but it was revolution.

It was revolution on the broadest imaginable social and economic levels. It was revolution in government—in *existing* government. It was revolution in thinking. It was revolution in the whole concept of the state's relation to the citizen—and *responsibility* to the citizen—in a free republic.

The Lawless Decade set the stage for it. The Lawless Decade brought us up to it—willing, eager and in dire necessity. Say that about a time that was wild and whacky and finally tragic but never dull. The twenties weren't wasted at all; the wide and wonderful land came of age.

INDEX

INDEX

Page references in italic indicate illustrations.

St. Pierre, 94
St. Valentine's Day Massacre, 204, 206, 207, 212
Sapiro, Aaron, 181
Sarazen, Gene, 97
Sarnoff, David, 39
Scalise, John, 205, 207
Schultz, Dutch, *187, 202*
Scopes, John T., 120, *121*
screen, 69, *see* movies
Seabury, Samuel, 217, 218
Shapiro, Jacob (Gurrah), *189*
Sharkey, Jack, *211*
Shaw, George Bernard, 56
Sheik, The, 66, *138*
Shelby, Montana, 88
Sinclair, Harry F., 53, 84, 86, 227
Smith, Gov. Alfred E., 199, *200,* 201, 202, 216
Smith, Jess, 53
Smith, Moe, *119*
smuggling, 90
Snyder, Albert, 158
Snyder, Ruth, 158, *160,* 161
socialism, 62, 234
socialists, 27, 28, 29, 63
soup kitchens, 230
Sousa, John Philip, *44*
Southern Methodist Church, *26*
speakeasies, 19, 24, *24,* 191, *192, 194,* 195, 198
Spirit of St. Louis, The, 162
sports cars, 73
Stanwyck, Barbara, 182
Stege, John, *211*
Stevens, Henry, 142, *et seq.*
Stevens, Willie, 142, *et seq.*
Stillman, Anne, 79
Stock Exchange, *see* Wall Street, 220
Stone, Irving, 199
Stork Club, *195*
strikes, 29
Sumner, John S., 79, 166
Sunday, Rev. Billy, 21
Swanson, Gloria, 73, 74, *136*
Syndicate, 208

Talmadge, Norma, 75
Tammany Hall, 201, 216
Taylor, Estelle, *59,* 60, 173
Taylor, William Desmond, 70, 71
Teapot Dome, 53, 84, 86
Thaw, Harry K., 66
Thayer, Judge Webster, 177, *179,* 180
Thomas, Olive, 74
Thompson, William Hal (Big Bill), *114,* 208, 210, 211, 217
Tinney, Frank, *108*
T-Men, 214
Torrio, Johnny, 37, 105, 107, 111, *112, 113,* 114, 208
Trader Horn, 203

Tresca, Carlo, *28*
True Story (magazine), 45
Truman, H. S., *50*
Tunney, Gene, *173, 174,* 175

Unione Siciliano, 106, *114,* 205, 207, 208
U.S. Coast Guard, 91
unknown soldier, 61

Valentino, Rudolph, 66, *138,* 139, 140
Vallee, Rudy, *41, 42*
Van Loon, Henrick Willem, 79
Vanderbilt, Cornelius, Jr., 50
Vanzetti, Bartolomeo, 51, 66, *176, 177,* 178, *179,* 180
victory parade, *17*
Volstead, Rep. Andrew J., 26

Wagner, Senator Robert, 216
Wales, Prince of, 109
Walker, Mayor Jimmy J., *132,* 203, 216, 218, 219, 226
Wall Street, 221, 224, 225, 226, 229, 230
Wallace, Henry C., *54*
Waller, Fats, *43*
Warner Brothers, 136
wartime prohibition, *23*
WCTU, 25, 26; *see* Women's Christian Temperance Union
Weaver, George (Buck), 33
Weeks, John W., *54*
Weiss, Hymie (The Polack), 105, *106,* 204, 210
Whalen, Grover, 191
White, Alice, 48, *49*
White, George, 51
White, Major J. Andrew, 39
White, William Allen, 53
White Sox, Chicago, 33, 34
Whiteman, Paul, *42, 43*
Whitney, Richard, 225
Wild Bull of the Pampas, 89
Willard, Frances E., *25*
Willard, Jess, 56, 57
Willebrandt, Mrs. Mable Walker, 227
Williams, Hannah, *59*
Wills, Harry, *58,* 60
Wilson, Imogene, *108*
Wilson, Woodrow, 19, 20, 63, 64
Winter, Dale, 37, 37
Wittenmyer, Mrs. Annie, 24
Women's Christian Temperance Union (WCTU), 24

Yale, Frankie, *106,* 107
Yankees, the New York, 168, 169, 170, *171*
York, Sergeant Alvin C., *18*

Zero, Mr., 66
Ziegfeld, Florenz, 76, 80, *108*
Zwillman, Longy, *188*